HMS WILD SWAN

HMS WILD SWAN

One Destroyer's War
1939-42

PETER C. SMITH

WILLIAM KIMBER·LONDON

First published in 1985 by
WILLIAM KIMBER & CO LIMITED, 100 Jermyn Street,
London, SW14 6EE

ᐰ Peter C. Smith, 1985
ISBN 0-7183-0542-6

Photoset by Tellgate Ltd, London WC1
and printed in Great Britain by
The Garden City Press Limited,
Letchworth, Hertfordshire, SG6 1JS

For
EDDIE MILL
Guardsman; Sailor; Telegraphist; and always
a damned good friend

Contents

List of Maps and Diagrams

List of Illustrations

Foreword
by Bob Burns

It is traditional in books of this nature that the Foreword is written by a famous Admiral or a well-known personality. Peter Smith has changed that by allowing me, an ordinary member of the ship's company of the gallant old *Wild Swan*, to introduce his detailed and sympathetic study of a 'V' and 'W' at war. That's how it should be because she was a working warship, unpraised and unsung in other history books despite the fact that she was at the forefront of the naval war and went down in action in one of the most gallant battles of the Second World War.

I was serving at the shore establishment HMS *Excellent* when I heard the news of her loss and that dreadful casualty list, including many old friends with whom I had served for two years. Even after forty years many memories crowd in on me about *Wild Swan* and her crew. The following cameos of mine give some idea of the picture of this gallant little vessel whose story is so accurateley portrayed in these pages.

A tropical night in the warm South Atlantic ocean somewhere off Freetown, Sierra Leone. Our captain, Lieutenant-Commander Sclater, requesting that a Liverpool lad, Danny Rossiter, who had a lovely baritone voice, sing 'How Deep is the Night' from 'B' Gundeck. Despite his distinctive 'Scouse' twang his song came over through the still night to entertain the crew on watch, far removed from the horrors of war all about them. Danny survived the sinking and is still alive and recently retired from a printing company.

I doubt whether our captain ever fully realised just how close the ship's company came to near-mutiny at Christmas 1940 after months in the grim North Atlantic wastes without any respite at all. I recall we arrived at Liverpool just before the festive day after another harrowing convoy period, with one watch already changed into their 'tiddley' suits for a well-deserved four days boiler-cleaning leave. However, instead of gliding into Gladstone Dock, we oiled at Tranmere Oiling Jetty then went alongside Princess Pier to collect orders. Lieutenant-Commander Sclater then had the unenviable task of breaking the news that an ex-American four-funnel destroyer had

collided with the dock gates on leaving convoy duty and that we had
to return to sea to take her place. I recall Lieutenant 'Dutchy' Holland, our No 1, trying to console two of the lads who until then had
been on their way home to see their offspring for the first time.

The same Lieutenant Holland (later to command a 'Hunt' Class
destroyer) had a miraculous escape in those evil waters that winter.
Leaving Liverpool in foul weather in a hurry due to a U-boat sighting in the Irish Sea I was Petty Officer on the 12-pdr AA gun amidships when he ordered me to send two of the guns crew to help him secure the Wardroom Hatch. I recall vividly the two 'Hostility Only'
ratings that I despatched, Gordon Watson, a furrier from Edinburgh
and Norman Shinwell, a printer from the *Daily Herald's* northern
office. An enormous wave washed all three men over the side and
only a desperate hand from Lieutenant Holland grasping at a broken
guardrail saved him. On the next roll of the ship he was washed back
inboard but the other two lads were swept away within seconds and
we never even stopped to search for them; it would have been hopeless in those conditions.

Gordon Watson, a brilliant artist, it had been who, during the
evacuation of Boulougne amid the hell and roar of our guns and the
enemy's firing at point-blank range alongside the quay, had
remained cool enough to draw a charcoal sketch of the scene on a
Pussers chart. Lieutenant-Commander Younghusband was so thril-
led with its precise detail that he cadged it from Gordon and hung it
in his cabin.

Such are the fragmented memories over forty years, but turn the
pages and the whole story is carefully unfolded for you. Read it with
pride for *Wild Swan* was typical of the overworked and overburdened
destroyers of that tragic period and their story deserves telling while
there is still time for such recollections. For myself I am more than
pleased that the Old Lady has at last found a niche in history for she
and her crew contributed so much.

Bob Burns, Thornton, Liverpool, February 1985

Preface

This is the story of one British destroyer at war; it is a remarkable story of one small warship and her crew and how they endured two-and-a-half years of total war. She was not a famous ship, nor did she catch the headlines as did other, sometimes less worthy, vessels with famous captains. When her exploits are examined in detail, however, it will be seen that she played a full part in the frontline for most of her wartime career and her death was as gallant and heroic as any warship in the Royal Navy.

HMS *Wild Swan* was an ancient vessel before the war commenced, one of the famous 'Modified W' class ships which were built at the end of the Kaisers war. She should have gone to the scrapheap eight years before she began her final commission. Since her launch in 1919 she had seen service in the Baltic, Mediterranean and Far East; had touched the troubled fringes of war in areas as diverse as the Bosphorus, the Yangtse-Kiang and Latvia; had outbluffed one dictator at Malta and witnessed at close hand the work of a second at Huleva. She had a long and honourable peacetime service and by all rights her work was done by 1936. But there came a stay of execution and an extension of life as a part of the 'Second Eleven', or so it was thought.

In fact when war *did* become a harsh reality with the coming of the Blitzkrieg and the fall of the Low Countries and France, *Wild Swan* was in the forefront of battle, not the reserves. So it remained for the rest of her life, until her epic last battle.

Her tale here is based on official records and signals; Reports of Proceedings and documents. But her story, as is fitting, is also seen through the eyes of her crew, the 'Frantic Ducks' as they were known. The story of *Wild Swan* also sheds new light on many little-known episodes of the war at sea.

Peter C. Smith, Riseley, Beds. 1985

Acknowledgements

Personal papers, documents,letters and interviews were supplied for use in this book by a great many individuals and organisations; to all I give my grateful thanks for their time, generosity and kindness, in particular to the following:

Former crew members of HMS Wild Swan (periods, ranks and dates in brackets): William E. Aveling (Leading Seaman 1926-28), Commander W. D. Leslie King, DSO*, DSC, RN (Midshipman 1929), Captain E. N. Pumphrey, DSO, DSC, RN (Midshipman 1929), T. G. Treadwell (Leading Seaman 1931), Arthur Manton (Able Seaman 1934-36), Edmund J. J. Rice (Writer 1934-36), E. W. Edds (Able Seaman 1934-36), Frank Skidmore (Able Seaman 1934-36), H. J. 'Florrie' Ford (Leading Stoker 1939-42), A. V. Hassell, DSM (Leading Stoker 1939-42), Patrick G. Satow (Lieutenant 1939-42), Wally K. Harrison (Yeoman of Signals 1939-42), C. E. L. Sclater (Lieutenant-Commander 1940-42), A. G. Linford (Stoker Petty Officer 1940-42), F. H. D. Hutter (Surgeon Lieutenant 1941-42), G. Marsh (Leading Seaman 1940-42) (Posthumously via Mrs A. E. Townsend), Donald Lingard (Telgraphist 1941-42), Andrew H. Rippon (Engine Room Artificer 1941-42), Owen S. Pugh (Sub-Lieutenant 1941-42), F. R. Burrett (Torpedo Gunners Mate 1942), Albert J. H. Timpson (Gunner (T) 1942) (Posthumously via Mrs Beryl Sandal), Hiram W. Morgan (CPO Steward) (Posthumously via Mrs G. Sankey and Mr T. T. Morgan).

Other former naval personnel: C. D. Howard-Johnston CB, DSO, DSC, RN (Commander, St Malo Demolition Party, 1940), Darby Kelly (GMHMS *Whitehall* 1934-36), P. Russell Dickson (Surgeon Lieutenant HMS *Boreas* 1941-42), Ron Howell (Able Seaman, HMS *Vansittart* 1942).

Military, Aeronautical and Naval Informants: Captain M. Gomez-Miranda, Spanish Navy, Captain Claude Huan, French Navy, Rtd., Commander F. C. van Oosten, Royal Netherlands Navy, Rtd., Commander H. J. Grefe, Royal Netherlands Navy, Lieutenant-Commander J. V. Watson, RN, ARNO, Colonel J. F. E. Pye, O. St. J, FCIT, Assoc. I. Mech. E., FSCA, Lieutenant-Commander D. A.

Nicholson, RN, HMS *Vernon*. M. le Colonel Chef du Sirpa, 4°Division
Bureau AVPH, Paris, Captain Francis De Winton, RN, Rtd., Group-
Captain T. C. Flanagan, MSC, BA (Hons), RAF, Rtd., Air Historical
Branch, London.

Historians and Authors with specialist knowledge: The Hon Ewen E. S.
Montague, CBE, QC, DL, London. Senor Rafael Gonzalez Echegaray,
Santander, Spain, Jak P. Mallmann Showell, Telford, J. Richard
Smith, *Luft Archiv* Aviation Research, Stroud, Pierre Herveaux,
Sainte Adresse, Alfred Price, F. R. Hist. S., Uppingham, Edwin R.
Walker, Great Bookham, Douglas Clare, Secretary 1st D. F. Associ-
ation, Newent, Patrick Ehrhardt, Ostwald, Geoffrey P. Jones, Lon-
don, Chaz Bowyer, Norwich.

Organisations and Companies: R. Suddaby, Keeper, Depart of
Records, Imperial War Museum, London, D. F. K. Hodge, Historic
Photograph Section, National Maritime Museum, London, P. Reed,
Department of Document, Imperial War Museum, London, T. J.
Curl, Admin. Manager, Swan Hunter Shipbuilders, Wallsend, F.
W. Manders, Local Studies Librarian, Newcastle Central Library,
Mrs L. Moore, *Illustrated London News* Picture Library, S. J. Cox,
Naval Historical Branch, London, J. R. McAvoy, Naval Office,
Canberra, Neil Somerville, B.B.C. Written Archives Centre, Read-
ing, D. Quinn, General Medical Council, London, John Thorn and
A. King, Divisional Librarian, Portsmouth Central Library, Miss
K. Langrish, Information Officer, Shipping Information Services
Group, Lloyd's Register of Shipping, London, Tony H. H.
Richardson, Library & Records Department, Foreign & Common-
wealth Office, London, Staff of the Public Record Office Depart-
ments, Kew, London, Harry E. Riley, Modern Military Headquar-
ters Branch, Military Archives Division, National Archives and
Records Service, Washington, DC, Jaime Lloret, Hijos de J. Bar-
reras, S. A., Vigo, Spain.

CHAPTER ONE

New Wine in an Old Bottle
May 1919 – April 1940

On 16th May 1919, a bright spring day on the grimy river Tyne, a
new destroyer was launched. In the aftermath of the 'war to end all
wars' and with a life expectancy of fifteen years at best, it was not
thought she would ever see battle or action of any sort. When Job
Number 1105 at Swan Hunter's yard had the traditional bottle of
champagne broken over her bows by Mrs R.M.R. West, wife of
Commander West, RN, the District Superintendent of Torpedo Boat
Destroyers building by contract, and became HMS *Wild Swan*, latest
warship of King George V's powerful Navy, little employment other
than training and peaceful exercises could be envisaged for her.

Twenty years passed and the world changed considerably. The
Royal Navy was ruthlessly cut back by uncaring politicians; while
dictatorships arose and democracy and freedom were threatened. In
those twenty years *Wild Swan* had seen much of war and death and
the threat of war.* In the Baltic she witnessed the emergence of the
States of Finland, Lithuania, Latvia and Estonia, three of them to be
brutally blotted out in 1940 by one dictatorship of the left. In the
1920's she saw war between Greece and Turkey in the Mediterranean and between left and right in China; in the 1930's she witnessed
the rise and posturing of right-wing dictators in Germany, Italy and
Spain and sensed the menace of Japan in the Far East. She had seen
Baltic refugees fleeing one enemy, Greeks another, Chinese fleeing
each other's armies, witnessed Fascist Italy's troops on their way to
crush Ethiopia and finally had evacuated refugees from Franco's
armies. When she returned to England in the summer of 1936 those
two decades of 'peace' had, for *Wild Swan*, been merely rehearsals of
war.

By 1938 she was a very old lady, beyond her time and destined for
the scrapheap. But at last the menace was seen. Every ship, even an
old ship, became doubly precious. Instead of the scrapheap plans
were made to refit and re-boiler the old vessel. Give her new engines,
equip her with the submarine detection device, Asdic. Hold her

* See Appendix Four for outline of service 1919-39.

ready for the second line in case of war. . . . Initially a refit only had been planned, just to fit the Asdic, and it was hoped to complete by mid-July 1938. However, once the preliminary examination had been done, it was announced that she was to be paid off into reserve on 23rd August and placed in state of readiness for major work.

In order to fit the Asdic dome and associated equipment extra space had to be found below decks. The original arrangement ruled out the conversions being done as to earlier V & W destroyers, turning them into useful AA destroyers with extra range fuel tanks. Instead, once the Asdic was fitted, both she and her sister ship, *Whitshed*, were docked and placed in a state of preservation pending what were termed 'large repairs' to them both, 'on completion of new boilers'. The full re-equipping, scheduled to be carried out by the Royal Dockyard itself, was due to be completed by the autumn of 1939, a fitting choice as it transpired! On 20th July 1938, Commander Engineering H.H.Swayne was appointed to oversee this vital work and *Wild Swan* was officially listed as tender to the Reserve Fleet cruiser *Effingham* for accounts and manning while the major work was carried out.

To house the Asdic dome required three feet from out of the hull and that space had to be found from the existing boiler rooms. The hull had also to be strengthened in the vicinity of the dome and the weight of the dome and equipment was five tons, with another six tons for hull weight. The weight of a basic set of throwers and depth charges came out at a further five tons. The costs were £1,700 for a set, plus the installation expense, although the Asdic equipments themselves were manufactured by the Royal Dockyards and fitted by them. The boilering work was also done in drydock at Portsmouth.

All this involved the virtual gutting of the midships portion of the ship. Her mast and funnels came out, her iron deck was opened up and the giant sheerlegs lifted out her old equipment and lowered in the new. The once 'Queen of the China Fleet' now looked more like a derelict hulk than a fighting ship. Although work was being done on both destroyers, *Whitshed* was actually commenced first, with work on *Wild Swan* following three months later. The Munich crisis passed, then in 1939 followed the sacrifice of Czechoslovakia, tensions in the Far East, frantic re-armament and the German ultimatum to Poland. There is some evidence to suggest that the growing crisis saw speeding up of work on the two ships in a desperate attempt to get them ready in time, but it was not to be.

When, on 3rd September 1939, the war against Germany finally began, *Wild Swan* was still an inert hulk in dry dock. *Whitshed* was closer to completion but a contemporary description of her gives a very good idea of just how World War II found *Wild Swan*: 'She had literally been dragged off the scrap heap; was without boilers, guns, funnels or masts, and merely consisted of a hull which just managed to keep afloat.*'

*

On the last day of July 1939 a new captain for *Wild Swan* had been appointed. The mobilisation of the Reserve Fleet had already taken place once, at the time of the Munich crisis. It had not then affected *Wild Swan*, which at that time could not even remotely be considered ready for duty. But in July 1939, although far more ready and still listed as a paid-off tender to *Effingham*, her completion for war service was only months away and a skeleton crew *could* be allocated. Thus, on 13th July, the Admiralty informed all relevant naval authorities that the major proportion of the Reserve Fleet was to be placed in full commission and crewed with Reservist and Naval Pensioners. The word 'mobilisation' was deliberately kept from the wording, giving some indication of the trepidation felt by a still hesitant Government about going over the brink until every option had been exhausted. Appeasement died hard. Nonetheless all such men called upon were to report to their depots on 31st July. This followed the actual issue of appointments to all officers on the Reserve list, telling them of their allocations,† which had taken place on 14th July. Among the hundreds of naval officers on the Reserve List who received such notifications through the post was Lieutenant-Commander J. L. Younghusband. His instructions were to take command of HM destroyer *Wild Swan*, completing for service at Portsmouth Naval Dockyard. However, there was little that Lieutenant-Commander Younghusband could do until the work being carried out was at a far more advanced stage. Work was, of course, given added priority with the coming crisis, but although this enabled *Whitshed* to be rushed to sea early, *Wild Swan* still needed time. Corners *were* skipped, as was to be discovered later but when the final telegram indication went out to the Fleet on 3rd September 1939, for 'TOTAL – Germany,' *Wild Swan* was still not a fighting ship.

---

* *HMS Wideawake; Destroyer and Preserver*, by Lieutenant-Commander George Stitt, RN, George Allen & Unwin, London, p. 10.
† CW. 13047/39, 14th July, 1939. (ADM 205/1)

She was merely listed as 'Unallocated Destroyer', Portsmouth Command.

And so the nation went to war; at sea two major tragedies soon took place: the loss of the battleship *Royal Oak* and the aircraft carrier *Courageous*. The convoy system was organised and *Wild Swan*'s sister ships began attacking submarine 'contacts' and claiming imaginary victories. The Germans began to utilise the magnetic mine and merchant ship losses began to climb. But all this passed by the little destroyer in her dry-dock at Portsmouth harbour. The clamour of the builders' hammers filled the air, the banshee wailing of the sirens heralded air raids that did not materialise.

By October the re-boilering was advancing enough to appoint the next officer to the ship, another pensioner from the Reserve List, a very experienced man to whom the new engines and the old ship's mobility were entrusted and found a sympathetic and highly-efficient response. This was Commissioned Engineer C.J.C. Derbyshire, a great man who reflected the heart of the rejuvenated destroyer. By 1942 he was to be rewarded for his diligence and hard work with the MBE. But on 16th October 1939, when his appointment was made, little but damned hard work faced him to get the ship ready for sea. Ultimately all the conflicts and final difficulties *were* overcome, largely by the solid relationship and teamwork of Younghusband and Derbyshire, a fine, efficient and stable base of experience around which the rest of *Wild Swan*'s crew of new young officers and mixture of pensioners and 'Hostilities Only' ratings could gell and form a effective team.

By the beginning of December the work was nearing completion and due to finish by the 16th. She was listed as refitting and re-boilering and assigned to Portland to work-up fully before joining a new Western Approaches Command flotilla to be based at Plymouth, the 18th Destroyer Flotilla, along with others completing refits, namely *Veteran* and *Whitshed*. On 1st December the First Lieutenant joined the ship, Lieutenant M.J. Lee. As 'Jimmy-the-One', he was to be responsible for licking the new crew into shape under Younghusband's directions. Another important appointment made on 4th December was that of her Gunner (T) Commissioned Gunner G. Casey. His responsibilities were the twin banks of torpedo tubes, the depth charges and associated equipments and most of the electrical installations of the ship. On 16th December another member of the wardroom was appointed to the ship, Sub-Lieutenant H.G. Vere.

By this time the greater part of her crew was on board and settling

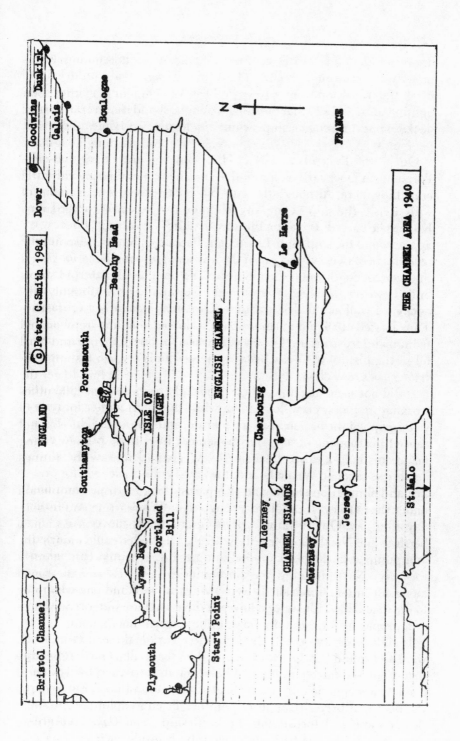

THE CHANNEL AREA 1940

© Peter C. Smith 1984

ENGLAND

Bristol Channel
Plymouth
Lyme Bay
Portland Bill
Start Point
Southampton
Portsmouth
ISLE OF WIGHT
Beachy Head
Dover
Goodwins
Dunkirk
Calais
Boulogne

ENGLISH CHANNEL

Alderney
CHANNEL ISLANDS
Guernsey
Jersey
St.Malo
Cherbourg
Le Havre

N

FRANCE

in and at 0900 on 16th December the official commissioning ceremony was performed aboard. The White Ensign again unfurled to
mark the transition from a Reserve Fleet vessel to an active service
fighting unit. At 1120 that morning Younghusband cleared the lower
deck and addressed the ship's company for the first time as a complete unit.

On 19th December 1939, His Majesty the King visited
Portsmouth Dockyard on a morale-boosting trip and inspected several ships there. Although the little old *Wild Swan* was not favoured
with a visit, the ship's company fell in on the jetty and cheered the
King as he passed. It was on this day that the Navigating Officer was
appointed to the ship, Sub-Lieutenant Patrick G. Satow, who, at the
tender age of twenty, was given the awesome responsibility for plotting her course through the unknown and dangerous waters of war.
Still, however, *Wild Swan* remained a stationary object beside the
dockyard wall as the first wartime Christmas was duly celebrated.
Thus passed 1939 and in came 1940. If the old year had been one of
tedium and frustration, the new year was to be one of the most eventful in the history of Great Britain and certainly for the majority of
Wild Swan's new crew.

It did not seem like that at first. The daily routine of a ship slowly
working up a new crew continued, while the worst winter for many
years gripped the nation in an icy mantle, and, across the North Sea,
caused postponement after postponement in Hitler's plan to commence his long-awaited offensive. New Year's Day saw the ship's
gun crews taken to Whale Island, the naval gunnery school, for practice and simulation shoots and this painstaking learning continued
under the hard eyes, and harder tongues, of 'Whaley's' petty officers
day after day. On 5th January *Wild Swan* actually moved out of her
berth to the North Corner jetty where a Fleet oiler came alongside
and pumped in the black oil fuel into her hungry tanks throughout
the day. Next morning an ammunition lighter took her place
alongside and 4.7-inch shells were swung inboard and passed down
to the magazines. She settled lower in the water; she was girding herself, preparing for the supreme test that awaited her.

If *Wild Swan* was not in the war, then war, or the results of war,
were all around her. On 8th January the great bulk of the battleship
Nelson entered harbour astern of her, high in the water, badly damaged by a magnetic mine in the Scottish fastness of Loch Ewe where
the fleet had been driven after Günther Prien's exploit in entering
Scapa Flow and torpedoing the battleship *Royal Oak*. Two great
ships, one sunk, one badly damaged, both inside their own bases.

Truly, the war was not 'phoney' at sea! The cold, clammy hand of death touched others close to the *Wild Swan* and cast its shadow over them. For example some of the D class destroyers, which she had last seen in China in 1934, finally arrived at their home bases. On 9th January *Wild Swan* had held off the old minesweeper *Saltburn* by tug and made fast again alongside the jetty and one of the D's, *Delight*, shifted berth from her port side. Her companion, the *Daring*, secured alongside also next day, and both D's remained in close company while they re-commissioned for their new duties. How could anyone imagine that within three weeks all aboard the *Daring* save one young sub-lieutenant, would be lost when she was torpedoed while turning at speed under helm at night, the ship rolling over and going straight to the bottom. The lottery of chance, which took one ship and her crew and spared another, was something they fortunately had little time to worry about during this thorough work-up. The effect of the new German 'secret' weapon, the magnetic *mine*, was already being painfully felt in the fleet. Not only had the fleet flagship suffered at the hands of this weapon; other fighting ships had also succumbed; the brand-new cruiser *Belfast* had her back broken, the destroyers *Blanche*, *Gipsy* and *Grenville* had all been sunk in the Thames Estuary. Clearly an antidote had to be found to this hidden menace.

The German magnetic mine was actuated by an increase in the vertical component of the magnetic field. If it was subjected to a field of 50 mg for a minimum period of five seconds it was detonated. The average total vertical magnetization of ships around the British Isles was around 90 mg so that by pre-setting their mines at 50 mg the Germans would achieve the desired explosion right below the ship's keel (mg = *milli-gauss*, one-thousandth of a *gauss*, which is one line of force per square-centimetre.).

Once this setting was unlocked the remedy was clear. But a trials vessel was required, and quickly. Just across the harbour from HMS *Vernon* an entirely suitable vessel was available: *Wild Swan*!

Patrick Satow describes what took place:

> Measures were taken in January 1940 to minimise the risk of our ships setting off magnetic mines which might be lying upon the sea bed. *Wild Swan* had some heavy duty electric cables wrapped around the outside of her hull. A powerful current was passed through these cables, which were slowly raised and lowered verti-cally to reduce the strength of the ship's magnetic field.
>
> Specially designed detection loops were placed on the sea bed of the Solent, between Portsmouth and the Isle of Wight, to assess

the effectiveness of this treatment, or 'wiping' as it became known. The ship had then to be steamed on a very accurate track across the loops, and the results obtained were studied by experts from nearby HMS *Vernon*. If they were not satisfied with the way a ship had been wiped, the process would be repeated using a different strength of current through the big cables.

Although warships had gyro compasses upon which they depended almost wholly for their navigation, it was essential also to have a dependable old style magnetic compass with which to check the gyro. It would also be needed in any emergency such as action damage or a power failure.

As the wiping of a ship had a considerable effect on her permanent magnetic field, it was necessary for the compasses to be re-checked before going out to sea. The intensity of these degaussing trials, and the thoroughness with which they were conducted, may have been instrumental in ensuring that *Wild Swan* had a somewhat charmed life over the next two years, during which she was working in many hazardous areas subjected to mining by the enemy.

The initial loop course was laid along the old torpedo firing range at Stokes Bay and it was up and down this beat that *Wild Swan* sped to test the effectiveness of her degaussing coils.

Tests of a more realistic nature were now demanded and a second loop course was laid across the Solent. Such was the secrecy of these trials that, to conceal them from the enemy air reconnaissance, they were ordered to be run at night with an escort of Coastal Command aircraft as added insurance. In addition to these special trials normal trials had to be fitted in during the daylight hours to prepare her for more usual duties. The crew were now beginning to work as a team but, although her weapons systems had yet to be evaluated, her new boilers and engines needed a proper run to settle them in. Thus at 0815 on 16th January *Wild Swan* proceeded out of harbour again with no attempt at concealment and at 1003 she commenced a full power speed trial on the measured mile off St Catherine's Point, Isle of Wight. Three runs in all were required by British destroyers, the main average being taken as her best speed. She was over twenty years old, no longer a racehorse, but she put on a brave enough show for a veteran. Her second run was delayed for a time due to the hazard of a floating surface mine, one of the many which littered the Channel after every storm.

While the trial had been completed, loading of ammunition and other essentials had been interrupted, and the completion of this now took place, a tug towing her round to B lock on 19th January for the coils to be examined, and from there she moved to No 3 basin in berth 6 to complete working up. The final members of her complement were still arriving at this period, among them, on the 21st, her 'Doc', Surgeon-Lieutenant J.M. Couchman, BM, BCH, MRCS, LRCP, and she remained at Portsmouth for the rest of the month.

It was not until the middle of February that *Wild Swan* headed out down Channel towards Portland to undergo yet more trials and degaussing tests. By this time she was carrying a new Gunner (T), Acting, A.B. Clark and a young midshipman, or 'Snottie' as the service charmingly christens them, a Royal Naval Reserve 'Middie', R.R. Tett, who was appointed on 2nd February. He proved a popular addition to the mess in a period marked by yet more intensive effort by everyone aboard. *Wild Swan* was at Portland from 16th to 25th February and each day was a hard slog, as W.K. Harrison, at that time a young signalman, recalled:

My recollections of this period are ones of sea trials, gunnery exercises and generally getting the old ship seaworthy and fighting fit. I worked alongside such people as Chief Yeoman of Signals Charlie Burton, Signalmen. Plant (known to us as 'Signalman Plant'), Ted Maronie and Wolfe –

Patrick Satow detailed just what working-up at Portland involved thus:

This comprised a number of days at sea in coastal waters, testing all the machinery, equipment and armaments to ensure correct and efficient operation. It usually includes a trial of the engines running at full power, coupled with the ship making severe alterations of course. Also in the programme would be some emergency stops by ordering the engines to full astern. Guns are fired, and then maybe a telephone fails to work. All these problems have to be located and put right to ensure as far as possible that nothing goes wrong on the day, when everything is needed in action.

With all the modern aids now fitted in ships, it has to be remembered that there was no radar onboard at the start of hostilities. During this mid-winter of working up, the ship had to return to harbour one day in dense fog. The tidal streams around Portland Bill are strong, and the ship had to creep along close to the shore, using her siren to obtain an echo off the sheer cliffs, and so determine the distance. It was an eerie experience for the Navigating Officer, only twenty years of age, and in his first appointment with this responsibility.

Leading Stoker H.J. 'Florrie' Ford recalls:

She was a grand old ship and her crew were splendid. I thought life aboard her was great and we all worked well together and made things as happy as they could be in the circumstances. I thought the officers were very good and most of them helped the crew in many little ways. Life was very overcrowded, she had a far larger crew than originally built for and we had to sleep where we could when at action stations. But we managed to pull through even in the really bad weather of that winter.

The new boilers served her well and her engines did not let her down very often despite her age. She could still steam along quite happy at 26 to 30 knots although she rolled her guts out in any kind of sea.

Finally came the day when even the Admiral in command of the Portland base expressed satisfaction with *Wild Swan* and her crew. She was as ready as she would ever be now to face the enemy. On 25th February she left Portland for Plymouth to join the 18th Destroyer Flotilla.

*

And so to war! The war in the South-Western Approaches was an anti-submarine war. The Commander-in-Chief, Western Approaches, was based ashore at Plymouth and had several flotillas of old destroyers and some sloops under his control, of which the 18th Flotilla was one. The general area in which they operated at this period of the war lay south of Ireland out beyond Bantry Bay and Land's End, and covered the approaches to the Irish Sea through St George's Channel and Bristol Channel. Convoys had been organised to protect the shipping plying these routes, but only limited protection could be given owing to both shortage of numbers of destroyers and their lack of endurance.

Convoys of ocean-going vessels proceeded out from the major

port, London, passed down-Channel in OA convoys from Southend, as did those bound for Gibraltar, OG convoys. Another series of such ships started their journeys from Liverpool, passed down the Irish Sea and out through the same funnel south of Ireland; these were the OB convoys. The limited protection which *Wild Swan* and her consorts could offer to such ships extended only to the longitude of 12½° West and latitude of 47° North if heading down across the Bay of Biscay. Generally the destroyers would take convoys out to these parameters and rendezvous with inward-coming convoys, taking them back towards Britain, in a continuous shuttle.

In March there were six U-boats active in the South-Western Approaches, three attacking shipping, three laying minefields. Western Approaches Command tried several times to locate and destroy these U-boats, but without success. *Wild Swan* herself took part in many of these abortive hunts. But what took its toll more than any enemy action was the wicked North Atlantic weather.

The ship rolled so much that even on the bridge I would secure myself to the stays with a halliard. The daily routine was to wake up in the morning – count the ships in your sector of the convoy and report to the Captain how many were missing. We would periodically leave the screen to hunt U-boats. We would get good 'pings' and bad 'pings' and would drop depth charges. It was the Captain's decision as to how long we would carry on with an attack. Lieutenant-Commander Younghusband had to weigh up in his own mind what confidence he could place in each echo from the Asdic against the desperate need for us to return to the screen and plug up the gap we had left.

So recalls Signalman Harrison. He goes on:

We always had to seek Captain (D)'s permission to leave the screen so that the destroyers left could adjust the pattern to stop U-boats slipping through. We were aware that submarines might deliberately lure us away in order to leave such a gap for their comrades. But, U-boats apart, the weather always seemed atrocious with the ship wallowing and the lower mess decks two feet deep in water all the time. The communications branch and the stokers who occupied these mess decks had to live in our hammocks for the duration of many such trips, when not on watch.

It was quite normal to move about the mess by walking on the

mess tables! We even ate our food in our hammocks. I have never
suffered from sea-sickness but many of my comrades did. This
sometimes benefited me in bad weather as they would happily
give me their tot of rum. This helped keep the cold and damp out
on occasions. I usually had to collect the food from the galley on
behalf of my messmates as they would be under the weather.

While she was battling homeward in such atrocious conditions that
Wild Swan suffered her first tragic loss. The young midshipman from
South Wales failed to arrive on the bridge for the Middle Watch
(0001-0400). By the time it was evident that he was missing, the ship
had probably gone ahead for some five miles, and perhaps twenty
minutes had elapsed. Even if the ship had then been turned through
180 degrees, it might have been 45 minutes from the time he went
overboard until they were back at the approximate position. In the
heavy seas prevailing, a search at night would have been utterly
hopeless.

> We asked permission to leave the screen the next morning and
> went back to look for him. We all knew it was hopeless. Nobody
> could have survived in those seas for that long.

Midshipman Tett was lost on 1st March while *Wild Swan* was returning from escorting an armed merchant cruiser to the westward.
Within a day she was back at sea again from Plymouth hunting submarines. A report had been received from the steamer *Ackland Star*
that she had sighted a U-boat in position 49°. 26′ N, 7°. 27′ W. This
position, some fifty miles WSW of the Scillies, was close enough for
the sloop *Leith*, escorting a convoy, to be detached, and the
destroyers *Wild Swan* and *Versatile* were also sent to hunt at 1907 that
evening.

Leith, meanwhile, had obtained a firm contact and attacked. The
contact then appeared to settle on the bottom and remained stationary. The sloop held this contact throughout the night and on the
morning of the 5th another destroyer, *Venetia*, joined her, followed a
little later by *Wild Swan*.

More destroyers were detached by Western Approaches Command – the *Veteran*, *Volunteer* and *Whirlwind* – in response to yet
another sighting report. This time it was from aircraft N9028 which
reported dropping eight bombs on a U-boat, only one of which
exploded, at 1835. After the aircraft landed its crew were questioned

about this attack and at 2320 the destroyers were informed that in the view of Western Approaches this was considered a very doubtful contact – it was probably a whale. *Whirlwind, Volunteer* and *Veteran* were therefore diverted to join a convoy leaving *Wild Swan* to continue the attacks on the other, stationary, target. These attacks had continued throughout the whole day with little to show for it, as the following signals indicate:

Wild Swan to C-in-C, WA: Attacked U-boat 1400 today in 49°26′N, 07°20′W, photographs taken. Also attacked a contact at 0024 with *Leith* in 49°27′N, 07° 33′ W. Diesel oil reported on surface.
   Wild Swan to Leith: 0647. Target is moving. Am attacking.
   C-in-C, WA to Venetia: 0746. Are you still in contact?
   Venetia to C-in-C, WA: 0845. Still in contact. Target has not moved. Intend dropping two more patterns. Leaving vicinity to rejoin convoy at 1200. Oil still coming to surface.
   Versatile to C-in-C, WA: 1000. Four more patterns dropped this morning. Target is stationary, leaking oil.

When the others had departed a bucket was lowered from *Wild Swan* and samples of the oil were brought abroad and analysed by Mr Derbyshire to see if they could be confirmed as U-boat diesel or not. Younghusband was convinced that they had damaged a U-boat and vigorously pressed his claim later, but C-in-C, Western Approaches, Admiral Sir Martin Dunbar-Nasmith, .., was not convinced as was indicated in his signal later that day: '2358. Contact is considered to be a wreck.'

Two false trails in as many days. It seemed as if the South-Western Approaches were alive with submarines at that time, and there was another false alarm the next day.

Wild Swan reached Plymouth late on the 6th and refuelled but almost at once the hue-and-cry recommenced. There was report of a contact some eight miles from the Eddystone Light, *Wild Swan* was ordered to raise steam, 'With all despatch', and with *Eskimo* and *Vanessa*, also informed, to join the anti-submarine yacht *Maid Marion* in the attack. Again they took over the hunt from the yacht and dropped one depth charge on a possible contact but had reluctantly to conclude that this was yet another 'non-sub'.

Wild Swan returned to Plymouth, refuelled again and then they were off up the Channel once more with the flotilla leader *Broke* to pick up a convoy of eighteen ships sailing from St Helen's Bay, Isle of Wight. During 9th March they were joined by a further seventeen

ships from Milford Haven escorted by *Winchelsea*; the combined mass
of shipping was painstakingly marshalled into an OG convoy and
escorted by the three destroyers to about 47° N where it was taken
over by a French destroyer escort from Brest. On their way in the
usual appalling weather the inevitable signal arrived. A U-boat had
been reported to the south-west of Land's End, *Broke*, *Wild Swan* and
Winchelsea to hunt.

> *C-in-C, WA*: 2300. 49°N, 8°W (230°Scillies, 85 miles).* Possible contact,
> indefinite.
> *C-in-C, WA to destroyers: Broke, Wild Swan, Winchelsea*. Attack.

They were off again. There was no doubting the fact that there were
U-boats operating in these waters at this time, principally on
minelaying missions though with torpedoes to use on targets of
opportunity. The Atlantic convoy HG21 was in the area, escorted by
the destroyers *Velox* and *Vidette*, but the U-boats steered clear of these
and searched for easier targets. In the early hours of 11th March, at
0317, the *U-28* (Lieutenant-Commander Günter Kuhnke) sighted a
lone merchantman in 48°35'N, 08°22'W and slammed a torpedo into
her. Satisfied, he crept away. His victim was the neutral steamer
Eulota, a 6,236-ton Dutch motor tanker proceeding in ballast about
her lawful affairs. Although mortally hit and broken in half she did
not immediately sink.

For the whole morning the crew fought to save their ship but there
was no hope. At midday an aircraft was sighted overhead. Fortunately it was French and they signalled their plight. At 1240 the news
that a Dutch freighter was sinking some 120 miles south-west of the
Scillies was passed on by C-in-C, Western Approaches to the
destroyers and, while *Winchelsea* continued to the original contact
position, *Broke* and *Wild Swan* swung round on their errand of mercy.
At 1725 that evening, they found the victim. The main section of her
hull had sunk but her bows section was still afloat and, in heavy seas,
Younghusband skilfully rescued the entire crew before *Broke* sent
the bows to the bottom with gunfire. Patrick Satow still has a sou-
venir of that first rescue, a lifeboat from the *Eulota* presented to him
by her grateful captain and inscribed by the officers and men of the
tanker.

Joined by the French destroyers *Capricieuse* and *Frondeur* the

* On a bearing of 230°, 85 miles distant.

destroyers searched carefully for the submarine but without success. Then it was back to Plymouth to refuel, and up to St Helen's Roads to collect yet another OA convoy. At Plymouth they were joined by Midshipman L.W. Green, who arrived to replace the ill-fated Tett. He quickly fitted in and was soon to prove his mettle.

Earlier in the month the submarine *U-29* (Lieutenant-Commander Otto Schuhart) had been playing havoc with coastal shipping sinking three ships and claiming (falsely) a fourth before laying a minefield off Portsmouth. When *Wild Swan* arrived on the 14th this U-boat had been reported off St Catherine's Point on the extreme southern tip of the Isle of Wight and the destroyer *Hero* was busy hunting her. *Wild Swan* was at once ordered to go to her assistance but although again she searched diligently, no trace of a submarine was found. That afternoon *Wild Swan* left to refuel at Portsmouth before joining her convoy and that night she escorted it down-Channel on the first part of its journey without incident.

We know now that most of the U-boats had been recalled but as they left they were reported and the alarms and excursions continued in the Channel unabated. Early on 15th March *Wild Swan* arrived at Portland from Plymouth to carry out yet another set of degaussing trials to improve the equipment in the light of further research but a report came through that a U-boat had been reported at 1054 some 17 miles due south of the Needles. The destroyer *Isis* and the anti-submarine yacht *St Modwen* were already following this up. The original report had come from a civilian aircraft and *Wild Swan* and *Hero* were despatched at 1157. They were rewarded by a possible contact by the latter south of the Isle of Wight that afternoon and an attack was duly carried out by both destroyers. The only result was 'a slight trace of oil' and *Hero* lost contact. A night sweep was organised with *Isis*, *Wild Swan*, *Hero* and other anti-submarine forces sent out from Portsmouth. They combed the area between the Needles and Anvil Point but came up with nothing.

So the wild goose chases continued. They were kept at full stretch but the enemy was not there. On 28th March *Wild Swan* and *Havant* were sent to search for a U-boat reported in 50° 45′N 7° 0′ W. Plymouth signalled that this was, ' . . . an unreliable fix. May be returning up-Channel.' An Anson aircraft of Coastal Command was also sent out to co-operate with the destroyers, but nothing was found.

April came in. Nine days later Denmark and Norway were occupied in sudden thrusts by German forces.

At sea *Wild Swan* was still hunting ghostly submarines. On 7th April the steamer *Ulster Monarch* reported having sighted a surfaced U-boat some 37 miles north-east of Cape Barfleur. Although the report was considered unreliable by Western Approaches, it could not be ignored. *Wild Swan* escorting convoy OA124 and *Windsor*, escorting convoy SL25A, were both detached from their respective screens and sent to search. Nothing was found.

On the 15th a convoy was proceeding down-Channel in thick fog when two of the vessels, *Queen Maud* (Convoy number 41) and *Fort Hunter* (61) were in collision. The latter managed to head for Southampton, keeping close inshore, but *Wild Swan* was detached to keep close escort on the crippled *Queen Maud*. She reported at 0746: 'No immediate assistance required unless weather worsens.' It did not, but as the days grew longer the ominous stirrings on the Western Front grew greater. There seemed little doubt that Holland and Belgium were in Germany's way and that she would have no second thoughts about treating them in the same brusque manner as her Scandinavian counterparts when the time came. Plans had been secretly drawn up to prepare for the worst.

On 17th April *Wild Swan* received a signal from Plymouth which read: '1114. *Windsor* to escort OA.132 in place of *Wild Swan*.'

With *Whitshed* and *Verity* she turned her slim bows towards the Straits, and her destiny.

CHAPTER TWO

At The Hook
May 1940

Little has been written of the part played by the Royal Navy, and the Royal Netherlands Navy, in the fall of Rotterdam in May 1940. The Official Historian of the war at sea could only cover the role of the British destroyers there briefly. Other historians have tended to dwell on Dunkirk at the expense of other equally important operations at this time. *Wild Swan* was involved with all these hasty exits in the summer of 1940 and their story is told from her viewpoint here, but with much new information on these naval operations.

When *Wild Swan* joined the port of Dover on 18th April, she became part of the 19th Flotilla. Officially Dover itself was contained within the organisation of Nore Command under the control of the Commander-in-Chief, the Nore, Admiral Sir Reginald Plunkett-Ernle-Erle-Drax. But, in a typically British way, Dover itself had its own Flag Officer, Vice-Admiral Bertram H. Ramsay, who operated semi-independently. As a complication, when the plans for blocking the ports of Belgium and Holland had been drawn up and approved in October 1939, Dover had been detailed as responsible for the blocking of Dutch ports, while Nore remained responsible for minelaying operations off that coast, which were an integral part of the blocking scheme.

At Dover the signs of tension were reflected in the comment made in the War Diary of 1st May the day Holland went on full combat alert:

> There were also received from the Admiralty reports originating from the British Naval Attaché at the Hague which indicated possible developments in that area. Shortly after mid-day orders were received from the Admiralty that all destroyers were to be brought to immediate notice for steam. Captain (D) 19 in HMS *Keith* was recalled from patrol so as to be on hand to take charge of destroyers in case of developments, and was relieved by HMS *Wild Swan*.

Wild Swan took over what was known as the North Goodwin Patrol, which had been regularly carried out since the outbreak of the war. Convoys passed through The Downs in well-regulated series; many other coastal ships anchored there in the lee of the sandbars as they had done since time immemorial. The minefields laid to bar the U-boats were backed up by nets and screens of patrolling trawlers and drifters, much as with the Dover Patrol of World War I fame. To protect these ships against a surprise intrusion by the enemy two destroyers constantly maintained a beat up and down across the swept channels north of the Straits.

As a prelude to their planned assaults, the Germans were stepping up their aerial minelaying activities with operations by *Fliegerdivision 9*. Considerable air activity was reported on the night of 1st/2nd May and as a result of their labours the ports of both Calais and Dunkirk were closed owing to mines. Dover was left unmolested and although the sound of aircraft engines was loud overhead during the night, no planes were actually sighted by *Wild Swan* on her patrol. This pattern continued over the next few days but as the crisis point had come and gone without result and as *Wild Swan* had now been steaming hard for almost three months without a break, it was decided to give her a boiler-clean while there was still a lull. Accordingly, on 6th May, she entered the Submarine Basin at Dover with the minesweeper *Skipjack* to have this done. Never was there better timing.

May 1st may have been a false alarm, but time was indeed running out for the low countries and the Allies. *Wild Swan*'s boiler-cleaning took three days and she was undocked on the 9th ready for action once more. Action she was certainly to get, for that night the Germans poured over the borders of Holland, Belgium and Luxembourg. Although the Dutch had confidently expected that they could hold normal ground assaults by flooding vast areas of the homeland and retreating intact behind these impenetrable water barriers, in practice the modern German army, spearheaded by overwhelming air power which closely co-operated with the land forces, proved unstoppable. Here and there spearheads were held up, vital bridges held, counter-attacks launched, but overwhelming use was made of dive bombing in close support, to break any such resistance. Moreover positions considered impregnable were outflanked by the lavish use of parachute and glider troops which caused considerable confusion in rear areas.

On the morning of the 10th the bomber *Geschwader* KG.4 crossed the Dutch frontier at first light and struck hard at the airfields of Schipol/Amsterdam, Ypenburg/Hague and Waalhaven/Rotterdam. The Dutch defences were on the alert and ready for them in the air and on the ground. Some casualties were inflicted but the bulk of the bombers got through and delivered their deadly cargoes.

The attack was devastating and was almost immediately followed up by the 7th Airborne Division, whose job was to secure the airfield for the landing of the transport planes containing the tough troops of III/IR 16 under Lieutenant-Colonel Dietrich von Cholititz. Once Waalhaven was secured they were to advance into the heart of Rotterdam and secure the vital Maas bridges for the arrival of the 9th Panzer Division attacking from the Rhine at Duisberg.

Even as the airfield fell further German reinforcements were on their way by air. This time they flew up the New Maas waterway into the centre of Rotterdam itself, six seaplane aircraft from each direction, hugging the water to avoid detection, and, with breathtaking audacity, landed close to the vital Willems bridge. Quickly they landed sappers and storm-troopers in rubber boats and the Willems, Leeuwen and Jan Kuiten bridges were seized and held along with the rail viaduct. Here they resisted counter-attacks with III/IR 16, fighting their way up from Waalhaven to take the other bridges to Maas Island. So much for the audacious German invasion moves at Rotterdam. The objectives had been seized, but could they be held long enough for the Panzers to come up in support?

Efforts had to be made to dislodge the 1,200 troops holding the airfield and the handful at the Willems bridge. And all the while fresh troops were being continually flown in by the Luftwaffe. Not surprisingly there was considerable chaos and confusion. Communications between the Hook and Rotterdam and between both places and The Hague were mainly by phone, but as street fighting was taking place in both cities the situation was totally confused. Speculation of attack and counter-attack, of new enemy landings and of false victories all filled the airwaves and led to a weird atmosphere of 'controlled panic'.

It was into this bedlam that *Wild Swan* sailed later that same day.

The operational plans to carry out blockings and demolitions at The Hook had been issued by Vice Admiral Ramsay at Dover as late as 7th May, although earlier plans had been laid the previous October. Four destroyers were earmarked to carry demolition parties, codenamed Operation 'XD': *Brilliant, Verity, Whitshed* and *Wild Swan*. The latter was destined for The Hook and she had, in addition, to carry over a British Military Mission to co-ordinate events with the Dutch army.

The objectives of the demolition party 'B', led by Commander J.A.C. Hill, were to destroy vital installations like oil tanks, gun emplacements, mine and torpedo stores and lock facilities at The

Hook before the arrival of the enemy. In all there were 96 men, both naval personnel and men of the Royal Engineers who were to divide their attentions between The Hook and Rotterdam itself. These, and their stores, were embarked at Dover and their equipment was struck down below to avoid confusion with the Military Mission's stores, which had to be stowed on deck. The Mission itself, however, had failed to arrive by midday. The other three destroyers had already sailed, and, not wishing to delay any further, Younghusband sought, and received, permission to sail without them. Their passengers were given a hot meal on the way over, probably the last good meal they enjoyed for several days. By 1630 after an uneventful passage, *Wild Swan* had reached the point of arrival off the long moles that stretch out into the sea forming a half-mile entrance to the Hook itself.

Younghusband had already received a series of signals from V/A, Dover, informing him of what was known of the continually changing events ashore. Magnetic mines had been laid in the entrance, Waalhaven airfield had been occupied, German troops were reported advancing alongside the left bank of the Maas. It was not an encouraging picture.

A German reconnaissance aircraft was sighted, and, a little later a large squadron of dive bombers. They ignored *Wild Swan* and directed their attacks against *Whitshed* who was further out to sea heading up to Ijmuiden. Younghusband's decision was made immediately, 'I decided to attempt to enter the Hook'. Patrick Satow recalls that:

> This was the first of many missions of great urgency, which taxed the physical endurance of all onboard to their limits. Arriving alongside in broad daylight, a word was seen painted in huge white letters on the wharf; it was 'VELKOMMEN', or of course, 'Welcome'. Unfortunately there was no time for any fraternisation with the friendly Dutch people, because the Germans were already dropping parachutists within sight of the ship, and just outside the port of Rotterdam. A warning had been received that some of them were dressed as women, nuns or even as clergymen!

As they neared the Whistle Buoy that marked the entrance to the harbour, a Dutch pilot boat (*Loodsboot 9*) arrived alongside and the pilot was duly embarked along with a Dutch Naval Officer who enquired who they were. Younghusband duly informed him adding that they were bringing a party to assist the local authorities and he

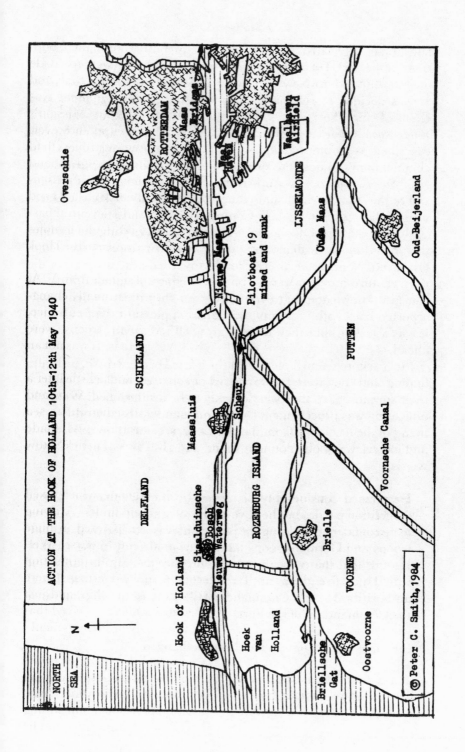

ACTION AT THE HOOK OF HOLLAND 10th–12th May 1940

NORTH SEA

N

Overschie

ROTTERDAM

Maas Bridge

IJsselmonde

Oud-Beijerland

Oude Maas

Waalhaven Airfield

SCHIELAND

Nieuwe Maas

Pilotboat 19 mined and sunk

PUTTEN

Schour

DELFLAND

Maassluis

Hook of Holland

Steelduinsche Bosch

Nieuwe Waterweg

ROZENBURG ISLAND

Voornsche Canal

Hoek van Holland

Brielle

VOORNE

Briellsche Gat

Oostvoorne

© Peter C. Smith, 1984

left, apparently satisfied. The pilot was then quizzed about conditions in the port. He confirmed that magnetic mines had been laid in the harbour and the New Waterway, but said he knew their location. It was decided to rely on their degaussing protection and take a chance before the Stukas spotted them. At twenty knots therefore, *Wild Swan* made a spectacular and what her captain himself described as 'somewhat hair-raising' entry the wrong side of the channel buoys to miss the suspected mines. Nothing happened and *Wild Swan* secured bows up-river to the Harwich (LNER) Quay where the train ferries usually docked. Ahead of her lay the Dutch torpedo boat *Z5* (Lieutenant-Commander W. van Lier).

Despite the ominous sight of German aircraft circling the harbour the unloading of the demolition party and their stores proceeded at full speed. None of the aircraft made any attempt to attack, nor did they venture into gun range, but the feelings of vulnerability, the constant knowledge that everything that they did was being duly reported back with impunity, was far from pleasant. Unfortunately it was a feeling that they were to grow all too used to in the weeks ahead.

Most ashore seemed pleased at the arrival of the British, no doubt hoping that they were the vanguard of considerable forces come to their succour. If so they were quickly to be disillusioned! While the unloading was proceeding a Dutch commander, the second-in-command of the local fort, Commander Logger, came aboard *Wild Swan* and interviewed both Younghusband and Hill. In Younghusband's words:

> He seemed considerably disturbed by the fact that we carried demolition parties but he gave us the local situation. He appeared to be confident of holding the place, but was worried by parachute troops and German troops landing from aircraft in the vicinity. He was told that we had come to prepare demolitions only, and would not fire them until requested to do so by the Dutch authorities. He and Commander Hill went ashore to confer with the Commandant of the Fort.

Meanwhile further signals had been exchanged:

> *V/A, Dover to Whitshed, Wild Swan*: 1720. Situation ashore at Ijmuiden and Hook obscure. German troops may be in vicinity, approach with caution.

It was certainly too late to comply with the latter request! Younghusband duly responded:

Wild Swan to V/A, Dover: 1752. Parties landed. Certain amount of aircraft activity from fighters and reconnaissance aircraft. No bombing locally. Northern side of channel is reported to be blocked by magnetic mines. Parachute troops in vicinity.

The saving of the Dutch gold reserves was high on the British Government's list of priorities, along with the rescue of the Dutch Royal Family, the saving of what shipping could be got away and the blocking of the harbours. The laying of the minefields was already in hand, by the *Princess Victoria* and the minelaying destroyers of the 20th Flotilla. The other parts of the scheme were put in hand immediately. From Harwich the 2nd Cruiser Squadron sailed under the command of Vice Admiral Sir G.F.B. Edward-Collins. They were to rendezvous with two Dutch merchantmen, with the gold bullion duly embarked, off Ijmuiden next day and escort it back to Britain. Unfortunately, during the confusion at The Hague, the exact identities of these two ships were not made clear but eventually the steamers *Iris* and *Titus* were duly found by *Arethusa* and two destroyers and brought safely in.

However this was not the sum total of the gold bullion at risk. There were no less than 36 tons of it lying at Rotterdam at the Netherlands Bank, under guard by worried Dutch officials and a detachment of Dutch Marines! Anxiety was felt for its fate and this was duly passed on down the line. . . The result was a signal from the Admiralty:

DOD (H) to Wild Swan: 1831. Dutch Foreign Minister states large amount of gold at Rotterdam. Estimated weight 36 tons. Essential to get gold away tonight. Make all arrangements in co-operation with local authorities. Gold to be loaded in merchant ships or *Wild Swan* as convenient.

Put like that it seemed a simple enough matter. No doubt in the bowels of Whitehall it seemed a simple enough request for Younghusband to comply with without further ado! The Admiralty expected all its captains to be resourceful, yet in the conditions then prevailing in Holland this request amounted to an invitation to suicide for *Wild Swan* and her crew. Divorced as they were from the realities of the situation, the Admiralty's further signals only added insult to injury.

Nonetheless Younghusband did his best to comply, within the dic-

tates of commonsense. Before the signal arrived at 1930 he had been
concerning himself with more immediate problems. No motor transport had arrived to take the Royal Engineers party to Rotterdam to
carry out their part of Operation XD. It was therefore suggested that
they be taken there by boat, since *Loodsboot 9* was available with a
pilot who knew the New Waterway and the location of the mines
readily on hand. It seemed the perfect answer. As none of the Army
officers was conversant with ships it was arranged that Commander
Hill take charge, handing his own team over to his second-in-command, Lieutenant J.W. Whittle. Both Hill and the Royal Engineers
commander, Captain Goodwin, departed to make the necessary
arrangements forthwith.

The Royal Naval party meanwhile was busy about their affairs
and started to place demolition charges under rolling stock at the station. *Wild Swan* also disembarked three of their depth charges fitted
for electric firing, with the necessary gear, to aid their efforts, and
plans were also made for the destroyer to fire torpedoes into the
northern breakwater if driven from the port by bombing or the arrival of German troops in force.

On arrival of the signal concerning the bullion another conference
was held aboard and it was decided, 'that in view of the time, tide
and known disposition of German troops, mines and the large numbers of enemy aircraft now about, that the pilot boat would have a
better chance of getting through.' Accordingly Commander Hill
took three of his naval party with him and, at 2015 that night, the little vessel chugged away up the Waterway. The plan was to tranship
the gold from the pilot boat to *Wild Swan* on her return and then sail
for England with it. Fate was to decree otherwise.

Problems were now descending on Younghusband's head thick
and fast. As soon as one crisis was surmounted, another arrived out
of the blue. Signalman Harrison describes the arrival of the next:

There appeared a party of what were clearly rich, or very highly
placed persons, either diplomatically or socially. They seemed to
be leaving with just what they had and most had heavy, bulging
suitcases. They were dressed in expensive coats with fur collars.

I walked over to the starboard side of the bridge and on the far
side of the harbour, about half-a-mile away, I could make out
what appeared to be German soldiers with rifles over their shoulders. There were perhaps two hundred of them in the field but

they showed no interest in *Wild Swan* and we let sleeping dogs lie and did nothing.

It is more likely that these were Dutch soldiers taking up positions against the German paratroops reported moving down the Water-way towards the Hook in large numbers. The party on the quay was a Dutch Naval and Military Mission, headed by Major-General J.W. Van Oorschot and consisting of Colonel Zegers, Lieutenant Voss, RN and Sub-Lieutenant Clay, RNVR. They asked Younghus-band for passage to England and he agreed to take them when he sailed. They had had a nightmare journey down from the Hague, having been travelling since 0500 that morning, and were exhausted hungry and thirsty. Their story only added to the general picture of confusion. Subsequent signals received at this time, did little to make things clearer as they were distorted. When re-sent they added yet another problem to Younghusband's list.

V/A, Dover to Wild Swan: 2136. *Wivern* arriving Hook at daybreak with Military Mission. Request for assistance from Dutch authorities against enemy landing by air at Waalhaven should be complied with by one or both destroyers as you think fit.

In view of the fate of the Dutch destroyer *Van Galen*, sunk by stukas at Rotterdam on the 10th, Younghusband had quite a lot of thinking to do.

Meanwhile the pilot boat had arrived at Lekhaven harbour at 2200 after a tense two-hour journey through German-held territory. Once ashore Captain Goodwin and Commander Hill set about establish-ing contact with the Dutch authorities to commence their respective tasks. This proved far from easy, as firing and fighting were going on and the whole of the southern bank of the river and the eastern part of Rotterdam seemed to be in German hands; the jitteriness of the Dutch authorities concerning the 'disguised' paratroops infiltrating their defences; all combined to frustrate their purpose.

The reason that their expected transport had not arrived at the Hook in the first place became apparent after they were both placed under arrest several times and then, finally, got to see the Dutch Commandant. Nobody locally had troubled to pass on to the Dutch news of their mission or indeed that they were coming! Leaving his engineers with his second-in-command, Goodwin had finally made his way round all his objectives but was unable to get permission to place his charges by any of them. All were protected by troops with machine-guns and unclimbable fences. Eventually the Dutch authorities told him to return to the Hook and that they would send for him if they required him. He commandeered some vehicles and, at 1030 on the morning of the 11th, set off.

Meanwhile Commander Hill and his three ratings convinced the wary officials that the 300-ton *Loodsboot 9* (Lieutenant Y. Smit, RNLNVR) was in fact to embark the gold bullion on the first part of its journey and loading commenced. The gold was packed in small crates and, even with the assistance of the Dutch Marines and the pilot boat's crew, it took a long while working through the night, to get it all stowed safely aboard. By 0430 on the 11th it was done and the little vessel cast off from Lekhaven again. Commander Hill and his ratings, along with many of the others, were totally exhausted and went below to get a little sleep, as did the captain and many of the 16-man crew.

Back at the Hook the situation in the early hours was that the Dutch Supreme Commander, General H.G. Winkelman, had expressed firm opposition to any large-scale demolitions being carried out at this time. He suggested spoiling the oil in the tanks rather than blowing them up and objected strongly to British plans to wreck the sluices and lock-gates as this would cause widespread flooding, with appalling results for his own people rather than the enemy. Nonetheless the Germans were pressing in closer and he allowed the naval party to start preparing. This was enough for Whittle who got his team to work right away.

Meanwhile there was a great deal of enemy air activity all through the night. This kept *Wild Swan*'s crew on their toes. They kept a close watch on the harbour entrance to make sure no fresh mines were laid, and, in the event, none were, but the night air was full of the sound of aero engines and flares, and it was believed that further reinforcements of paratroops were being dropped along the river bank. There was little bombing, although the pom-poms did engage one German aircraft which bombed a factory some 500 yards up-river.

For Younghusband, the ether was alive with messages from all quarters, which all finally ended up on his bridge for implementation! At 0215 on the 11th he received the following: '*DOD (H) to Wild Swan*: 0029. Contact Consul Rotterdam to ensure sailing of all British and Norwegian shipping forthwith.'

The only means of doing this was via the Dutch Commandant's direct phone link with Rotterdam. Younghusband went to the fort and, with the help of Lieutenant Voss, he got through to the Consul-General and passed the message on. He also asked that it could be passed on the link to the Naval Attaché at The Hague. Younghusband also made enquiries about Commander Hill but when the Consulate rang back to confirm the messages had been passed on he could give no news of the demolition or bullion party.

At 0300 another long signal came in, which reflected considerable agitation in high places:

VCNS* to Wild Swan: 0143. Following recently from Naval Attaché, The Hague. Urgent. No news of the two British destroyers promised to co-operate with Dutch. Street fighting in Rotterdam, situation precarious. Dutch ask that destroyers should go up and assist. Can instructions be given to *Wild Swan* to do what she can if local Dutch naval authorities advise that this is possible? Fighter aircraft should be in attendance.

Shrugging off his tiredness, Younghusband returned to the fort and, again with the help of Lieutenant Voss, got a direct call through to the Dutch Naval Authorities, both locally and at The Hague, and again offered to carry out a bombardment of Waalhaven airfield. After some delay Younghusband was politely told that this was not necessary as a Dutch counter-attack had being delivered from 0230 that morning and the situation was in hand. In any event there could have been no possibility of carrying out an accurate bombardment during the dark hours and a daylight attack was suicidal, 'they had seen what had happened to one of their own'. Nonetheless Younghusband put in a call to the Rotterdam Harbour Master asking for a pilot to standby in case such a mission was ordered later. From this worthy he received the welcome news that Commander Hill was loading the gold in the pilot boat at Lekhaven.

No sooner had the captain returned to *Wild Swan* than more immediate problems faced him. The Germans were moving in force on the Hook and at 0330 there was heavy firing by artillery and machine-guns on the right bank of the Waterway and at the back of the Hook itself. The possibility that *Wild Swan* would have to make a quick move necessitated the landing of the Dutch Mission. German soldiers were, at one stage, reported as being within 500 yards of the ship, but none was seen and nor was there any fire directed at her.

* VCNS = Vice Chief of Naval Staff. At this time this was Rear-Admiral Sir Tom Spencer Vaughan Phillips.

Dawn on this endless night was now fast approaching and Younghusband fully expected to be bombed to blazes at first light. Surprisingly no such air attack took place, possibly, he reasoned, because
the Germans expected the port to fall soon and wanted to preserve it
intact for their own use.

At 0415 the destroyer *Wivern* arrived off the harbour entrance but,
because of the heavy fighting ashore, Younghusband recommended
that the Military Mission ought to be landed in a safer place, and
Wivern was duly sailed to Flushing to complete her duty. At 0455 two
destroyers of the 2nd Flotilla arrived off the Hook Whistle Buoy from
Harwich; *Hyperion* and *Havock* were under the command of Commander H.St.L. Nicolson in the former, who now assumed the position of
Senior Officer and took some of the weight from Younghusband.

In order to prevent them suffering the same indignity as a Dutch
gunboat which had run aground earlier Younghusband signalled for
them to await the arrival of pilots before entering the harbour. Once
they had berthed, the pilot informed Nicolson that six magnetic
mines had been laid in the entrance and that two had exploded prematurely. Younghusband went aboard *Hyperion* and gave a full
report of events as far as he knew them in this fluid situation. A little
later the Dutch Commander J. Van Leeuwen and his staff also went
aboard *Hyperion* and stated that, despite the situation, the only support they required was AA fire.

At around this time there were grim tidings from up-stream. The
pilot boat had just reached that part of the Scheur marked by the tip
of Rozenburg Island off Vlaardingen when she detonated a magnetic
mine. There was a depth of water of about 14 feet at this point but the
explosion was confined by the narrow banks. The result was devastating and the little boat was split asunder and sank very quickly.
Lieutenant Smit, asleep forward in his cabin, the river pilot and the
steersman on the bridge, Commander Hill and his three volunteers
and the majority of the crew died instantly. The only survivors were
the mate, thrown from the ship's deck by the force of the explosion
and found unconscious later, and five young apprentices asleep in
the bunk-room right aft, away from the initial explosion. The bodies
of the rest went down with the remnants of the pilotboat and the 250
boxes, each of which held 1,000 gold ingots. The estimated value of
the gold was 22 million guilders – nobody put a value on the men who
perished trying to rescue it.

Loodsboot 9 was not the only victim of the magnetic mines in this stretch of the Waterway, however. Of the four ships at Rotterdam under British flags, two managed to get clear and sail to safety, passing down river and out through the Hook safely. The third was the steamer *Roek* (1,041 tons). She had sailed on the 10th, but had come to grief in the same way, almost at the same spot. Fortunately her crew survived, made their way back to Rotterdam, and then to the Hook and finally were evacuated to Britain aboard the destroyer *Mohawk* much later. The last British vessel, the 2,435-ton steamer *St Denis*, could not get clear and was scuttled to prevent her falling into enemy hands at Rotterdam docks on 12th May. Two Dutch destroyers building there shared her melancholy fate.

Back at the Hook events continued to unroll with bewildering rapidity. At the first opportunity Younghusband had informed Their Lordships of some of the realities of the situation yet again.

> *Wild Swan to V/A, Dover, C-in-C, Nore*: 0541. HMS *Wivern* is proceeding to Flushing to land Mission. Parachute troops are in close vicinity and communication with The Hague impractical. Dutch authorities have cancelled request to bombard Waalhaven airfield.

Fighting ashore was still continuing at full daylight. Lieutenant-Commander van Lier took *Z5* up-river, bombarding various buildings thought to have been occupied by the paratroops but, by around 0700, the firing had died away and there was little aerial activity either. All communication with the Hague and Rotterdam was most erratic, and the phones were reported to be 'tapped' by German sympathisers. At 0745 the first news came in from the Dutch of the tragedy off Rozenburg Island and Younghusband passed this on.

> *Wild Swan to Admiralty*: 0801: Dutch pilot steamer sunk. Struck magnetic mine off east end of Rozenburg Island. Believed gold was on board. No survivors located yet. Commander Hill was on board, proceeding from Rotterdam with evacuated gold. The wreck lies, as well as that of the SS *Roek*, near the entrance to Noord Geul. Major-General J.W. Van Oorschot, leading Dutch Military and Naval Mission is at the Hook awaiting transport to England.

The rest of the morning was relatively calm. The fight with the paratroopers had eased the Dutch attitude to the demolition party and Lieutenant Whittle and his party got steadily on with their work of preparing charges to be fitted at an instant's notice in the forts and

gun batteries on both sides of the Waterway. One of these gun batteries was bombed but most of the German air attacks were concentrated up-river in support of their troops still holding on in the city.
Any aircraft that strayed into range of *Wild Swan*'s AA weapons were
engaged, but without effect.

At 1230 yet another signal was received, from C-in-C, Nore,
instructing *Wild Swan* to bombard Waalhaven airfield. Once more
Younghusband attempted to comply. He notified Nicolson of his
instructions and again got in contact with the local Dutch
authorities. He was told firmly that such a bombardment was *not*
required as the airfield was re-taken and safely back in Dutch hands.
This however, proved *not* to be the case. Instead he was requested to
carry out a bombardment of the Staalduinsche Bosch, a large wood
some two miles up-river, where it was believed German parachute
troops had dug themselves in. This was duly reported to V/A, Dover.

Wild Swan to V/A, Dover: 1324. *Hyperion, Havock, Wild Swan* alongside.
Placing the parcels charged for local demolition should be completed by
1600. Little air activity. Local isolated groups of Germans in vicinity. No
details of Rotterdam party available. Am proceeding to bombard wood
to eastward of town at request of Dutch authorities.

Early the previous day German transports had been observed dropping parachutists in this area and another six transports had landed
in a polder south of the Staalduinsche Bosch, which was taken under
fire by army artillery. The Dutch estimated that about 200 to 250
men were entrenched there. *Wild Swan* took aboard a Dutch commander to direct fire and proceed up-river at 1345. Off the wood her
gunners were able to open fire for the first time in real anger from her
main armament, *Wild Swan* firing off some 66 rounds of high explo-
sive at a range of 2,500 yards. No sign was seen of the enemy during
this bombardment but during her return to the Hook more German
transports were observed dropping paratroops, about fifty in all, out
towards the coast to the north of the town. When he learned about
this Nicolson despatched *Havock* to patrol up the coast and engage
any enemy troops sighted on the sands to the north.

By teatime on the 11th the naval demolition party had completed
their preparations completely satisfactorily. The Dutch still
appeared confident of holding on despite being cut off from the
Hague and only partly in contact with Rotterdam. They were convinced that they were regaining control of that city. The Luftwaffe

was constantly active and *Wild Swan*'s pom-poms were in use from time to time, but no direct attacks had been made on the two destroyers berthed alongside, although *Havock* underwent a fierce assault while on patrol outside. About this time the military demolition party arrived back after their long journey from Rotterdam and for the first time the confusion and farcical conditions prevailing there during the night were revealed by Captain Goodwin, RE. This put a different complexion on the rosy picture still held by the local Dutch authorities.

Havock having returned to harbour for food, the officers were divided between the three destroyers and fed while the soldiers and stores were accommodated in a large shed on the Fruit Wharf. The Engineers were able to confirm that magnetic mines had been strewn liberally across the entrance to the docks at Rotterdam. Younghusband, Nicolson and Goodwin considered sailing the destroyers out from the Hook overnight, rather than risk being bottled up, or overrun by German troop advances after dusk, but finally decided that *Havock* alone should maintain a patrol outside leaving the others to support the Dutch.

Meanwhile other events were in train. In order to rescue the Dutch Royal Family and the Dutch Parliament from the Hague and carry them to safety in Britain, C-in-C, Nore had sailed Captain (D) 1st Flotilla, in *Codrington*, with other ships of that unit and he was concentrating all available destroyers in readiness for the attempt, codenamed Operation 'J' (for Juliana) next day. Accordingly Captain G.E. Creasy expected Younghusband to join him, but *Wild Swan*, having originally sailed from Dover, was not aware of these operations.

Meanwhile another request had been received from the Consul-General in Rotterdam, via the Naval Attaché, for two destroyers to proceed there at once to help the Dutch. In view of the further reports of magnetic mines Nicolson, as Senior Officer, was loth to risk his ships in this manner. He accordingly signalled the Admiralty to that effect, stating he had no intention of complying with that request, without approval. The reply, from Rear-Admiral Phillips, was received shortly afterwards: '*VCNS to Wild Swan, Hyperion*: 1640. *Wild Swan*, who is extra well degaussed, is to proceed to Rotterdam to communicate.'

This left Younghusband trying to figure how to place his ships in two different places at the same time. Further telephone conversations with the Dutch naval authorities in Rotterdam were hastily arranged.

Meanwhile fresh ideas were flowing from London in the face of growing evidence of Dutch collapse.

> *DOD (H) to Hyperion*: 1743. Could troops with light equipment be landed at Hook or thereabouts, with enemy opposition, at dawn?
> *Hyperion to Admiralty*: 1930. Yes, unless situation deteriorates rapidly. *Havock* will patrol off entrance during night. *Hyperion, Wild Swan* remaining in harbour.
> *DOD (H) to Hyperion, Wild Swan*: Object of force is to hold landing place at Hook so that further landings can take place unopposed.

In response to these signals a Royal Marine guard was quickly embarked at Dover and sent over to the Hook. A more substantial force of a battalion of Guards was to follow. The arrival of the Royal Marines aboard the destroyers *Verity* and *Venomous* was duly notified by London, giving Younghusband yet a third job to carry out.

> *VCNS to Wild Swan*: 1936. Landing of Marines: two destroyers from Dover to embark 200 RM's and take them to Hook, to arrive if possible, at dawn.

While this flurry was taking place the Dutch Military Mission returned on board *Wild Swan* again seeking accommodation for the night! Younghusband passed them along to Nicolson as he had enough problems of his own at that time. Nicolson later reported that the Mission, led by Major-General J.W. Van Oorschot, 'was glad to be aboard.' Meanwhile two minesweeping trawlers, *Arctic Hunter* and *St Melante*, fitted with 'LL' sweeps to detonate magnetic mines, had been sent over from England and duly arrived at the Hook. Nicolson sent another signal out which confirmed earlier decisions: '*Hyperion to Admiralty*: 1835. Naval Commander, Hook, has now cancelled request for destroyers to proceed to Rotterdam after communication with Chief of Naval Staff, Rotterdam.'

That was one headache out of the way again for a short while, but at 1900 that evening the Dutch Naval Attaché gave Nicolson an alarming résumé of the situation. Paratroops were active, dressed as Dutch troops and even women, he luridly stated. Another major attack was expected at any moment. Nicolson wasted no time. The *Hyperion* and *Wild Swan* prepared for action. Armed sections were positioned with rifles and Bren-guns both forward and aft aboard

HMS *Wild Swan* in her heyday. 3rd Destroyer Flotilla, Mediterranean Fleet.

(Left) Looking aft from the bridge, 'General Quarters' sounded off on a sunny Mediterranean day. Pom-poms crew closed up, with torpedo tubes trained both port and starboard; whaler on davits and carley floats in foreground. 1935.

(Below) Exercises off Malta, 1935. During the Abyssinian crisis the 1st Flotilla prepared to take on the Italian Fleet and continual torpedo-firing practice at high-speed targets was the order of the day.

each ship, the ship's Lewis guns were positioned so they could sweep the entire jetty. B and X mountings in both destroyers were fully manned, as were the close-range weapons which were above the level of the jetty. Both ships were duly warped out into the channel a few feet to prevent them being rushed. There was quite a considerable rise and fall of tide in the harbour and *Wild Swan* had been lifted and dropped several feet while alongside. Little was thought of this at the time but there was a horizontal rubbing strake fixed to the quay just under the water at high tide. Unknown to her crew the destroyer's starboard propeller had been badly damaged by the ship's motion up and down over this and twisted badly out of true in addition.

Meanwhile signals continued to be exchanged:

Hyperion to Admiralty: 2025. Your 1936/11. *Wild Swan* will be at Hook Whistle Buoy by 0400 Zone -1, tomorrow, Sunday, to meet destroyers. Air protection considered most advisable during disembarkation.

Those aboard *Wild Swan* had not yet seen a single Allied aircraft in the sky. Nicolson then clarified orders for Younghusband a little.

Hyperion to *Wild Swan*: 2231. Cancel previous verbal order. Be at Whistle Buoy at 0400 Zone-1, Sunday, to meet destroyers mentioned in Admiralty 1936/11. Lead them into harbour or transfer Pilot to Senior Officer whichever you consider advisable. While they are turning to bows out, support their landing.

At 0340 on 12th May *Wild Swan* finally slipped and proceeded to comply with above instruction; the pilot had failed to appear as requested and Younghusband sailed without him. At 0515 the *Venomous* was sighted and a signal was received that *Verity* would be delayed until 0600. Younghusband took *Venomous* in to the pilot ship and followed her in to provide her with cover; in the dawning sky two British fighters appeared for a few moments before vanishing to the west.

Wild Swan was then told to join *Havock* and maintain an AA patrol up the coast, between the Hook and Ijmuiden to protect Dutch shipping. Accordingly she turned yet again and headed out towards the harbour entrance. The time was 0625 and, as she reached the narrowest part of the entrance, one Stuka from a formation of three which appeared overhead out of the clouds, put in an attack dive. It was, in Younghusband's own words, 'beautifully timed and would have sunk the ship in a very tricky position in the channel.'

The destroyer was steering a course of 288° at a speed of twenty knots and was between the 1 and 2 Red Conical buoys at the harbour entrance when the bombs were released. There was only slight cloud, in which the Ju 87's had taken advantage to hide, with patches of alto-cumulus at 6,000 feet. The wind was north-west, force 3, the sea conditions dead calm and surface visibility a good fifteen miles. Even so the dive bomber was not sighted until he had commenced his dive, detaching himself from a *Kette* of three in clover-leaf formation and diving at an estimated angle of 65° from the starboard bow.

The angle of attack was too steep for the main armament to engage, but the pom-poms and Lewis got off a whole belt, without effect. In those confined waters there was no question of taking avoiding action; all Younghusband could do was ring the engine room telephone to 'full ahead' and put the ship's wheel hard to port, in order to take her clear of the main channel so that she would not block it if hit.

The Stuka released his bombs at 1,500 feet, a salvo of four small bombs, estimated at 100-lb weapons. They struck the water about fifty feet away abreast the bridge on the port side. Their delayed-action fuses detonated them under the water at a distance of about thirty feet from the ship, abreast of A gun. There was no direct damage caused, the splinters being absorbed by the sea, but the shock effect was considerable.

All the stay bars of both condensors started to leak at once and continued to do so steadily. The lead to the Asdic training motor under the hull was broken, but was repaired within half-an-hour. Several low power (LP) fuses were blown due to the close proximity of the explosion to the LP switchboard. Unharmed, but shaken up, *Wild Swan* proceeded out of harbour. Below decks the Mess Deck furniture and crockery were found badly smashed up and one or two rivets in No 2 Boiler Room started to weep. She had had a lucky escape.

As they left the harbour entrance Captain Creasy's destroyer *Codrington* was sighted and Younghusband closed him to ascertain the patrol zones, as his own lack of signal books made communication difficult. Creasy again ordered her to reinforce *Havock* which was then off Scheveningen.

Wild Swan had meantime intercepted signals from the Dutch gun boat *Van Nassau* reporting she was being bombed and as the position given was some nine miles north of her, Younghusband ordered *Havock* to continue her patrol while he went to investigate. It was when speed was increased to fifteen knots that severe vibration was felt all over the bridge; there was no time to investigate the cause, which was initially put down to the bombing. By 0855 *Wild Swan* had reached the position broadcast but the ship had continued northward and there were no signs of wreckage, only two Dutch torpedo boats heading north. Younghusband therefore turned back towards the coast and in so doing, it quickly became apparent that the starboard propeller was severely damaged. At a speed of twenty knots all the instruments on the bridge were made inoperational and damage was caused to the W/T office. Slowing down Younghusband decided to return to the Hook and report to *Hyperion*. As she proceeded down the coast once more there was little sign of fighting ashore by armies but the Luftwaffe was everywhere in the low cloud and several times *Wild Swan* opened fire. One bomber appeared to be frightened off by a burst of pom-pom fire, 'A rare feat for this weapon!' wrote Younghusband later.

In the interim *Hyperion* had signalled twice to the destroyers on patrol:

Hyperion to Havock, Wild Swan: 0935. Close Whistle Buoy with despatch.
Hyperion to Havock, Wild Swan: 1014. Stop *Zeeland* passing outside Whistle Buoy and order her to disembark troops at Hook into Pilot Vessel. Protect disembarkation. Orders from Naval Staff, The Hague.

But again, it was not *that* simple! Like most other messages during that frenetic period the details were incorrect. At 1010 *Wild Swan* steadily heading south passed the steamship *Prinses Juliana* which was carrying Dutch troops from Flushing to Ijmuiden. Twenty minutes later, as *Wild Swan* neared the Whistle Buoy, *Prinses Juliana* was seen to be under very heavy dive bomber attack. There was no sign of *Zeeland*, but, as Nicolson later was bitterly to recall, the reason for this was that *Zeeland* eventually turned out to be *Prinses Juliana*! There had been another mix-up in communications, and thus the *Juliana*, a twin-screw passenger ship of 2,908 tons, built in 1920 by Koninklijke Maats at Flushing, was caught by the Stukas without immediate protection.

She was laden, not only with troops, including a British military party, but also horses for she was transporting a pack-unit and cavalry troops as well. Built for the Cross-Channel packet trade and for European summer cruising, she presented a weird appearance thus laden, as Signalman Harrison remembers:

Eventually we got close to the sinking ship. She had an odd, square shape, similar to a Mississippi paddle-steamer. There were lots of dead and alive horses in the water, bodies and many survivors.

On seeing the attack, Younghusband altered course to close at the best speed he could which left the bridge habitable and as they closed they opened fire with both long-range 4.7-inch barrage and pom-poms at the Stukas that hung vulture-like above her and kept swooping down on her defenceless decks. As they closed so did other destroyers in the area, *Codrington, Hereward, Havock* and *Valentine*, the latter an old destroyer specially converted to an AA escort. The Stukas were diverted from their prey and turned their attentions to the newcomers, both *Hereward* and *Valentine* being heavily attacked, with no result. The Stukas then transferred their attentions back to the merchant ship. Captain Creasy wrote in his report:

> The unfortunate ship was the sole target. Destroyers closed her at high speed and tried to protect her as best they could by AA fire. The first four or five bombers missed her, but then she suffered a near miss to starboard and two or more hits to port.
>
> Dive bombers came in at a steep angle of 70° from 6,000 feet. Five bombs dropped from 1,000 feet. Such attacks made difficult targets but at least three aircraft were well shaken by our fire, one 'rocking' heavily and disappearing with the black smoke, so beloved by BBC Broadcasters, pouring from her tail.
>
> The sea was calm. *Prinses Juliana* abandoned ship, lowering boats, but as there were several Dutch trawlers nearby in the immediate vicinity destroyers continued to steam around *Princes Juliana* to protect her from further attacks. I ordered *Wild Swan* to rescue survivors and he* correctly interpreted my wishes by placing his bows alongside *Prinses Juliana* and taking off all the remaining survivors left aboard, and later picked up more from rafts and floats in the water. *Wild Swan* then proceeded to the Hook with her passengers.

One heavy bomb had hit the ship, but the main damage appeared to be caused by a salvo which had burst under her port quarter as she was making water aft. All her boats were lowered and filled to capac-

---

* In the Royal Navy signals and references always refer to the Captain by the name of his ship. Thus Younghusband was the *Wild Swan* mentioned in all signals while he was in command. If he were injured the same mode of address would apply to his successor in command automatically.

ity and these Younghusband told to pull for the shore as several trawlers were approaching. About thirty troops were left on the sinking ship with no way of escaping. Without hesitation Younghusband took *Wild Swan* in and, in a beautiful movement, laid his bows against the steamer's weather bow and the troops successfully jumped onto *Wild Swan*'s fo'c'sle. The two bows ground together briefly but the only damage the destroyer received was one small dent at deck level, which, commented the captain later, was '. . . fortunate in view of the conditions'.

Wild Swan then approached the men in the rafts and swimming, and picked up about forty. Some were non-swimmers, others in a bad way, and there were plenty of volunteers who went over the side and into the water to rescue these unfortunates. Chief Petty Officer A.E. Meadus, Petty Officers L.T. Howard and F.J. Pitcher, Leading Seaman R. Jackson, Able Seaman R.G. Townsend, Artificer J.G. Faulkner and Stoker W. Jackson, all showed what Wild Swans were capable of. It is thanks to them, and Younghusband's skilful ship-handling, that all seventy survivors were brought aboard. They only lost one, a Dutch engineroom fireman who was picked off a raft in a state of collapse. Despite artificial respiration and all that the ship's doctor, Surgeon-Lt Couchman, could do, he subsequently died.

Tugs and pilot steamers were arriving by the time Younghusband had completed this humanitarian task, although the ship herself still floated well. Leaving the work of salvage to them *Wild Swan* signalled the fact that the ship was intact and that horses were still aboard and that he intended to land the survivors at the Hook forthwith.

Among those rescued was Captain J.H.G. Goodwin, another officer and three 'other ranks' from the British Military Mission landed by *Wivern* at Flushing the previous day. Goodwin asked for some messages to be transmitted to the War Office and, when they disembarked, reported to *Hyperion* before leaving for the Hague. He informed Nicolson that certain confidential papers had been left behind in cabins 4, 5 and 6 of the *Juliana*, and *Havock* later boarded and retrieved these. But, in Nicolson's words, 'the papers were Dutch and not very confidential.'

When the survivors were safely put ashore at 1230 Younghusband was able to report his propeller troubles to Nicolson, but while doing so they received yet further signals from Britain.

C-in-C, Nore to Wild Swan: 1154. Proceed up-river and bombard Waalhaven Aerodrome if Dutch authorities concur. Armed drifters to sweep ahead of you if available.

Yet again Younghusband made his way to the Commandant of the Dutch defences. Again General Winklemann listened politely to his offer and for the third time he repeated that the Dutch authorities did *not* require Younghusband to hazard his ship on such an impossible mission. What they *did* require was the continuation of the coastal patrol. Younghusband stated that merely carrying out a bombardment of the airfield was an impracticable operation unless it was accompanied by permission to shoot up the oil tanks and other essential targets as arranged with Captain Goodwin. The Dutch Commandant again insisted that the time for this was not yet at hand. Younghusband reported the results of this conversation to Nicolson and returned to *Wild Swan*, to snatch a few brief hours of rest.

Hyperion to C-in-C, Nore, Wild Swan: 1335. Dutch authorities do not, repeat not, concur. This operation is not being carried out.

Hyperion to C-in-C, Nore: 1545. *Wild Swan* has developed a very severe vibration at 20 knots and excessive enough at greater speeds to cause damage to material. Trouble is in starboard shaft or propeller, cause unknown.

Out at sea Captain Creasy was beginning to concentrate his destroyers in readiness to carry out Operation J, the rescue of the Dutch Royal Family. He accordingly signalled: '*Codrington to Wild Swan*: 1638. Join me off Whistle Buoy at 1840, tonight, Sunday.'

Not understanding what this last part of the signal meant, Younghusband sent Lieutenant Whittle to *Hyperion* to get his orders before sailing. As he did so Captain Goodwin's Military party was seen passing up-stream aboard a tug on their way back to Rotterdam for a second attempt to carry out their orders. In view of the fate of the predecessor their bravery was admirable and happily they *were* successful in setting the oil tanks ablaze on the afternoon of 13th May.

CHAPTER THREE

Battle at Boulogne
May 1940

At 1830 on 12th May *Wild Swan* steamed out of the harbour at The hook for the last time and one strange interlude was terminated. She was complying with Captain Creasy's orders for her and *Hyperion* to concentrate with his other units in readiness to carry out the salvation of the Dutch Royal Family. Once, however, Captain Creasy was told of *Wild Swan*'s disability, he immediately detached her with orders to return to Dover forthwith.

As the *Wild Swan*'s captain wrote later:

I very much regretted being ordered away from the Hook without completing the job I had been sent for. It is however possibly fortunate in one way, for, as a result of strained condensers, boiler water was getting to a dangerous density.

In fact just getting *Wild Swan* back to Dover placed considerable strain on the engine room staff, and Younghusband was full of praise for Commissioned Engineer C.J.C. Derbyshire, Chief Petty Officer Meadus, TGM Petty Officer Howard, G.M., Artificer Faulkner and Leading Stoker 'Florrie' Ford, as well as the tireless efforts of the First Lieutenant, M.J. Lee.

They finally reached Dover at 0700 on the morning of the 13th and, as *Wild Swan* was going alongside the depot ship *Sandhurst* at 1430 that same afternoon, the machinery had to be stopped completely. Divers were sent down from *Sandhurst* and they reported that *Wild Swan* had broken the blade of her starboard propeller. This was a dockyard job; it could not be done by the depot ship. This meant a rest, no matter how short, for her bone-weary crew. But there was no rest for her captain yet. He repaired ashore and made a detailed report to Vice Admiral Ramsay. The gist of it was filed but one signal was made to the Admiralty in case there was any thought of holding on to the Hook.

V/A, Dover to Admiralty: 1143. *Wild Swan* reports that AA gun defence of Hook is essential if port is to continue to be used. Heavy air attacks would quickly decimate piers and vessels alongside would be very vulnerable.

On the 'Condenseritis' which finally brought his ship to a standstill Younghusband was forthright. 'Had the stay nuts been faced properly when the condensers were re-tubed by Portsmouth Dockyard in 1939 this trouble should not have occurred'. It would be expected that old boilers which had seen hard service over many years and many climes would become prone to this, but *Wild Swan*'s boilers had only just been replaced in the Royal Dockyard, hence Younghusband's exasperation at his ship being out of service at a crucial time.

Little time was spared, once her boiler's problems were patched-up, in getting *Wild Swan* away to the nearest dockyard capable of replacing her damaged propeller. It was to the friendly and efficient firm of Stone Manganese Marine of Blackwall on Thames that *Wild Swan* sailed on 14th May. By the 16th the job was done, the destroyer undocked and sailing back down-river. She rejoined Vice Admiral Ramsay's command on the 17th, good, if not better, than new.

During her brief absence Holland had fallen. Queen Wilhelmina was taken to safety aboard the destroyer *Hereward* at the Hook on the 13th, *Codrington* embarked Juliana and her family the same day and the Dutch Cabinet and Allied Legations reached safety aboard the *Windsor*.

One little nation had gone under, others were threatened. Worried eyes began to be cast at the French Channel ports, which were looking less and less secure.

Patrick Satow describes what Dover was like in these strange but stirring days:

The port of Dover, on the very south-eastern tip of the English mainland, was to become the scene of frenzied activity for several weeks, whilst the Germans continued their rapid advance westwards on land, through Belgium and right across France. Standing high up on the cliffs and overlooking the harbour, was the headquarters of Admiral Ramsay and his staff, who issued most of the orders to ships. Flashing lamps would call for the attention of the signalmen on watch. Many of the warships in Dover at this time were kept at very short notice; perhaps thirty minutes or less.

One or two might be at immediate notice to go to sea. All this meant that a ship had to be ready to leave harbour within the time stated. Everyone had to keep on their toes for instructions, such as; 'Proceed with the utmost despatch to . . . '

By 19th May, of the six Dover Command destroyers that had been sent over to assist the French in the blocking of and evacuations from Flushing and Antwerp only two remained operational.

On the night of 18th/19th it was the turn of *Keith* and *Wild Swan* to patrol the Goodwins beat once more. The Luftwaffe was fully aware of these regular exercises and duly paid them a visit right on schedule. At 0035 on Sunday morning, the 19th, a solitary aircraft attacked *Keith*, commanded by Captain D.J.R. Simpson, Captain D.4 and the senior officer of all Dover Command flotillas. The attack shook up the flotilla leader, but caused no serious damage. Either the same aircraft or a friend returned to the assault at 0605. The light was by then good enough for both ships to get good sight of him, and he was identified as a Dornier 17, nicknamed in Britain the 'Flying Pencil'. This bomber made a deliberate feint bombing run towards *Keith* and only at the last moment did it suddenly switch target to *Wild Swan*. This violent alteration in direction three off the aim of ship's gunners but also almost brought the German to grief, for his wingtip grazed the sea! His bombs all missed and he made a wobbly get-away back towards the Belgian coast.

On conclusion of the patrol *Keith* returned to Dover harbour, where she embarked the Chief of the Imperial General Staff (CIGS), General Sir Edmund Ironside, and took him to Boulogne. This left just *Wild Swan* to cover any emergency, and, sure enough, one was waiting for her. Earlier the *Saon*, one of a group of very excitable French armed trawlers that had a habit of depth-charging everything and anything, had reported a U-boat contact. She was busy attacking with everything she had and was joined by a host of other trawlers trying to get in on the act. On her way back from her patrol *Wild Swan* was ordered by Ramsay to join in the search and organise a proper hunt.

It is known that the *U-9* (Lieutenant-Commander Wolfgang Lüth) was active in the northern part of the Straits at this time, but a prolonged search by *Wild Swan* failed, in the end, to flush him out. Eventually the hunt was abandoned after 24 hours activity and *Wild Swan* returned to harbour leaving one trawler in the vicinity of *Saon*'s attack of the previous day. By the time *Wild Swan* had berthed and oiled and her crew cast their bleary eyes around the anchorage, other, greater, events were stirring.

Because of the uncertain position in France, from where the most alarming stories were circulating with German tanks reported here, there and everywhere, the passage of troop reinforcements was speeded up. As an additional measure, in order to have some kind of reliable link with the other side of the Channel, Ramsay despatched the armed yachts *Gulzar* and *Grey Mist* to Calais and Boulogne respectively to act as radio links. Meantime a brigade of Guards was embarking at Dover in two cross-Channel steamers, *Biarritz* and *Queen of the Channel*. Without waiting for them the *Wild Swan* was rushed across to Boulogne at full speed on 21st May. Some of her crew were allocated tasks as emergency demolition men with orders to help in the dock area as they could. Also embarked at this time were two medical officers from the Royal Naval Barracks, Chatham. They had been hastily rushed to Portsmouth and each officer had a section consisting of a sick-berth attendant and six stretcher-bearers.

At 0525 on the 22nd the *Biarritz* and *Queen of the Channel* followed her over with the first section of the Brigade of Guards and some material, being escorted by *Whitshed* and *Vimiera*, while the transport *City of Christchurch* with a cargo of tanks sailed later escorted by the destroyers *Vimy* and *Wolsey*. Finally, the personnel ship *Mona's Queen*, with the remainder of the Guards, sailed at 0948 under escort of *Venomous*. As well as the 20th Guards Brigade these ships had transported the Brigade Anti-Tank Company and one battery of the 69th Anti-Tank Regiment.

When *Wild Swan* arrived the port had been under constant air bombardment, but although *Grey Mist* had been attacked, she was not damaged. Ashore things were out of control. The scene that met the incoming destroyers and their Army passengers was almost indescribable. With the Germans pressing hard at their heels all discipline seemed to have collapsed among the defenders' ranks. The harbour was littered with abandoned cars and transport, the dockyard had ceased to function and the cranes could not be used to unload the cargo. Stragglers from all manner of French and British units, deserters and other such riff-raff, mixed with civilian refugees, all seeking sanctuary and safe passage to England. As the first ships docked there were some ugly scenes as this rabble attempted to storm aboard and they were only checked, and order restored, when the sailors from the destroyers and soldiers from the transports were organised by the Senior Naval Officer, Commander E.R. Conder, and the commander of the Guards into parties with fixed bayonets. Gradually they cleared the immediate area and the disembarkation of the Guards could proceed in an orderly fashion. Such a collapse boded an evil future for our armies ashore in northern France to Younghusband and his crew.

As soon as the troops had landed the two personnel ships were ordered back to Dover, taking aboard some of the 'unnecessary mouths'. Earlier that day *Wild Swan* herself embarked 150 British subjects for passage back to Dover almost immediately. The *Mona's Queen*, however, remained behind as it was not certain whether she would be required to unload her cargo or embark more refugees instead.

When she arrived back at Dover they found that the grave situation in France was fully reflected in the tension and activity there.

When the racing columns of German armour that spearheaded Army Group A's massive assault across the Meuse at Sedan and across the northern French plain, reached the English Channel at Abbeville at the mouth of the river Somme on the evening of 20th May, it cut off the bulk of the Allied armies.

The tip of this armoured juggernaut was General Edwald von Kleist's Panzer Group, operating under the command of Field Marshal Gerd von Rundstedt and supported by the Stukas of General Wolfram von Richthofen's *Luftflotte VIII*. By the 21st 2nd Panzer Division had reached the river Canche and, at midday on the 22nd, it crossed and crashed towards Boulogne in strength.

Opposing it by this time were the men of the Welsh Guards dug in along the town's perimeter. There was not much to back them up. The senior French naval commander had ordered his forces to evacuate the port on the 21st. On the 22nd the more resolute Commander Henry Nomy organised some defence with what artillery and garrison troops remained until General Lanquetot, with what was left of the 21st Infantry Division, took over. The arrival of the Guards brought about the stiffening required to hold the first German assaults but it could not stop them for long. Calais, to the north, was also threatened by a parallel attack by the 1st Panzer Division through Desvres and the Rifle Brigade was carried thither and ordered to fight to the last. All this was by no means clear to the men of the destroyers or to Admiral Ramsay and his staff trying to organise their limited forces against a series of conflicting instruc-

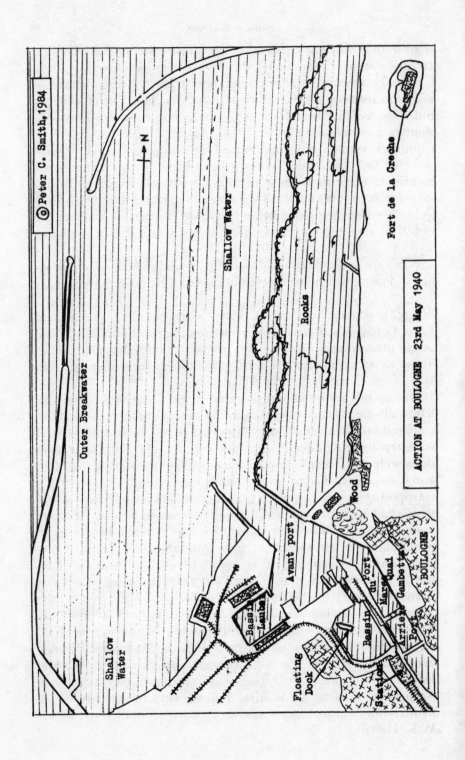

© Peter C. Smith, 1984

N

Outer Breakwater

Shallow Water

Shallow Water

Rocks

Wood

Bassin Loube

Avant port

Floating Dock

Bassin du Port

Maréchal

Arrière port

Station

Gambetta

BOULOGNE

Fort de la Creche

ACTION AT BOULOGNE 23rd May 1940

tions from Whitehall. It was the Rotterdam situation again, but on a far larger scale.

The first news Dover received of 2nd Panzers' advance was a signal from the *Grey Mist* at 2000 stating that enemy tanks were two miles south of Boulogne. This was followed by a second signal saying that she had been asked to bring away more refugees. As the Dover Command War Diary states:

> The situation in the vicinity of the French ports continued to be obscure and in varying degrees serious, the gravity of the situation being accentuated by an apparent demoralisation of the personnel, both British and French. At Dunkirk all confidential papers were burnt, an example followed by the BNLO; in regard to Calais the military authorities began considering complete evacuation and both service and civil refugees began to arrive; while at Boulogne evacuation continued and amongst other things the French coastal batteries were abandoned and troops were picked up from beaches outside the town and even from open boats away from the coast . . .
>
> Conflicting orders were received from time to time, first that Boulogne was to be evacuated entirely, and then that it was not; that demolition was to be carried out, followed by cancellation of the order.

It was against such a backdrop that the work of *Wild Swan* and her fellow destroyers should be viewed.

The initial need to evacuate non-fighting men and civilians was soon replaced by the need to ensure that all the French Channel ports were treated in the same manner as Rotterdam and the Hook and Ramsay's staff began planning new 'XD' parties and the ships to transport them. All these ports were now in range of the Luftwaffe which had been moving its airfields forward to accompany the German Army's advance and steadily the scale of air attack the ships were subjected to increased.

At Dover they found *Wolsey* and the hospital ships *St Helier* and *Solidarity*, and, on 22nd May the *Wild Swan* picked her way out of Dover harbour yet again and steamed towards Dunkirk where a large number of wounded were awaiting evacuation in these two ships. The destroyers had been carrying on for some days now at full stretch and there was to be no let-up, only ever-increasing intensity in operations. *Wild Swan* herself crossed and re-crossed the waters off Dover so often that they could have been running on tramlines. Accurate navigation under such conditions became increasingly difficult, but *Wild Swan* was never let down in this respect, as Signalman W.K. Harrison recalled:

We worked out of Dover for the various evacuations of French ports and for a period of many days were constantly shuttling backward and forward from Dover to France – 24 hours a day. Action Stations all the time – with the signalmen living and sleeping on the bridge. The ship's company were at continual action stations for about five days at a stretch in this period.

One man who gained the respect of the people on our bridge at this time was Sub-Lieutenant Satow, our Navigation Officer. On the continuous backward and forwards runs, bringing shiploads of soldiers back, we always seemed to pass close to a particular floating mine. On the way out it would be to starboard and on the way back it would be on the port side. We did not worry during the daylight hours as the lookouts would always spot it in good time, but at night there was some concern that they would not see it and would fail to warn us in time to prevent us hitting it. We always seemed to pass four or five feet from it (almost unbelievably).

The Captain would be sitting on his stool on the bridge in front of the binnacle with his duffle-coat on and he would say, 'Satow! We are coming up near that damned mine, are we not?' And Satow would reply, 'It's all right, sir.' Sure enough the lookouts would shout out, 'Mine on the port bow', and we would watch it glide by at the usual distance. Why we never gave it a wider berth I'll never know. Satow was, however, recognised as a very excellent navigator, even though the mine at night always gave the people on the bridge many secret worries!

Eventually, towards the end of the evacuations' period, when it seemed that, for once, we had a little time to spare, Younghusband decided to sink that mine. The ship this time pulled away to a safe distance and slowed down. The seamen were all lined up along the deck and shot at the mine with rifles until eventually someone hit one of the horns and it exploded with impressive force. It did, however, take about twenty minutes!

At Dunkirk they left the cross-Channel steamer *St Helier*, waiting to give her escort back, when loaded with 1,500 French and British evacuees. The Germans had commenced shelling the roadstead with field artillery, which caused some casualties. Gradually these light pieces were replaced by heavier calibre guns until, eventually, the southern approach route was made untenable. At this stage, however, it was still being used and the destroyers put in some brisk counter-battery work to keep the fire down. They were joined by the *Wolsey*, but before *St Helier* could sail a greater priority arose and sent *Wild Swan* scurrying south through the Straits to Boulogne once more. Here the German attacks were being held off by a large concentration of destroyers. The French had assembled a strong force consisting of the *Chacal, Cyclone, Bourrasque, Foudroyant, Fougueux, Frondeur, Jaguar, Mistral* and *Sirocco*, under the command of Captain Urvoy de Prozamparc. To the weight of their guns were added the *Wild Swan, Vimy* and *Keith*. Their success in stopping the Panzers naturally soon brought down the wrath of the Luftwaffe and air attacks were heavier throughout the afternoon.

In one of these attacks *Wild Swan* suffered her first war losses since March. A large bomb scored a near-miss close alongside. Although only minor structual damage was caused to the ship itself by bomb splinters above the waterline, these same jagged slivers of metal sliced into the gun crews and others in exposed positions near the explosion area, killing three men and wounding another seriously. They buried the dead and carried on, but, towards nightfall, the need for their guns had lessened and they received an urgent recall to Dover to prepare for yet another duty.

During their time across the Channel plans had been finalised at Dover for the transportation of the XD parties and *Wild Swan, Venomous* and *Vimy* had been earmarked to carry these parties to Dunkirk, Calais and Boulogne respectively. *Wild Swan* was allocated party G for Dunkirk under the command of Commander Banks, RN. Younghusband first received orders to embark these men at 0130 on the 23rd and the operational signal arrived on *Wild Swan*'s bridge at 0300 the same morning. By 0800 the demolition stores had arrived and the various military and naval personnel arrived aboard between 0900 and 1000.

As with the previous parties for the Hook, mistakes arose. It was subsequently found that whoever had organised the demolition stores had sent insufficient primers but by that time *Wild Swan* was *en route*. It was not to be the first time that such sloppiness at home was encountered by the fighting men at the front. Younghusband also took care to see the Liaison Officer detailed in order to impress on that worthy that air cover would be nice to see on the way over. He added: 'My experience of the previous day in Dunkirk convinced me that my ship would be commandeered to evacuate parties, which I did not want to do without informing you.'

This proved a very accurate forecast indeed! The passage of the

Wild Swan back to Dunkirk was uneventful, the ship leaving Dover at 1026 and arriving alongside the Monitor Quay at Dunkirk at 1305. On the other side of the Channel, while passing Gravelines, a force of fifteen German bombers was observed but they did not attack. Visibility was poor with rain squalls and showers and they probably did not notice the lone destroyer. Once alongside, the demolition parties were quickly put ashore and Younghusband followed the pattern he had set at the Hook by unshipping six of his depth charges for Commander Banks to utilise as he saw fit at the lock gates. At 1400 the destroyer *Wolsey* secured alongside *Wild Swan*, having escorted the hospital ships *Isle of Thanet* and *Worthing* from Newhaven. They arrived in the middle of an air attack and both *Wild Swan* and *Wolsey* were heavily engaged with enemy aircraft over the harbour mouth at this time.

Younghusband took the opportunity to borrow as many spare detonators from *Wolsey* as he could and made them available to the demolition party. While awaiting the contingent of RAF personnel the Liaison Officer had gone in search of for passage home, some Army personnel also turned up and the STO authorised their passage home as well. With the 75 airmen, eight civilians and 72 soldiers *Wild Swan* cast off and returned to Dover at 1700 after reduced visibility and heavy rain along the French coast had slowed them down. They berthed alongside *Verity* at the Admiralty Pier, and disembarked their passengers. Due to the huge quantity of personal luggage and equipment brought away by these passengers this took a considerable time. While it was taking place urgent orders were received from Vice-Admiral, Dover to join Captain D19, in *Keith*, and his destroyers force at Boulogne. *Wild Swan* sailed again at 1820 on 23rd May.

The situation the destroyers had found at Boulogne was parlous in the extreme. The Germans had penetrated the town and several strategic strongpoints had fallen to them, including the Tour d'Odre which had been directing the bombarding destroyers' fire on the advancing Panzers, their slow progress soon prompted them to whistle up the Stukas to deal with their tormentors.

It was not until 1830, that the War Office finally came down on the side of evacuation and orders were issued to the 20th Guards Brigade and the assembled destroyers at that hour to commence embarkation. By then the situation had changed from perilous to almost hopeless.

(*) High-tempo exercises Mediterranean 1935. The flotilla, based at Malta, carried out warlike exercises almost daily in this period. *Wild Swan* passes close to her 'Chummy Ship', HMS *Whitehall*. 'In this instance she passed a darned sight too close to me,' recalled Darby

(below) *Wild Swan* in a heavy sea during the passage of the flotilla from Malta to Gibraltar prior to her involvement in the Spanish Civil War, 1936. Seen from HMS *Verity*.

Wild Swan on completion of her refit in 1940. Looking forward from the stern bank of torpedo tubes at the searchlight platform, port single Pom-pom, another destroyer along-side to starboard, either *Daring* or *Delight*.

Portsmouth Harbour, 1040 – Monday, 8th January, 1940. Seen over the stern of *Wild Swan*, with her smoke-making equipment (CSA) and depth-charges on their racks, is the battleship HMS *Nelson*. She is arriving at Portsmouth under tow from Loch Ewe where she had been heavily damaged by a magnetic mine a month before. She was under repair for six months. *Wild Swan* at this time was herself undertaking special and secret 'Degausing' trials to counter such mines.

It was around this time that the destroyers *Venetia, Venomous* and *Vimiera* arrived from Dover and *Whitshed* commenced her return journey. *Keith* and *Vimy* lay alongside the quay and *Mona's Queen* was still loading inside the harbour. Two large formations of dive bombers appeared over the harbour area and, brushing aside a weak fighter patrol, commenced attacks on the town and shipping there. Simultaneously heavy mortar fire was opened on the two berthed destroyers in conjunction with another German assault. Bombs crashed into the quay close alongside the destroyers and shrapnel and splinters sliced through their thin bridge and upperworks plating causing heavy casualties, even though neither ship was actually hit. Captain D.J.R. Simpson was killed by machine-gun fire on his bridge, and Lieutenant-Commander C.G.W. Donald of the *Vimy* received fatal wounds.

With the death of Simpson, command dissolved upon Commander E.R. Conder of *Whitshed* whose own vessel had been attacked offshore suffering casualties from a near-miss bomb. Conder at once returned to Boulogne to see if he could help and met the *Keith* and *Vimy* backing out of harbour still engaging shore targets with the forward guns. Conder was determined to continue the evacuation if he could, but first he requested air cover. After a fifty minute wait some British fighters put in an appearance and *Whitshed* and *Vimiera* re-entered the port. It was now low-water but both ships managed to reach the quay and together they embarked more than a thousand men of the Welsh Guards. By this time *Wild Swan* had arrived on the scene.

On their way over they had been intercepting signals which spelt out the dire situation, thus they knew about the loss of Captain (D) and indeed met the retiring *Keith* on the way across. Younghusband was not sure who remained in charge of the remaining destroyers as a signal from *Whitshed* had stated her captain was wounded, but as they closed the port they observed both her and *Vimiera* entering. This was at 1920.

By a peculiar mirage effect I actually thought at that moment that *Whitshed* was sinking and was beaching herself. *Venomous* and *Venetia* closed me and asked what was happening. I told them to keep to seaward until I could find out. I closed the entrance and *Vimy* who was just off it. *Vimy* told me that her Captain was seriously wounded, that she had some soldiers on board, and also some casualties. I ordered her to return to Dover at full speed and report the situation . . . At this time I was still under the impression that I was the Senior Officer and I could not get *Whitshed* to answer. However soon after W/T signals from *Whitshed* were intercepted from which I gathered she was in charge and that an evacuation was in progress.

The signal in question was actually transmitted at 2025 and read: '*Whitshed to Admiralty*: 2025. Fighter escort gone, enemy aircraft over town.'

Soon afterwards the *Whitshed* and *Vimiera* were seen backing out without apparent opposition so Younghusband signalled Conder asking if any more destroyers were required and received the order to go in taking another with him. Younghusband told *Venomous* to follow him in, and signalled *Venetia* to wait as he was uncertain whether there would be room enough for her as well at low water. No sign was seen of German troops or guns as *Wild Swan* slowly entered but British soldiers could be seen on the north-western spur of the Quai Chanzy with some stretcher cases on the low tide stage on the quay's south-western face. Younghusband decided to go alongside at that spot, port side to, and *Venomous* followed a few moments later and berthed on the north-eastern face. Younghusband found that, owing to the very low water and lack of bollards, he had great difficulty in keeping his ship's bows alongside. He could not get hold of anything aft and the ship's bows went aground when he tried to get the full length of his hull alongside. While he was thus engaged in this tricky manoeuvre a sudden crash of gunfire and flash of flame on the hills overlooking the town to the north, heralded an intense bombardment from German artillery.

What signalled this barrage was the *Venetia* (Lieutenant-Commander B.H. de C. Mellor) entering the harbour behind them some 300 yards astern. It was an obvious attempt to sink her in the entrance to the harbour and thus block it, trapping all three ships and the remaining troops ashore, and it almost worked. Having entered the trap like flies into a spider's web all three ships were now in a perilous position. 'Frankly', admitted Younghusband later, 'I never expected that any of the three ships would get out . . . '

The initial bombardment was sighted almost exclusively on *Venetia*, with tracer shell arcing in from the direction of Fort de la Crèche and from the ridge below it. It was deadly in its accuracy. Younghusband wrote:

I saw her [*Venetia*] hit on the bridge and searchlight platform. At first I thought it was another air raid.

As Signalman Harrison recalls:

One direct hit caused terrible damage. I saw a frightful explosion with debris flying and an enormous quantity of smoke. Soon we could just make out that her fo'c'sle and bridge had been blown away. What was left of the ship was still slowly moving through the harbour mouth. We thought that the Germans were trying to sink her in the mouth of the harbour to block the entrance and stop our escape.

Aboard *Venetia* the carnage was enormous. Her captain was killed and most of 'B' guns' crew were wiped out by this hit. Almost all the officers were either dead or wounded and she ran aground with her engines stopped until young Sub-Lieutenant D.H. Jones, RNR, the only uninjured officer, took control of the ship. Although she was at a standstill with her bows ashore against the jetty on *Wild Swan*'s starboard quarter, her surviving guns were all heavily in action throughout. Gradually she got underway astern and backed out and down the channel, getting clear.

Meanwhile the artillery had shifted target to the two ships alongside the quay and the pace became very hot indeed. The screech of the incoming shells, the crash and roar of the destroyers' guns, large and small, making continual and spirited reply, the cries of the wounded, the hiss of escaping steam, all turned the night into a seething cauldron of noise and action. *Wild Swan* found that her director on the bridge was masked by a crane on the quay and the view of enemy batteries from the bridge was similarly masked. The two sternmost guns, X and Y 4.7's, however, had a clear shoot and Sub-Lieutenant H.G. Vere was sent aft to control their fire in 'Quarters Firing'.

Venomous was closer to the enemy and all her batteries were unmasked. She was returning the fire with interest from all her four 4.7's and what small arms would bear. Meanwhile shells from the German field guns continued to fall all round *Venetia* and down the starboard side of *Wild Swan*, although the latter, by some miracle, was not hit.

In the midst of this uproar Younghusband continued to try to get his ship alongside correctly with a view to getting the wounded aboard, but he found it very difficult to get the ship's bows alongside. Lieutenant M.J. Lee was then sent forward from the bridge, where he could perform no further functions while the director was masked, and when the First Lieutenant got to the fo'c'sle he tried to get the ship's bows secured. As he was joined on the fo'c'sle by Sub-Lieutenant Patrick Satow, a spring parted under the pressure of the engines and the *Wild Swan* surged forward and grounded. It looked grim until a timely shell burst under the starboard bow and lifted the ship off again. Younghusband and his team then managed to nose her in once more in the position he required, leaving her stern jutting out so the two after guns could keep engaging the enemy. This they did with a will and Sub-Lieutenant Vere got the two gun crews well onto several targets and maintained a very creditable rate of fire for the whole period.

In charge of X gun was young Midshipman Green who did well in getting his gun onto machine-gun posts and keeping his crew firing – despite casualties – from light arms fire which wounded the sight-setter on this mounting. Green took his place and, with equally efficient work by the trainer, Able-Seaman A.J. MacDonald, kept the gun going. 'Full of guts and initiative,' was how his captain later described Green. On Y gun the trainer, Able-Seaman J. Noble and the loading number, Able-Seaman J. MacDonald (no relation to the trainer) were also commended.

Nor should the work of the men below go ignored. Commissioned Engineer Derbyshire and his team had, in Younghusband's words, 'as usual, all the anxiety and none of the excitement . . . Mr Derbyshire's department produced what was required accurately and quickly. One small slip on their part would have meant the stranding of the ship, there was little room for error.'

As Patrick Satow points out:

Seagoing ships are not often deliberately run aground; but then a ship's main armament is not often fired when she is berthed alongside in harbour. The effect of firing her guns straight into the town was that *Wild Swan* started to drift away from the quay, making it difficult for the troops to clamber aboard from the slippery timbers exposed by the low tide.

It would have been nothing short of suicide for any member of the crew to go onto the quay to secure hawsers to the bollards. So the ship was eased cautiously ahead to put her bows aground. She was then slewed back alongside by using the propellers, and held there.

Right from the start soldiers had been trying to get aboard. Not surprisingly some were close to panic and wanted to jump down onto the ships fo'c'sle from the top of the quay, a drop of about twenty feet or so! Signalman Harrison recalls the desperate scene:

We were not even secured before the soldiers were clambering and jumping aboard. They were dishevelled, clearly demoralised in a few cases and had obviously been through a lot. Our captain was shouting above the gunfire, 'Tell those bastards to wait!' It was difficult controlling them but they were all able to walk and get aboard by themselves, there being only a few stretcher cases among this particular group.

As the troops were filing aboard heavy fire was still coming in from the other side of the harbour. I myself could not see where the fire was coming from, although I did not really have much time to watch what was happening as there was so much activity on the bridge. I do recall that some of the fire was heavy and that our sister ship was hit. She had shouted over just before this, using her loud-hailer, that she was full up with troops and requested instructions. Captain Younghusband told them to proceed out of the harbour.

Patrick Satow's viewpoint from the fo'c'sle was similar: 'The quayside area became so dangerous with cross fire, that many of the soldiers climbed down amongst the slippery timbers of the quay, which had been exposed by the low sea level, and they scrambled aboard as best they could.'

In his report Captain Younghusband mentions the good work of the Brigade Major of the Guards stating that without his control loading operations would have been complete chaos. In all *Wild Swan* embarked 403 and *Venomous* 500 troops, seamen and Royal Marines.

It had been 2042 when *Venetia* had been abreast of the Harbour Master's Office and had been hit. It was a further thirty-five minutes before *Venomous* commenced pulling out. In that period the Germans had subjected the vessels to a constant barrage, not only of artillery fire, but also some heavier weapons, from the abandoned guns of the French fort, and considerable small-arms fire from machine-gun nests, rifles and snipers in the building of the town and docks. Luckily much of it was tracer, which gave away the positions of those using it and this enabled some excellent counter-fire work by the destroyers which caused some considerable havoc among the enemy.

During this intense period of bombardment the destroyers

remained unscathed, incredible as it later appeared. Nonetheless the intensity of the fire did not leave them without casualties, but the serious injury to the trainer of X gun, Ordinary Seaman P.S. Middleton, who was hit by a piece of shell which burst off *Wild Swan*'s starboard side and entered the gun shield from the rear, was her only loss *Venomous* had one officer and three men slightly wounded. Younghusband wrote:

. . . the noise was terrific in that confined space. Six 4.7" guns were going full blast in addition to Pom-Poms and enemy shell fire. A shell hit the edge of the jetty abreast my bridge and another carried away my main aerials. Neither caused any casualties. Very fine work by my W/T staff had us in communication again in one minute. Engines had to be worked the whole time as the recoil of X and Y sent the ship bodily out.

This brief action was as divorced from the text books as anything could be. X and Y guns fired mostly at suspected gun positions in the fort, when not taking shots at suspected machine-guns concealed in the houses. I sincerely hope that there were no civilians left in this district for the destruction wrought was extensive, and we left the place in flames. To this I think we can attribute our escape. The gunlayers stated that they saw machine-gun fire and tracers coming from several houses up the hill. This did not last long. Y gun saw a tank coming down on the quay opposite. The second shot was a direct hit and the tank vanished. The port pom-pom had an effective burst at snipers on the front before it had to cease fire due to proximity of the quay.

Able-Seaman G.A. Morgan, the layer on this pom-pom, got special praise for his work that day, while Leading Telegraphist R.C.E. Clement and Telegraphist R.F. Anstey got the aerials repaired in grim circumstances. Once this was done *Wild Swan* got away two signals while still alongside the quay: '*Wild Swan to V/A, Dover*: 2055. Have commenced evacuation. Being bombarded by artillery.' And she sent another just before she pulled out: '*Wild Swan to V/A, Dover*: 2114. Request more assistance.'

Earlier *Whitshed* had signalled: '*Whitshed to Admiralty*: 2025. Fighter escort gone, enemy aircraft over town.'

The only reply received at this time was: '*NOIC Dover to Destroyers*: 2123. S.O. destroyers take charge and use discretion as to appropriate action.'

By 2127 it was *Wild Swan*'s turn to back out of this death trap and try and reach the safety of the dusk sea outside Boulogne harbour. Patrick Satow again:

> Because of the low tide, and the proximity of the other ships assisting with this operation, it was not possible for *Wild Swan* to turn around to leave harbour. She had to be brought out by going astern in pitch blackness, and with everyone on the bridge trying to keep their heads down to avoid the shells and bullets still being fired from the shore.

Signalman Harrison remembers events like this:

> The Captain called the Engineering Officer and the First Lieutenant to the bridge to tell them his plan. Captain Younghusband first wanted the ship 'trimmed', as the soldiers were still all massed on one side of the ship and around 'A' gun on the fo'c'sle, which we would need to use.
>
> On the First Lieutenant organising this effectively, the Captain then wanted the fore-and-aft lines to be eased gently and, once the ship was at a sufficient distance from the jetty, he told the Engineering Officer that he would call for 'Full Speed Astern'. He told Mr Derbyshire to go and get full power in the engines ready for that order. He wanted everything the engines could offer.
>
> By this time *Venetia* had limped clear of the outer mouth of the harbour. The ship was trimmed and slowly and gently she was eased away from the side of the jetty. I think this was partly done by people pushing the ship away by hand! Once she was about ten to fifteen feet away Younghusband gave the order to the engineroom, 'Full Speed Astern'. There was a terrific shudder and the stern of the ship seemed to sink down into the water two or three feet.

She had grounded just as she reached the inner pier heads of the harbour! The destroyer was deeply laden now and the water was fully slack. She took on a list to starboard. Since leaving the jetty A and B guns had had their arcs unmasked and now they eagerly joined in the battle, director salvos were fired into the fort and fire was kept up by all guns until clear of the breakwater. The gunlayer on A mounting, Able Seaman J.E. Weston, and the No 2 on B gun, Leading Seaman A. McLeod, both got praise for their work at this time, as did the layer of the starboard pom-pom, Leading Seaman J. Callaghan. He saw some men with machine-guns hiding in the trellis-work of the southern inner pierhead which he demolished before they had a chance to use them against *Wild Swan*. Then she came free!

X and Y guns were not to be outdone in this last furious exchange. They directed most of their fire against suspected gun positions up by the fort, after knocking out the tank and machine-gun nests. The supply party that kept the shells arriving at these insatiable guns also got a deserved mention, in particular Petty Officer Steward H.W. Morgan and Leading Seaman W.J.R. Wells, while up on the bridge, dodging the sniper fire, Yeoman of Signals C.W.G. Burton, Lewis Gunner Able Seaman H. Patchett and Ordinary Seaman M. McRae all did stirling work. At the ship's wheel all through these crucial manoeuvres was the TC, Chief Petty Officer Fletcher. For long periods he had to deal with a continuous string of wheel and tele-graphic orders. 'He never made a mistake under appalling condi-tions of noise. A very worthy upholder of the true tradition of Destroyer TC's', wrote Younghusband of this man.

Down below the stretcher cases embarked lay in the darkness lis-tening to the carnage of battle above and unable to move or do any-thing other than lie and listen. The ship's doctor, Surgeon-Lieuten-ant Couchman, divided his time between caring for them and deciphering signals. The damage to the ship itself was luckily slight or else casualties below among their passengers might have been ghastly. The bursting shells alongside the starboard side made a series of holes in the hull but caused no internal damage. The voice pipe from the bridge to the after guns was cut, a serious handicap but they coped splendidly on their own. Many circuits and fittings were severed but quickly repaired.

The chief damage to the crew was utter weariness. They had been on the go continually, as we have seen, day and night for several days and were all tired *before* this battle commenced. The added strain and tensions took from them the last reserves they had. But even when clear of the harbour they still had to get their ship home to Dover. Behind them in the blackness the German guns continued to pound away, but there was now little or no response.

Thus *Wild Swan* came clear of Boulogne.

CHAPTER FOUR

Non-Stop
May–June 1940

Behind them in the darkness the shroud of night fell over Boulogne. Ahead *Wild Swan* sighted the *Venomous* and *Venetia* and quickly closed with the former. Her captain soon was able to re-assure Younghusband that she was all right and able to proceed to Dover without assistance. *Venetia*, however, was obviously in some considerable difficulty and appeared to be steering rather a dangerous course over the sandbanks and bars outside the harbour mouth, probably because her charts had been destroyed. *Wild Swan* came up alongside her at 2200 and led her back to Dover. Signalman Harrison recalls:

> Once inside the harbour we made contact with *Venetia* and stayed in her company all the way home. What was left of her could only travel at six or seven knots and it seemed a terribly long, slow journey back to England. We did learn later that the captain and all the officers were lost when the ship was hit. It was a young sub-lieutenant who brought the crippled *Venetia* home by using the after steering. He was a young RNVR officer and we always considered this a wonderful achievement on his part.

Meanwhile Younghusband was asked by Dover about the situation at Boulogne and replied with the following signal:

> *Wild Swan to NOIC, Dover*: 2234. Harbour is under field-gun fire from heights to northward, destroyers should not enter without covering fire from seaward. Consider a number of military left. Regret consider further evacuation impracticable.

Around the time this signal was being sent, the destroyer *Windsor* had arrived off Boulogne from Calais and, unknown to the others, had entered the harbour with great difficulty and confusion and berthed at the Quai Chanzy they had just vacated. She was unmolested due to the darkness and managed to embark a further 600 soldiers and 30 wounded. Not content with this, two more destroyers were sent over, but one was diverted to Calais on the way. It was the *Vimiera*

(Lieutenant-Commander R.B.N. Hicks) that arrived on her own in the early hours of the 25th and secured to the outer jetty. There was the absolute silence of defeat over the town and she was about to leave when yet more refugees, civilians and French and Belgian troops appeared from the buildings they had been hiding in. There also appeared a Guards officer who told Hicks that about 1,000 men still remained in the area! *Vimiera* took all these, and, incredible as it may seem, this little ship left the jetty at 0245 with no less than 1,400 passengers aboard, just as the German artillery and bombers made yet another attack. Happily she survived and reached Dover.

Wild Swan and *Venetia* had arrived at Dover 2255, the former securing alongside the *Whitshed* at No 1 berth at Admiralty Pier and commenced unloading her passengers. Both crew and soldiers were so weary they could hardly walk or stand. Younghusband paid tribute to the Guardsmen thus:

> Having seen the somewhat shattering effect of our fire on our own troops on the quay, I can understand what it must have been like at the business end of our guns. All ashore thought we were being bombed. However, once on board and realising that the noise was being made by us, various soldiers helped our ammunition supply party forward, for which we were very grateful.

Before taking leave of the Boulogne epic record should be made of the medical officers from Royal Navy Barracks at Chatham whom *Wild Swan* had taken over earlier. They found themselves attached to a party of the destroyer's seamen helping with demolition work and soon were busy with casualties around the ruins of Boulogne Railway Station at the docks. Each MO was accompanied by a sickberth attendant and six stretcher-bearers and each contrived to set up a regimental aid post with what assistance he could muster. Joining up with some men from the RAMC they formed a casualty reception centre in the station's debris-littered corridors and the wounded and the occupants of two hospital trains, which had been routed into the besieged town, owed much to their devotion.

On the 24th the Admiralty had signalled to Vice-Admiral Ramsay that his damaged ships, *Keith, Wild Swan, Whitshed, Venomous* and *Venetia*, could all be taken in hand for repair work at their home ports and were to be sailed thither 'at the first opportunity!' For some of the more badly damaged ships this was complied with, but for the others, including *Wild Swan*, such was the desperate need for

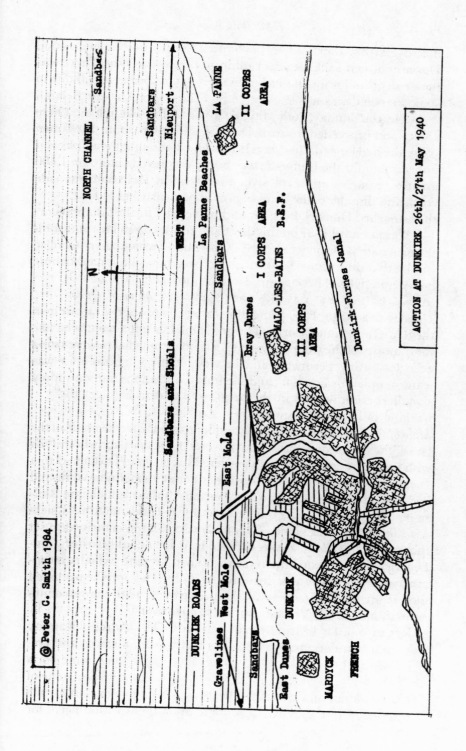

© Peter C. Smith 1984

ACTION AT DUNKIRK 26th/27th May 1940

destroyers that they had to be content with a quick patch-up at
Dover and then back into the cauldron. For by this time Calais was
under siege and only Dunkirk remained accessible to the BEF and
some French divisions.

At 1430 on Sunday, 26th May, *Wild Swan* slipped from her berth at
Dover and proceeded towards Dunkirk once more. The demolition
party she had landed a few days before had found that their work was
unnecessary for the Luftwaffe was busily employed doing it with far
greater resources and explosives than were at their disposal. The
crash and thunder of the bombing could be clearly heard at Dover as
they smashed Dunkirk harbour and pulverised the installations.

It was not until 1857 on this day that the final orders to commence
the evacuation of the whole BEF, Operation Dynamo, were issued.
But by that time some 28,000 men had been brought home or would
be by midnight. These again, were in the main part, non-fighting
troops. Earlier that day the passanger-ferry *Maid of Orleans* had
sailed with a cargo of 600 two-gallon cans of water, and 250 men from
the RASC and Signal Corps. The need for fresh water was great with
the majority of the troops being away from the normal facilities in an
ever-decreasing perimeter and in view of the wreckage of mains
water supplies by bombing and shelling. The medical parties and the
signallers were needed in the town itself and to help get the port
working full out once more. On her arrival at Dunkirk, however,
Maid of Orleans found the harbour undergoing a heavy air attack. She
lay off the moles for a period, but it would have been suicidal to dock
with no protection and she was ordered to return to Dover.

Half way across, the *Wild Swan* met her at 1503, and asked if she
had unloaded her vital cargo and was told she had not. This fact was
signalled to Dover and Younghusband was told to return with the
Maid forthwith to England. They had no sooner made fast once more
than, at 1709, *Wild Swan* was ordered to sail at once with the ferry to
Dunkirk and subsequently return with her, keeping well clear of the
port while the *Maid* was loading. At 1726 *Wild Swan* slipped and
picked up *Maid of Orleans* off the breakwater, told her follow her
across and set off. Younghusband passed over to her captain his
orders to wait for her and escort her back. Off they set once more.
Younghusband seemed tireless. His navigation officer remembers
him thus:

He was a tall and cheerful officer, with a ship's company which
responded to the many calls made upon them with loyalty and

long hours of duty. During the numerous high speed missions made during May and June of 1940, he never hesitated to answer all the unforeseen calls made by the naval authorities upon his ship, many of which were carried out under conditions of considerable danger.

The Navigating Officer recalls standing behind his Captain on the bridge, in daylight, with everyone wearing tin hats. The ship was on a steady course in quiet weather and the sun was hot. Due to sheer exhaustion, more than once, the 'pilot' nodded off, and his head tilted forward. The leading edge of his steel helmet caught his commanding officer at the back of his neck, and he came to abruptly when Younghusband snapped, 'Don't do that!'

The Germans had now mounted batteries of guns around Calais, which fell on the 26th, and this made the route very much a 'gauntlet running' excercise, but, on this trip at least, the guns remained silent and they continued on past Gravelines. Here a signal was received from Dover instructing Younghusband to escort the personnel ship *Canterbury*. As this signal was timed 1749 and *Canterbury* was due to sail from Dover at 1800, Younghusband decided the best thing to do was carry on with his first order to see *Maid of Orleans* safely to Dunkirk and then return for *Canterbury* as soon as possible. He could not be in two places at once despite Dover's apparent opinion to the contrary. It was as well he did remain with *Maid of Orleans* for as they were entering Dunkirk at 1929 that evening they were subjected to a bombing attack by a German aircraft.

This plane was first spotted coming in from astern out of the smoke and murk of Dunkirk's burning oil tanks. It flew round to the port bow and made a determined attack from that direction a minute later, dropping four bombs which exploded about 100 yards on the port beam. No damage was done and the aircraft was then chased away by three British fighters.

Yet a third signal had been taken in at this juncture, timed 1852, instructing Younghusband to embark General Eastwood, two other generals and their staffs, from Dunkirk. Having seen *Maid of Orleans* tucked safely away in Dunkirk, *Wild Swan* turned about and proceed back westward in search of *Canterbury*, which she met off Gravelines and she then escorted her into Dunkirk where she berthed alongside *Maid of Orleans* at the Monitor Quay. Here both ships started embarking troops until filled to capacity. Bombing continued and both ships received near misses but were not harmed. *Canterbury* embarked 1,340 men and *Maid of Orleans* a further 988. The French cross-Channel steamer *Rouen* was also present and she took 420 wounded French troops on to Cherbourg. Another departure was their old friend from Boulogne, *Mona's Queen*, who had also loaded to capacity with troops. She had earlier been subjected to both bombing and shelling off Gravelines, but had carried on. Now fully laden she pulled out for Dover once more and *Wild Swan* took her place alongside *Canterbury*.

It was now 2040 on the evening of the 26th and the Army officers arrived to board. Patrick Satow recalls this well:

> One distinguished general who we picked up from the coast at this time was General Sir Thomas Eastwood. I believe he became the first Commander of the Home Guard in Britain. Later, in 1944, he was the Governor of Gibraltar when I was going out to the British Pacific Fleet. He came to sea for a day in the flotilla leader HMS *Kempenfelt*, and when he discovered that I had taken him back to England at night four years earlier, I received an invitation to dinner with him on The Rock!

These guests aboard *Wild Swan* sailed at 2145. While alongside, the master of the *Canterbury* informed Younghusband that his vessel had been shelled off Gravelines on the way in and so *Wild Swan* patrolled up and down the coast in that general area to give help to any other vessels similarly attacked, while awaiting the sailing of *Maid of Orleans*. When, by 0324 on the morning of the 27th, no sign of that vessel had been seen Younghusband decided the order must have been cancelled and took his destroyer back to Dover to disembark the generals.

On her return to Dover *Wild Swan* found that her turn to sail for Portsmouth, to repair her many small injuries and generally refit to face the war again, had come and she sailed thither on the 28th. That afternoon she entered the dockyard and was placed in their hands for a whole week. It was a week that saw her altered in many ways, a week which saw the completion of the Dunkirk saga and a dark turn in the war situation with the imminent fall of France. A week in which destroyer losses assumed catastrophic proportions which made *Wild Swan*, ancient as she was, even more valuable to the Navy. But most of her crew can only remember that week as a brief respite and a chance to snatch a few days' golden rest before returning to the fray. As Patrick Satow states:

Dodging in and out of the channels littered with newly sunken ships, and carefully avoiding the adjacent minefields, the ship ran back and forth at full speed, taking onboard men from boats and from beaches. The long hours of daylight brought many threats of attack by German aircraft, who were operating within such easy reach of their own bases. Repeated calls to action stations meant that few members of the ship's company got any proper rest.

During these desperate and hectic days and nights, the ship might berth at Dover, and stay for a few hours to land the troops and take on fuel and provisions. As soon as the hawsers were secured to the quay, the men just lay down and slept on the deck; they could not muster enough strength to get below to their own quarters.

Largely as a result of these weeks of high speed steaming, and all that had happened, *Wild Swan* earned a nickname from her own ship's company, which stayed with her for the rest of that wartime commission. She was known affectionately as 'The Frantic Duck'!

On completion of this period the ship was sent to Portsmouth, where a stand-by crew from the barracks was placed on board. Virtually the whole ship's company was sent on special leave, and the navigating officer can recall arriving at his home to fall asleep for no less than twenty-seven hours!

While her crew dispersed to take brief respite from the nightmare that was unfolding across the Channel, work commenced on 29th May to put their ship back in full fighting trim. A proper boiler-clean and work on her engines was carried out to compensate for the days on scurrying around at top speed. Her guns were maintained and some armament changes were carried out in a hurried attempt to re-equip her with some weapons more suitable for the type of war she was now fighting. Two pairs of torpedo-tubes for example now appeared a needless luxury for a destroyer who, it was thought, would be unlikely ever to face a large German battleship or cruiser. What she *had* been facing almost every day, were German bombers and dive-bombers.

Accordingly the after torpedo mounting was taken out of the ship and from the dockyard depot at Whale Island was transported an ancient, but perfectly preserved anti-aircraft gun and platform. This was a 12-pounder weapon, built in the Great War. It was a 50-calibre weapon which fired a 14½-lb shell with a 5¾-lb charge at a rate of thirty per minute, and it had a better range than the pom-poms, which were retained, as were the Lewis guns. However, to supplement close-range weapons, two Bren-guns were fitted aboard, which, considering the dire needs of the army and home defence units, was a considerable achievement. They were only light-weight weapons it was true but every extra barrel that could point skyward was welcomed at this time.*

Two extra anti-submarine mortars were also embarked aft during this refit. Her pendant numbers remained I.62 as they had since April, and she retained her dark-grey 'Home Fleet' paint over all after her honourable scars had been plated over.† There were not enough radar sets yet available for *Wild Swan* to be so fitted, and not until September did the Type 286M radar reach the destroyers of her flotilla.

Her crew, refreshed and heartened, re-joined *Wild Swan* at Portsmouth. All repairs had been completed by 4th June, the day the Dunkirk evacuation finished, and, after a brief period of fresh trials and working up the new equipment in the Solent, re-ammunitioning and refuelling, *Wild Swan* rejoined the hard-pressed 19th Flotilla at Dover once more on the 8th of that month, the first of the damaged destroyers to do so. She was not destined to stay at Dover for long however; there were too many other calls on her services.

Paris fell on 14th June, and Cherbourg, Brest and St Malo were all threatened. On the 17th the French asked for an armistice. There was clearly no further help the British army could give alone and thus, for the third time, hasty plans had to be made to get as many troops out as possible in the little time remaining. So, once again, as at Rotterdam and Boulogne, *Wild Swan* was to be caught up in the heroism, despair, confusion and gallantry of a retreating Army, for caught up in the Battle of France were still 1st Armoured and 51st (Highland) Division and the 52nd Division, the latter newly transported to aid French morale.

Even as these momentous events unfolded another threat appeared, that of the invasion of Great Britain herself. Although we know now with hindsight that the Germans had not seriously considered this at this time, from the British point-of-view in June 1940,

* It is interesting to notice in the recent Falklands war that the multi-million-pound, all-missile and electronics, super-warships also had to embark Bren guns!

† *Wild Swan* was never dazzle-painted, or camouflaged, like many of her sisters early in the war. Her dark paint gave way to a light grey for the tropics later but no 'splinter' or other pattern was ever used on her hull.

(Right) After an abortive depth-charge attach on a suspected U-Boat in the English Channel oil has come to the surface. The Commissioned Engineer, Mr Derbyshire, is taking a sample to test in order to determine if it is submarine oil or not. It later turned out to be a submerged wreck.

(Below) Again not a U-Boat, but suppertime! Some very happy members of *Wild Swan's* ship's company with their catch after an attack. For several days after this there was little else on the menu but fried cod, kedgeree and then fish cakes. But it made a welcome change from corned beef!

'Friendly' contact mines were one of the biggest hazards in the coastal waters in 1940. Scores of them had broken adrift in the winter gales and had to be destroyed by rifle fire. Here marksmen from *Wild Swan* take care of one such specimen in the Channel.

Convoy in the South-Western Approaches, March 1940. A peaceful sunset as *Wild Swan* escorts heavily-laden merchantmen through the dusk towards British ports.

and afterwards, the threat was very apparent and very real. Any invasion force must be prevented from reaching the coast. And the only ships available for this vital function were the destroyers and cruisers of the Royal Navy. But, as these self-same ships already had the two equally vital duties of evacuating our fighting troops and protecting our convoys with the very sinews of war, they had to be very thinly spread.

Thus although nominally allocated to Dover *Wild Swan*'s crew found that their 19th Flotilla was switched to Harwich, to act as the first-line of defence against invasion convoys and fleets, and then back to Portsmouth with the 18th Flotilla, to help rescue the troops. And so, throughout June, the little ship spent as much time steaming backward and forward *up-and-down* the Channel between Harwich, Dover and Portsmouth, as she had sailing *across* the same stretch of water in May!

The first stage of these evacuations, Operation Cycle, had commenced on 9th June, when the C-in-C, Portsmouth, sent across nine destroyers under the *Codrington* to Le Havre, along with a host of smaller craft. The subsquent Operation Aerial saw the evacuation of what troops remained from the ports of Cherbourg, St Malo, Brest, St Nazaire, and La Pallice. This was split between Portsmouth and Plymouth commands and commenced on 15th June. But casualties had so reduced the ships available to Admiral Sir William James that he could not organise a proper convoy system to protect the merchant ships involved. They had to sail independently with his few warships patrolling up-and-down the routes used to offer some sort of protection. Thus he employed the destroyers *Vega*, *Fernie* and *Sabre* and the old sloops *Foxglove* and *Rosemary*. Reinforcements were urgently despatched by V/A, Dover and, between 10th and 13th June, *Wild Swan* was working from Portsmouth. She sailed for Harwich late on the 13th and arrived at Harwich the next day after performing one last run across to Cherbourg with a troop-ship. Patrick Satow recalls:

After a brief respite *Wild Swan* escorted one of the regular cross-Channel steamers, now loaded with fresh troops, to Cherbourg. But the advance of the German Army westward was proving so rapid that there was little time for these men to disembark. Just as the ship and her naval escort reached the wharf, an urgent signal was received to put the operation into reverse, as the enemy was just round the corner and there seemed to be no prospect of stopping him.

Wild Swan was not specifically engaged in the evacuation of troops from Cherbourg. We rushed there with this ship carrying a full load of troops; possibly they were intended to hold the port area during the final stages of evacuation. I do not think that one of the soldiers set foot on French soil before we pulled out; but the occasion is clearly impressed on my memory . . . the ship was operating at this time on some very tight schedules, and we were racing up and down the English Channel at the best part of 30 knots, with very little sleep!

No sooner had she reached Harwich than the order came to refuel and sail at once back to Portsmouth. It was soon apparent why. St Malo was threatened and it had been decided at short notice, to send in another XD party to block the installations. Younghusband and his crew were now old hands at this and so were duly chosen. Sailing immediately they had taken on fuel, *Wild Swan* sped back down-Channel once more, arriving at Portsmouth on 15th June, a Saturday. The officer selected for the demolition mission was then a young commander RN. He is now Rear-Admiral C.D. Howard-Johnston, CB, DSO, DSC, and his story gives a good insight into how things were done in those desperate days:

At the time I had a desk job in the A/S Warfare Division of the Admiralty having just returned from service on the Greek Naval Mission in Athens. The St Malo demolition job was a temporary assignment given me by Commander Teddy Dangerfield who was trying to organise last-minute parties to help the French with their demolitions. Naturally the French had never thought of this aspect!

I had met Teddy in the Club and was telling him how I often had been to Jersey and knew Dinard well. He knew I could speak a bit of French and some hours later I had the job! A captain, Royal Engineers, was our expert for the demolitions. He had already done a similar job brilliantly in the evacuation of the Dutch ports. I collected £300 in cash and with this bulging in my inside pocket to pay for the sustenance of my party and for their getaway, I headed for Portsmouth. My orders were to do the

demolitions of the port facilities, lock gates etc. and to burn the
petrol in the tank-farm at St Malo.

I arrived eventually at HMS *Vernon* and early on Sunday 16th I
received orders from C-in-C, Portsmouth, to sail in *Wild Swan* as
soon as possible. I was sent for by Admiral James later on who told
me that the situation in France was very serious and that evacuation was now proceeding at full speed. My demolition party 'M',
with eight tons of explosives, proceeded to the Southern Railway
jetty and boarded *Wild Swan*.

Before they sailed the Chief of Staff came aboard and instructed
Younghusband and Howard-Johnston to call in at the island of Jersey and talk to the Governor there *en route*. Thus prepared, the *Wild
Swan* sailed from Portsmouth at 1400 that Sunday afternoon ready
for yet another exploit in the unknown. Up on the destroyer's bridge
the two officers discussed the situation.

I remember Younghusband as rather tall and thin, very calm and
balanced, with a nice sense of humour. He was a comforting sort of
chap to be with and one felt one could rely on him totally. He was
well-known and liked in destroyers and I had met him once or
twice before.

Wild Swan arrived at St Helier at 1930 and Howard-Johnston at once
proceeded to report to the Governor. As *Wild Swan* dropped anchor
they counted seven cargo ships in the little harbour, busy loading
cargoes of potatoes. The Harbour Master was told to hold these
ships ready for Admiralty service and for them to raise steam in readiness. At 2015 Howard-Johnston saw the Governor and the Baliff.
'They were all in a great stew!' recalls Howard-Johnston.

Having put them in the picture Howard-Johnston hurried back to
the harbour and, at 2050, boarded the cargo vessels in the port with
the Harbour Master and explained the position to them. There were
four 500-ton and three 1,000-ton ships available and the Jersey pilots
all agreed to help in his plan. By 23.30 that night the indefatigable
Howard-Johnston was back aboard *Wild Swan*, having temporarily
galvanised the island into some action, and she at once sailed for St
Malo leaving the steamers to follow later together with an advanced
guard of yachts. *Wild Swan* duly arrived at the French port at 0050 on
the morning of Monday, 17th June, went through into the inner locks

and berthed. The dockyard demolition party quickly disembarked and the stores were unloaded at the Gare Maritime Quay while they contacted the DSTO, Captain Jeffries, RN.

As at Rotterdam, they found the local populace most uncooperative.

> France fell after we had arrived in St Malo and the French were turning sour. We later listened to de Gaulle's speech, 'France has lost the battle but not the war', from a St Malo café which was feeding my party in two sittings each day. There was no bombing though German aircraft were about.
>
> Younghusband was a splendid chap and ready for anything. When he heard that I only had money for getting away he then said he would manage to patrol off Cape Fréhel in a few days' time to see if we needed picking up.
>
> After dropping my party and gear at St Malo the *Wild Swan* received orders to patrol elsewhere but before he left I asked the Captain if he could let me have some smoke floats and I think he gave me five. I had these placed up in the narrow streets and lit them when I heard the Germans were about to enter the town. With the prevailing north-westerly wind these gave a marvellous dense sort of fog all over the town, and perhaps made the Huns hesitate before they entered the town, and gave us time to blow up a few lock hinges and set hundreds of thousands of gallons of petrol burning, and get out of it.

Also before *Wild Swan* sailed on her patrol which took her off Dieppe, Howard-Johnston sent aboard a signal for C-in-C, Portsmouth, which *Wild Swan* later despatched on his behalf:

> *Wild Swan to C-in-C, Portsmouth*: 0545. French objecting to demolition. Armed guards preventing access all objectives including Dinanoil. Will do my best.

Dinan lies at the head of the estuary on which St Malo and Dinard face each other at the mouth. By 0730 the party had loaded the demolition charges, stores and everything else in lorries and moved them to the Quai de Rocabey to keep clear of the troops which were embarking and Howard-Johnston posted sentries to guard his equipment. There *Wild Swan* left them and sailed northward to comply with her orders. However their fate is not without interest.

It was only when the Germans reached the outskirts of St Malo that the French Commandant de la Marine withdrew his armed guards protecting my objectives from being demolished and told me to go ahead and, ' . . . do what you can.' He then went off to change into his best uniform to receive the Germans!

I thought we were going to get caught. By the time the Germans got to St Malo and the French caved in, my party, what with stragglers, Belgian nurses and others, had grown from about 32 to over one hundred. In the end we made our own way back to Jersey, some of us under oars aided by the Jersey Yacht Club which had sent all the craft they had to potter around St Malo harbour in case we needed them.

After more adventures ashore at Jersey in the last frantic hours of that island's freedom, Howard-Johnston and his men eventually arrived at Portsmouth once more aboard the Goole tomato-boat ss *Rye*. He got a well-deserved MD for his work which Their Lordships later described in glowing terms thus: ' . . . Howard-Johnston behaved throughout in an entirely level-headed and commendable manner . . . '.

The successful outcome of their mission was not known to *Wild Swan* of course, but she had played her part in that success. St Malo has one of the greatest rise and falls of tides to be found anywhere in the world, the difference between high and low water levels being almost fifty feet at spring tides. The timing of her arrival had to be perfect and this was done in the dead of night with the enemy close-by with an ease that made it appear simple.

After leaving St Malo *Wild Swan* patrolled off Dieppe to escort the *Manxman* which left Cherbourg at 1600 with 5th KOSB.* Younghusband was then ordered to rejoin his flotilla at Harwich and entered Dover at 2218 that night, it being too late to risk the crossing of the Thames Estuary at night where mining had taken a heavy toll of ships. A night's rest and, at 0535, she resumed her journey reaching Harwich later on the 18th to enter a new phase of her life.

The time of retreat was over. Now came the period of standing firm to repel invaders and, shortly, of offensive action to take the war back to the enemy.

After the heady life of the previous weeks Harwich seemed to offer a

---

* Kings Own Scottish Borderers, the last unit of the 52nd Division to leave.

more steady pace to *Wild Swan* and her crew. Since the mining of several of the 1st Flotilla destroyers earlier in the war, and the operations off the Hook, the war had largely by-passed this port but the conquest of Europe soon put Harwich back in the forefront of naval operations, and between June and October, it became the premier anti-invasion port for the Royal Navy.

The Harwich flotillas also had to give what protection they could to the minesweeper forces constantly engaged in keeping clear the narrow channels up the Essex, Suffolk and Norfolk coasts, and also to protect the fishing fleets as they tried to go about their business. To all these many chores were added the almost nightly defensive and offensive patrol against invasion, escorting minelaying forces on secret missions to the German and Dutch coastal waters and offensive bombardments of enemy-held ports to destroy the barges and tugs being assembled therein in pre-emptive strikes. There was no let-up for the Frantic Ducks at Harwich. The ship's navigating officer was to recall:

> In addition to a number of special operations much of the time at sea was spent in protecting our convoys off the east coast of England. This area was too close to enemy airfields for comfort, and in the long daylight hours of that summer, ships' crews had to be specially alert for surprise attacks by German aircraft. At night, the big menace was from E-boats which were very fast. They must have known that our shipping channels were greatly restricted by numerous shoals, by wrecks and minefields. So anti-E-boat patrols also featured.

There were also false alarms. On 20th June, for example, soon after her arrival back at Harwich a signal was received via C-in-C, Chatham, which stated that a number of our trawlers had been attacked and set on fire at 1009 that morning in position 52°40′ N, 2°12′ E, just off Great Yarmouth, and that a submarine was reported being seen submerging near to the scene of the attack at 1035. *Wild Swan* was sent off hot-foot to investigate this, but, like Old Mother Hubbard, when she got there the area was bare!

> *Wild Swan to C-in-C, Nore*: 1319. Your 1045. *No* burning trawlers in this position. Consider report erroneous. Two sets of four mine-sweeping trawlers near.

By this time the crew of *Wild Swan* were a hardened bunch of experts welded together by hard wartime experience. A new member of that team was Stoker Petty Officer A.G. Linford. This is how he remembers her then:

I joined *Wild Swan* at Harwich in July 1940, after leaving a minesweeper. We worked out of Harwich on North Sea escorts and attacks on the Belgian, Dutch and French coasts in company with MTB's and other ships.

The majority of the crew at this time had commissioned *Wild Swan* from reserve and quite a few were reservists and recalled naval pensioners. Some of the ship's personnel I remember: Jack Silsby, naval pensioner from Brighton, a postman when recalled to service; 'Nobby' Clark, Chief ERA,* another pensioner; Arthur Clayton, a Londoner; McCann, a Chief Stoker, from Liverpool; 'Florrie' Ford, Leading Stoker from Portsmouth; Charlie Kennet from Emsworth; Leading Seaman John Slowly, a reservist and ex-London Fireman. A character on his own (kept chickens on the searchlight platform!);† 'Chalky' Chalcraft, our Canteen Manager, a Londoner, who had never been to sea before the *Swan*. Mr Derbyshire, Commissioned Engineer from Purbrook.

Patrick Satow remembers others:

Petty Officer Steward, Hiram Morgan. A most cheerful and resourceful officers' steward, who kept us all well nourished, in spite of the immense difficulties faced by all catering staff at sea in those days. We all remember the hot jacket potatoes, especially provided for those on duty during the bleak Middle Watches from midnight to 0400.

Mr Derbyshire, Engineering Officer: A middle-aged man, who somehow managed to keep an ageing ship at sea throughout a long period of arduous service. He was in charge of his department for the whole 2½ years commission and lived just outside Portsmouth.

Old hands or fresh-faced newcomers, *Wild Swan* took them under her wing and knitted them into a happy and efficient team. Which was

---

* ERA = Engine Room Artificer.
† Not quite but John Slowly's deeds created a whole legend of tales, some of which we shall be recalling in these pages.

just as well for fresh battles awaited them, new tests of their endurance and fortitude under conditions of constant stress. Whether *Wild Swan* held together through these new strains and tensions would depend largely on how they pulled together.

CHAPTER FIVE

They Shall Not Pass
July–October 1940

On 1st July 1940, the Admiralty in London stated flatly that, if a sea-borne attack on the United Kingdom was to be attempted by the enemy during the month of July, there was reason to believe that it would be launched during the next ten days! The Commander-in-Chief, The Nore, under whose authority most of the threatened area lay, therefore issued detailed 'Anti-Invasion Instructions' to all naval forces concerned, under the designation of Operation 'Purge'.

Admiral Sir Reginald Plunkett-Ernle-Erle-Drax had his flotillas immediately reinforced by the ships of the 18th Cruiser Squadron, two of whose ships moved from the Humber to Sheerness, arriving at 0750 on 2nd July. These were the modern 6-inch cruisers *Birmingham* and *Sheffield*, while the older 'C' class 6-inch cruiser *Cardiff* was retained at Harwich.

In addition to *Cardiff* C-in-C, Nore had stationed at this port two destroyer flotillas, two so-called Striking Forces, made up of small coastal corvettes, and sundry light craft, trawlers, minesweepers, auxiliary patrol vessels, MTBs and the like. The principal ships were disposed as follows:

Base Ship: HMS *Badger*
16th Destroyer Flotilla: *Malcolm* (Leader), *Achates*, *Amazon*,
　　　　　　　　　　Ambuscade, *Antelope*, *Anthony* and *Arrow*.
18th Destroyer Flotilla: *Montrose* (Leader), *Venomous*, *Verity*, *Veteran*,
　　　　　　　　　　Whitshed, *Wild Swan*, *Wivern* and *Worcester*.
1st Anti-submarine Striking Force: *Mallard*, *Pintail*, *Puffin*, *Sheldrake*.
2nd Anti-submarine Striking Force: *Guillemot*, *Shearwater*, *Widgeon*.

As part of the standing plan to meet the possible invasion threat under 'Purge' the following dispositions were ordered to be maintained each night, commencing on 2nd/3rd July.

Patrol 'A': Three Harwich-based destroyers to patrol between Smiths
　　　　　Knoll and 54B buoy in position 52°27′ North, 2°06′ East.
Patrol 'B': The cruiser *Cardiff* and three more Harwich destroyers to

patrol the swept channel about seven miles each side of the Aldeburgh Light Float.

Patrol 'C': Two destroyers from the 21st Flotilla at Portsmouth, to anchor in the swept channel near the North-East Spit buoy during the hours of darkness with steam up on their main engines and cables ready to slip at instant notice. Their job was to repel any attempted enemy invasion in the Margate area or to reinforce the Dover flotilla if so required.

All these ships were to leave their patrols or anchorages at daylight and return to harbour except the two Harwich destroyers which were to carry out Patrol '0', between positions 52°45′ N, and 52° N by day while *Cardiff* and one destroyer returned to harbour. These patrols varied considerably according to circumstances and the ships available, and other patrols, M off Smiths Knoll, and T were subsequently introduced.

On the night of 5/6th July, for example, the C-in-C, Nore, received special information which led him considerably to reinforce the normal nightly patrols. The cruiser *Sheffield* was sailed from Sheerness at 1800 on the evening of the 5th to assist, returning at daylight next morning. Three Anti-Invasion Groups were then disposed to meet the German fleet thus:

From Harwich:
Group 3: *Achates, Verity* and *Venomous* on Patrol 'K' off Smiths Knoll.
Group 4: *Sheffield, Ambuscade, Arrow* and *Whitshed* on Patrol 'M' off Aldeburgh
Group 5: *Cardiff, Anthony, Malcolm, Veteran, Wild Swan, Wivern*; the corvettes *Mallard, Pintail, Puffin* and *Sheldrake*, Motor Torpedo Boats (MTB's), *14, 17, 18, 22, 24,* and *29*; Coastal Motor Boats (World War I MTB's); *104, 106* and *107*; Motor Anti-Submarine Boats (MASB's); *6, 7, 8* and *10*.

This massive force, together with Groups 1 and 2 from Dover and Portsmouth, was at sea throughout the night and had the expected invasion convoy run into this concentration of fire power it is difficult to see how it could have survived. But there was no convoy; the ships patrolled all night, then dispersed to their standby anchorages to await the next major alert. The next night a similar show of strength was mounted with *Birmingham* taking *Sheffield*'s place and returning to Southend, not Sheerness, on completion of the patrol.

What had prompted this massive defensive picket was reports of enemy invasion craft, tugs, barges and the like, on the move across the Channel. In this danger period the Royal Navy just continued with their task. On the night of 7/8th July *Cardiff* took patrol M. The following night this part was abandoned but instead the *Sheffield* and three Harwich destroyers carried out Patrol O. It was *Cardiff*'s turn next night, then *Birmingham* on 10/11th July, upon which she again returned to Sheerness. On the 11/12th *Sheffield* went out once more. On all these long searches throughout the night hours no incidents at all were reported, the eastern horizon remained empty of enemy vessels.

Such regular patrols by the big cruisers ran an element of risk of course, and the period of the half-moon which commenced on 10th July, increased the risk to these valuable ships from E-boat attack. C-in-C, Nore asked the commander of the 18th Cruiser Squadron whether he would prefer not to patrol on these nights and as the answer was in the affirmative these dispositions were cancelled and revised destroyer patrols substituted. The new cruisers were held in readiness but did not patrol until specially ordered. One of the new beats was known as Patrol T, and, as W.K. Harrison recalls, it was not the most popular of duties owing to its vulnerability:

We often seemed to be in the company of *Malcolm, Montrose* and *Wren* at this time and *Wild Swan* normally teamed up with one of these for what was known as T Patrol. For this duty the two selected destroyers steamed between two buoys, one close to the English coast and the other fairly close to the enemy coast. The idea, as we understood it, was to intercept any enemy vessels approaching southern England as at this time an invasion was imminent, or seemed to be.

T-buoy was the one near to the enemy coast. We always felt very uneasy approaching T-buoy as we felt like sitting ducks as we approached this marker each time. I could never understand why the routine was not varied a little to reduce the risk of our being surprised.

One night we sailed to conduct this patrol as usual but *Wild Swan* developed engine trouble of some sort and we signalled the C-in-C to this effect. We duly received a signal back that detailed our chummy ship *Wren* to replace us. That night *Montrose* and *Wren* went out on T patrol and we had a welcome night in harbour. Next morning I was very disturbed to find that only *Montrose* had

returned to the destroyer trot. I believe there were very few survivors from *Wren*. If we had not had that lucky break it would have
been us, not them.

What had happened was that after completing the patrol without
incident, the two destroyers were returning to Harwich when they
witnessed a heavy air attack being made on the minesweeper flotilla
off that port. In a gallant effort to protect the minesweepers the two
destroyers steered flat-out to their aid with all their AA guns firing.
They succeeded in their worthy objective but at heavy cost as the
enemy turned his attentions to them and the *Wren* (Commander
F.W.G. Harker) was hit and sunk.

Fate was kind to them on the next T patrol also and again a sister
ship took the brunt while the *Wild Swan* escaped. This was on the
morning of 30th July, again after a night's patrol in company with
Ambuscade and *Whitshed*. Once more the night had produced nothing
and, after keeping strictly to the War Channel for the first 50-mile leg
in line-ahead, they reached the notorious buoy and commenced their
anti-invasion sweep in line abreast south from the Zuider Zee.

Just as she turned for home there came a colossal roar, and a huge
column of dirty water erupted from *Whitshed*'s bows. She had struck
a floating mine which tore the entire bow of the ship off. All main
steam was instantly cut off to bring her to a halt and take the pressure
off the straining bulkheads below. While the other two destroyers circled warily, watching for more mines, the damage was assessed. Fortunately the bulkheads took the strain and were quickly reinforced.
Then *Wild Swan* went alongside bows-to-stern and prepared to take
her stricken sister in tow stern-first while *Ambuscade* positioned herself astern to provide AA protection. Again, it was a long, slow crawl
back to Harwich. When *Wild Swan* attempted to increase speed the
cripple proved uncontrollable and so the journey continued at a
stately ten knots until, in the vicinity of the Cork Light Vessel, the
tow was slipped and *Whitshed* entered harbour crippled but safe.

Their duties also included work of a more clandestine nature.
With the whole European coastline, from the North Cape to the
Spanish border, now enemy territory, opportunity was taken to land
agents from boats in an effort to garner knowledge of how the
enemy's invasion preparations were progressing.

Little is on record of these furtive missions but Signalman Harrison gives us a rare glimpse into this twilight world:

During this period there was a considerable amount of 'cloak-and-dagger' work. Out of the blue would come a signal from C-in-C, Nore, to raise steam 'with all despatch' and get ready to slip. Then a small group of people, always well camouflaged in battle-dress, would come aboard and the ship would sail at dusk and steam close to the coast of France. In the blackness of the night these people would normally be transported by the ship's motor-boat to the shore.

As a rule these mystery groups would comprise two or three men but on one occasion I particularly remember one solitary person disappearing into the cold, black inhospitable night. I remember feeling very sorry for this lonely man as we steamed away and I made my way towards my warm hammock.

Occasionally I recall the ship quietly approaching a jetty and the mysterious passengers, who always kept themselves apart during their voyages, jumping straight ashore before we quickly and silently backed away into the darkness. They sped away without looking back at the ship or waving back at us.

From time-to-time these night-time missions would be replaced by daytime escort duties. The 'FS' convoys had originally commenced from the Forth in Scotland and ran south to the Thames at Southend-on-Sea but after a while this was changed and they ran in two sections, the greatest danger being in the south. Therefore the southern sections commenced running from the Tyne and the normal escort was constantly reinforced from the anti-invasion forces flotillas as they passed southward, first from the Humber, then from Harwich and finally from Sheerness if required.

Typical of such 'bus-stop' escort services were the arrangements laid on for an important double convoy, MT26 (Methil-Tyne) and FS38 (Forth-South) which totalled some thirty-three vessels in all. All these ships would have to be concentrated in just two columns to pass safely through the swept channels and as a consequence were strung out over a large corridor of sea, sitting targets for the regular morning bombing. To try and offer some degree of protection for this gaggle of merchantmen there were the destroyer *Woolston* and the sloop *Fleetwood*. For this scanty escort help was provided. From the Humber, where Captain Lord Louis Mountbatten's 5th Flotilla was operating, were sailed the destroyers *Jupiter* and *Kelvin* and the coastal corvette *Shearwater*.

These ships joined the convoy south of the Tyne at 1010 on 1st

August and remained with it most of the day. At 2000 that night the two destroyers returned to their base. Early the following morning, at 0615 on the 2nd, *Malcolm, Wild Swan* and *Ambuscade*, returning from another uneventful T patrol, supplemented the escort to provide extra AA protection. They stayed until the time of greatest danger was over, *Wild Swan* and *Ambuscade* leaving at 1000 and *Malcolm* at 1115. Little time remained, once the destroyers had returned to Harwich, fuelled and re-stored, for their crews to grab some rest before night fell and they were off on another anti-invasion sweep following another scare. The night of 3rd/4th August saw them patrolling with the cruiser *Cardiff*, destroyers *Venomous, Verity* and *Wivern* and coastal corvettes *Puffin, Shearwater,* and *Sheldrake*. It was another false alarm.

And so this was the pattern during August: patrol, escort, patrol. As destroyers became due for refits they left the anchorage for a period and fresh faces replaced old friends for a time. Thus on the night of 15th/16th T patrol was conducted by *Wild Swan, Veteran* and one of the new Hunt class destroyers from the 1st Flotilla detached from Portsmouth, the *Berkeley*. Finally it became *Wild Swan*'s turn to undertake a boiler clean and general refit at Chatham and on 20th August she was taken in hand. This meant one week's rest, time enough for most of her crew to snatch at least a few days' leave.

There were several times during September when it looked as if the balloon really had gone up at last and that the Germans were actually at sea and heading for the coast as had long been expected. The height of this scare period was 19th-26th September, when the Admiralty considered that all conditions of time, opportunity and tide would be right. But there were any number of scares before that, in particular on the night of 7th/8th September. On the previous night there had been sightings of a large concentration of enemy ships off Calais, some sixty vessels in all. At once the Admiralty placed all cruisers, destroyers and patrol craft on immediate alert during darkness and all refits and boiler-cleans were hastily abandoned. Once again *Wild Swan*'s timing had been immaculate and *she* was ready.

In one very important respect, however, *Wild Swan* was not quite the *same* ship for now she was under the command of a brand-new skipper. . . .

It was known that a replacement for Lieutenant-Commander Younghusband had been appointed. In the *Gazette* for 22nd September that appointment had been confirmed as Lieutenant-Commander Claude E.L. Sclater, RN. It was typical of the man who had led them through thick-and-thin in so many tight corners since last September that, when the year's appointment from reserve was up, he left them quietly, almost apologetically. They came in from one operation and when they sailed again he was no longer there on the bridge, his tall form hunched over the chart-box, calm and reassuring.

It was only right that, after a year's service, Younghusband and his like, should be granted a respite. They had been called back from retirement to command, and it was upon their broad shoulders that the first shock of war had fallen. Far from commanding a destroyer in a quiet area he had found himself and his ship thrust into the very thickest of the fighting. He, and his contemporaries, had taken the strain and held firmly. Thanks to them Britain was still fighting back with determination. Now it was time to hand over to younger men, however eager, or reluctant, they might themselves feel about it. One of the younger officers aboard *Wild Swan* at this time was to write:

> He was aged about 46 on commissioning, and he had certainly had a basinful by the autumn of 1940. He left us quite soon after this, and it is quite possible that he went back into retirement at his own request. It seemed to me that a number of officers were recalled early in World War II to fill gaps caused by the sudden increase in ships going to sea. But, as the months went by, and indeed as the strain began to tell, the older officers were replaced by younger ones.
>
> I cannot recall him ever mentioning earlier appointments. After his leaving *Wild Swan*, he might have gone to a shore base, but I do not know. I believe the upper age limit for compulsory military service was then 42 years. I think he probably left the ship during a brief leave period for the ship's company, and when we returned Lieutenant-Commander Sclater was onboard. I did not see or hear again of Younghusband; but this was not unusual in wartime, especially for those who went overseas.*

The man who replaced him in command of *Wild Swan* was certainly younger, but was no stranger to combat either.

---

* As Commander Younghusband DSC he survived the war and enjoyed a long retirement before passing away in 1966.

By contrast with his predecessor, he was a very quiet man. He had a dark beard and used to stand for hours on the bridge, picking with his fingers at his whiskers. He was a survivor from the battleship *Royal Oak*, sunk early in the war by a German U-boat which penetrated the fleet anchorage at Scapa Flow.

He was cool and pensive, very much a loner, who did not suffer fools gladly. However he was held in respect by the ship's company, who carried on with the 'Dunkirk Spirit' until the end.

A lower-deck viewpoint of their new captain confirmed this view:

Aged approximately thirty, Lieutenant-Commander Sclater was bearded and a typical RN officer. He was generally both respected and trusted, but was very much aloof.

Sclater recalls:

It was in August, 1940 that I relieved Lieutenant-Commander Younghusband, and brought *Wild Swan* back to Harwich after boiler cleaning at Chatham. On arrival, I reported to Captain Halsey in HMS *Malcolm*, the flotilla leader. He explained the situation, and said that *Wild Swan* would have a stand-off that night. No sooner had I returned onboard than a signal was received ordering the whole flotilla to raise steam for full speed, and land confidential books, a sign that we were going into dangerous waters. As I learned shortly afterwards we had been ordered to attack a convoy off the Dutch coast.

Wild Swan was fifth in the order of leaving harbour, and, when we had slipped from the buoy and taken our place in the line for the first time under my command, my spirits rose as the yeoman of signals reported that *Malcolm* was flying the signal '*Wild Swan* manoeuvre well executed.' This was my first experience of Captain Halsey's gift of leadership.

After passing through a narrow gap in the mine barrier, we steamed towards Holland in single line at thirty knots. It was a clear night but our luck was out, the convoy had evidently put into a Dutch port for the night. After a sweep to the north, we turned for home to avoid being caught in the North Sea in daylight. On the way back a small dark shape was sighted in the moonlight. We were just about to open fire, when it switched on bright lights, revealing a trawler clearly marked with the Red Cross. On return

HMS *Wild Swan* The destroyer has been taken alongside the crippled troopship *Prinsis Juliana* off the Hook of Holland during the German invasion of that country, 12th May, 1940. Dutch troops are climbing over the bows of their ship and being assisted on board the destroyer before being taken to England.

At the entrance to Dunkirk on the North-east coast of France, during the massive evacuation of 338,000 troops of the British Expeditionary Force at the end of May 1940, showing a close up of the main lighthouse, with a pall of black smoke from burning oil tanks.

to harbour, we were told that these craft, which were used for other purposes besides picking up ditched German airmen, were not declared, or accepted as, hospital ships and were to be sunk. On later occasions we sank several of them.

Commander Sclater recalls the tense situation at the time he joined the 16th Flotilla:

> The RAF was heavily engaged in the Battle of Britain and fighters could rarely be spared for the protection of shipping. A keen look-out and a light finger on the trigger was the order of the day. Destroyers did their best to augment their inadequate AA arma-ment with Bren and Lewis guns acquired at Dunkirk and other evacuation ports.*
>
> It can readily be observed that seagoing in the North Sea was a hazardous occupation at this period, and bombs and magnetic mines soon took their toll. After the loss of HMS *Wren* and severe mine damage to HMS *Whitshed* it became apparent that the flotilla should not be risked at sea in daylight until the invasion actually began. Consequently the routine became to leave Harwich just before dark and return after the minesweepers had swept the approach channel at dawn. If a quiet night was expected, half the flotilla would go out on patrol, but, at any hint of enemy move-ments, the whole flotilla would put to sea, thus ships frequently had a succession of nights at continuous action stations.
>
> So the Navy maintained the offensive, leaving the German High Command in no doubt as to the reception that would face any attempt at invasion, while Britain feverishy re-equipped her armies and fortified her coasts.

When the concentration of German ships had first been sighted on the 6/7th, four MTB's had been sailed from Dover on an 'offensive recce' in conjunction with four destroyesr. They sighted nothing but the destroyer force was heavily shelled by the radar-controlled heavy guns which the Germans had set-up on the Calais coast to cover their invasion fleet.

The worst was feared. It was Saturday 7th September. A strong force of 300 German bombers and 600 fighters was seen on its way to deliver a massive blow to London's docks and the City area. At a

---

* Lieutenant-Commander Sclater had formerly been first lieutenant of the *Broke*.

tense meeting at No. 10 the Premier and his Chiefs-of-Staff decided
to place the nation on full alert that night and the codeword for invasion, 'Cromwell', was issued.

The Army stood-to in readiness ashore, the aircraft of Bomber
Command, hitherto on the sidelines during the Battle of Britain,
commenced their pre-emptive strikes with heavy bombers against
the French ports.* At sea the Royal Navy added its weight to the proceedings. If the German invasion fleet *had* sailed that night it would
have had a hot reception. It would have been bombed as it sailed,
shelled, rammed and torpedoed as it crossed and met on the beaches
by a fully-alert defence. Perhaps it was as well for them that they did
not.

C-in-C, the Nore, had already laid his plans, a powerful force of
cruisers and destroyers was to operate off Dunkirk and Ostend that
night. Under the codeword 'Rival' movements had already been put
in train. On the 6th the cruisers *Aurora* and *Cardiff* sailed from the
Humber at night for Sheerness. They were met off the Humber Light
Vessel by the destroyers *Wild Swan* and *Wivern* who escorted them
south. Again it was a false alarm, no enemy stirred. If the Germans
were proving reluctant to poke their noses outside their harbours at
this crucial period the Navy was determined to see that it remained
that way by bombardment and intensive patrolling.

On the night of 10th/11th September it was *Wild Swan*'s turn
again. The operation was initiated by a signal from the Admiralty:

VCNS to C in C, Nore: 1701. Three destroyers are to be sent to attack any
shipping observed off Ostend tonight.
 C in C, Nore to VCNS: 2020. Asking what route is suitable?
 C in C, Nore to D16, Veteran, Wild Swan: 2026. Sail so as to arrive off
Ostend at 0315/11. Route (given). Attack any shipping in Ostend Roads
and look out for E-boats. If movements or navigational difficulties
involve risk of grounding you must abandon attack at your discretion.
Return by same route. Air protection will be asked for from daylight.

For Wild Swans this exchange meant one thing, the period of defensive was at last over; from now on they were on the attack!

D16 was of course the Captain (D) 16th Destroyer Flotilla, Captain
T.E. Halsey, while *Veteran* was commanded by Lieutenant-Commander Jack Broome. Late on the evening of 10th September they

* Attacks by light bombers had commenced two nights earlier.

set off. The *Wild Swan*'s Navigating Officer remembered that:

> The destroyers taking part sailed from Harwich just after dark, so they would not be spotted by enemy reconnaissance planes. Threading our way through British defensive and known enemy offensive minefields, we steamed across the southern North Sea to within a few miles of the Belgian shore. Earlier checks made by the RAF had revealed large numbers of barges assembled in the harbour at Ostend.

Halsey himself reported:

> Courses were followed as ordered. As previously reported North Hinder Light Buoy was not sighted, but, feeling fairly certain of our position, course was continued and Kwint Bank Whistle Buoy was sighted on the expected bearing. As previously reported, Ostend Bank RB and RW Whistle Buoys and Wenduyne Bank Bell Buoy were burning correctly and on station. Ostend was approached on course 171 degrees, making good 175 degrees. Ships were in single line ahead in order *Malcolm, Wild Swan, Veteran*, speed 12 knots, on approaching the coast.

Malcolm was one of the first of the Nore destroyers fitted with a radar set, an Air/Surface Vessel model (ASV) which greatly increased their versatility in night operations of this kind. It could be used for both locating targets and ranging them and of course it gave a comforting degree of security against surprise by enemy surface forces. At 0316 on the morning of 11th September, *Malcolm*'s radar set picked up four objects off the starboard bow about three miles distant. The starboard lookout sighted a large barge in that direction shortly afterwards. They were in luck!

Eleven minutes after the first contact the flotilla altered course to 235 degrees, parallel to the enemy coastline and, at a range of only one thousand yards, fire was opened on this barge bearing Green 50. The second salvo from *Malcolm* scored direct hits and bits and pieces could be clearly seen, by the light of aircraft flares over Ostend, flying off it as her 4.7-inch shells smashed home. As they fired they increased speed to 20 knots keeping line-ahead formation.

> It appeared to be rather less than the length of a destroyer, with a slightly raised bow and low freeboard of 2 or 3 feet. It is thought to

have been self-propelled and under way at slow speed on a parallel
course to *Malcolm*. This barge was engaged and hit by each
destroyer in turn, *Veteran* reporting it awash and sinking when she
had passed.

When this unfortunate target passed astern the destroyers checked
fire and their gun mountings swung round towards a smaller barge
sighted about Green 60 a little further to the north-west. Two or
three 4.7-inch salvos were pumped into her but only one hit was
observed before their escort, a large armed trawler, was sighted on
the port bow and fire was immediately switched to her. For a brief
interval this trawler returned the fire but was soon heavily knocked
about, ' . . . more than one shell of a salvo hitting her just under the
bridge, which produced a spout of flame of some height. She was last
seen breaking up and sinking.'

It was now 0329 and, as nothing more showed up on the radar
screen or could be observed ahead of the force, course was altered to
035 degrees, and, soon afterwards they were again rewarded with a
fresh target when a small trawler or tug was sighted on the starboard
bow, towing another small barge, which was later reported as being
'about the size and appearance of a Thames barge without mast'.
They were steering east.

Again fire was opened with both main armament and the pom-
poms so close was the range and the barge was well hit, before target
was shifted to the tug. This vessel too was hit repeatedly by all calibre
weapons, one shell sending most of her bridge over the side. This
trawler was last seen very low in the water, apparently sinking. The
barge had been hit once by *Malcolm* with a 4.7-inch shell and by both
Wild Swan and *Veteran* in turn as they passed.

So far the response from the enemy had been muted but now the
shore batteries woke up to the fact that it was not just bombing that
was taking place at Ostend.

> There was a fierce engagement and our little ships came under fire
> from the shore batteries. The destroyer force made frequent alter-
> ations of course to avoid being hit, finally withdrawing at high
> speed to return to base.

So wrote Patrick Satow.

The enemy return fire from ashore consisted mainly of white

tracer which was thought to be of pom-pom calibre most of which was fired at the destroyers at the end of the run to the west and more after they altered course back to the east. Captain Halsey wrote:

> Some small shell of about 12-pounder or less and three or four splashes on *Malcolm*'s port quarter and *Wild Swan*'s port bow, estimated at 4-inch or 6-inch calibre was reported. I personally only saw the white tracer shell, some of which passed fairly close over the after part of *Malcolm*, the remainder is based on reports of officers in *Malcolm* and of ships of the flotilla and is considered reliable.

Malcolm's gyro had failed at the first salvo so the run westward had to be estimated as this was not immediately observed. When it was the ship was steadied on the magnetic course then being steered. As a result the flotilla steamed considerably closer to the hostile coastline than had been intended. *Veteran* reported hearing the Stroombank Whistle Buoy close to port. After retirement speed was increased to 25 knots to reach safety before daylight brought retribution.

Actions such as this were a great filip for the morale of the crew. There is nothing worse than waiting for the enemy to strike first. From the outbreak of the war it had seemed that Germany always had the initiative and the British had to respond, usually too late. It made a great change to take the fight to the enemy for a change. Unfortunately he proved an elusive target and actions like this were the exception rather than the rule. However the Royal Navy kept up the pressure during this vital period.

On the night of the 12th/13th they were off again down-Channel. *Wild Swan* sailed from Harwich at 1700 with *Malcolm* and *Venomous* with orders to proceed to the vicinity of Boulogne, then to sweep towards Cap Gris Nez. Their objective was, yet again, the destruction of any shipping or barges met off the French coast. But on this trip an interesting rider was added to the Commander-in-Chief's instructions, 'Prisoners are required if possible.' This raised visions of boarding parties swinging across to fight at cutlass point in the grand old manner, and, if this proved to be rather impractical for a force of destroyers in World War II, it certainly gave an indication of how desperate things were at this time. Prisoners meant information and for information on what her fate was Britain was desperate. Alone and unaided she now faced the whole might of Nazi Germany.

That Germany had taken control of the whole of Western Europe with comparative ease. It had Italy as an ally, a non-aggression pact with Soviet Russia and America remained isolationist.

Reports received earlier that day indicated that enemy invasion barges might be heading for Boulogne that night and the flotilla was instructed to sweep to 50 or 51°N before returning to Harwich and to take a course to pass south of Le Colbart to avoid troublesome shore-batteries. Again they complied but went unrewarded with sightings. There was some excitement of a different nature however, as W.K. Harrison recalls:

During the period described an incident occurred which highlighted the importance of good communications. We were on patrol off Boulogne seeking enemy shipping. Captain 'D' took charge of the operation in *Malcolm* and in the darkness of the night off France we received an order from him to 'act independently'. The three ships went in their own ways and during the alterations in course the W/T bell rang on the bridge and 'Sparks' got an order over the voicepipe, 'Orange Robert One'.

We grabbed the Fleet Signal Book because this was obviously a signal from the FSB coding. The book showed this signal to translate to 'Set ASDIC watch' on a certain frequency. Our astonished Captain asked for the signal to be confirmed and we went back to the 'Sparker'* to verify the signal. Back came the reply 'Orange Robert One-Definitely'. The perplexed captain just turned his back, shrugged his shoulders and ignored the signal.

About ten minutes later the captain asked if anyone could see *Malcolm* or *Venomous*. Neither of these two ships was in sight and after about another five minutes or so the Captain decided to make course home to Harwich. We saw no sign of the others *en route* but at dawn, as we entered harbour, we saw *Malcolm* at anchor and *Venomous* swinging at her buoy.

Before long a visual signal came across, 'Where the bloody hell did you get to last night?' The signal also requested that the Captain and the Yeoman were to be aboard *Malcolm* later that morning for an enquiry. When Yeoman of Signals Burton came back he was cursing all the signalmen and asking why they had not anticipated what the 'Orange Robert One' signal should have been.

It turned out that what had happened was that Telegraphist

* Sparks, Sparker = W/T, or Radio operator.

Jack Darling had received the signal from *Malcolm* but in so doing had missed the link sign out. The *actual* signal that arrived was 'Link Orange Robert One', which meant 'Order One'. 'Order One' in turn meant "Form single line ahead and follow". The link sign he missed was .^{A}-/.^{A}-. This simple DE-DA, DE-DA being missed could have left the *Wild Swan* in a great deal of trouble. The mistake was obvious to all in the cold light of the next day but at the time it came in nobody gave it a thought.

Another short, sharp action took place on the night of the 13th/14th, again off Boulogne and this time they ran into some more enemy trawlers. Once more they inflicted some damage on them before breaking off the action under shore fire. This little brush lasted from 0115 to 0135 on the morning of the 13th. The pace could not last for ever, once more the strain was beginning to tell. They had escaped any damage from the enemy but on 16th September in Harwich harbour they suffered a slight collision with the destroyer *Worcester* which left them with their port flare holed two foot below the fo'c'sle by the mess deck after bulkheads. Neither ship was badly hurt and a hole some five feet by one-and-a-half feet in her bows did not prevent *Wild Swan* sailing on patrol again at 1909 on the 17th in company with *Venomous* and *Wivern*.

Perhaps it was a warning not to be too complacent. Certainly the luck of the 'Frantic Duck' continued to hold out. Perhaps it was her special degaussing early in the war; perhaps her guardian angel working overtime, but again she escaped by the skin of her teeth. It was the morning of 18th September. The flotilla was proceeding in line-ahead at 20 knots in the order *Wivern*, *Venomous*, *Wild Swan*. The destroyers were some two cables apart in position 51°59' N, 1°44' E when they set off a magnetic mine at a distance of about 3 to 4 cables from *Wivern*. The upheaval was tremendous and the shock-wave considerable, but all destroyers escaped without damage, other than to *Wild Swan*'s crockery which was smashed up completely!

On Sunday the 22nd they were at sea patrolling off the Dogger Bank in position 55°47' N, 2°55' E. *Veteran*, *Venomous* and *Wild Swan* were acting as part of the covering force for a force of minelaying destroyers from the 20th Flotilla who were carrying out a 'PR' operation off the Dutch Coast near Oost Gat. This job required a particular brand of courage. Just two weeks before the flotilla had lost two of their number and had another damaged when they had run into an enemy minefield, but the surviving ships carried on. For *Wild Swan* the trip was uneventful.

The middle of September was to mark another landmark in *Wild Swan*'s career. The enemy was curiously reluctant to venture from his harbour and bombardments and patrols had failed to lure him out. Plans were therefore being put in hand to go in after him. Once more the old seafaring traditions of Drake and Raleigh seemed to be resurrected in World War II, for the talk was of 'Fire-Ships'. Instead of floating blazing hulks into Cadiz to thwart the Armada the modern version was to send in oil tankers ablaze and steer them into the French ports to wreak havoc among the packed barges and lighters there. Thus was born Operation Lucid (formerly 'Lucifer').

On 8th August a meeting of the Petroleum Board had revealed that a special mixture could give a very fierce flame, enough to 'set the sea alight'. This concept appealed to the Prime Minister, ever alert for some form of offensive action and the project was given the go-ahead. In charge of the naval aspect of the operations was placed Captain Augustus Agar .., a very apt choice for he had the reputation as a 'fire-eater'. He could now live up to it with a vengeance!

Plans were made to obtain old tankers, fit them out at south coast ports and fill them with a mixture of 50 per cent heavy oil, 25 per cent diesel and 25 per cent petrol. This cargo could be easily ignited with cordite fuses, gun-cotton and depth charges. The idea was to tow them across the Channel at a time of favourable moon and tide and blow them up off the ports of Boulogne, Calais and Ostend. The blazing oil mixture would then be carried into the harbours by the tide and the resultant holocaust would wipe out the laboriously-assembled invasion fleet.

Naturally the Ministry of Shipping was not going to sacrifice its best ships for this task, and, as a result the tankers Agar was eventually allocated were, in his own words, 'cranky and slow'. He only managed to get four, *Mytilus*, *Oakfield*, *War Newab* and *War Nizam*, in time to be seriously considered.

The first attempt was fixed for the night of 25th/26th September. The forces for Lucid were organised into three groups, thus:-

Force A: *War Nizam* escorted by *Campbell* (D.21, Captain Augustus Agar), and *Garth*, minesweepers *Sutton*, *Salamander* and *Selkirk*, plus MTB's and ML's for smoke-making.

Force B: *War Newab* escorted by *Beagle* and *Wolverine*, minesweepers

Niger, Elgin and *Selkirk,* plus MTB and ML's for smoke-
making.

Force C: *Veteran, Venomous* and *Wild Swan* from the Nore to act as a
covering force.

Wild Swan and the rest of Force C sailed from Sheerness at 2130 on
the night of the 25th and steamed up as far as the North Goodwin
Light Vessel before taking up their covering position. But all was far
from well with the fireships. The *War Newab* was only good for a
speed at best of six knots. She left Portsmouth at 0930 on the 25th
escorted by *Wolverine* and *Beagle* for Southend but she was leaking in
many places and was considered unfit for service.

The *War Nizam* had, due to unforeseen delays, only been able to
load 2,850 tons of fuel. She sailed at 1830 from Sheerness with the
destroyer *Garth* as escort. The rest of Force A followed at 2100, with
Agar himself embarked aboard *Campbell.* Even as they headed to
their start positions it was clear the operation was foredoomed to failure. The wind was coming from an unsuitable quarter for Boulogne
and the MTB's were unable to operate in such conditions.

With *War Newab* out of the running it all now rested on her ancient
sister. As *Campbell* passed *War Nizam* on the way to the Edinburgh
Channel in the Thames Estuary she could be clearly seen making
thick, black smoke and wallowing slowly in the seas that were running. It appeared her patched-up boilers were giving trouble and
soon *Garth* signalled a reduction in speed to 5½ knots, and later to 4½
knots. It was painfully obvious to Agar that she would never have
made the rendezvous position. In the event she did not have to for the
Admiralty called the whole operation off. Officially it was because
the fireships could only be used successfully once with any chance of
surprise and Their Lordships were reluctant to waste such a promising weapon by utilising just one in poor weather conditions. Actually
it was obvious that the work, hastily carried out, was not correctly
done. More time was required.

The next favourite period was the night of 3rd/4th October, but,
another emergency was to send them hurrying to sea.

It was just before midnight on the night of 30th September/1st
October when reports came in that a German destroyer force was at
sea off the South Foreland. Destroyers were already at sea searching
for them off Dover but *Eglinton, Venomous* and *Wild Swan* were rushed
to sea from Sheerness to reinforce them. The enemy unit concerned
was the 5th Torpedo Boat Flotilla commanded by Commander

Henne with the destroyers *Falke, Greif, Kondor* and *Seeadler* and they were conducting another of their regular minelaying sorties with the codename 'Werner'. Time and time again German destroyers had slipped into British coastal waters and sewn their deadly cargoes since the outbreak of war. With the opening up of the French ports to them their range of activities increased, from the East Coast and Thames Estuary, to the South Coast and the Bristol Channel. They operated almost with impunity for, although often sighted and chased, they were rarely caught and usually had the extra speed to escape serious mishap. This night was no exception, for although *Wild Swan* and her consorts quartered the Straits, the German flotilla dropped their mines and headed swiftly for home without being brought to book.

Frustrated the destroyers returned to Sheerness to await their next assignment. This time Agar was hopeful of having three tankers available, and during the day on 2nd October they loaded with fuel. *War Nizam* had had some of her most glaring defects remedied at Sheerness Dockyard and the *Oakfield* had been completed by Chatham Dockyard. Both loaded their deadly mixture at Port Victoria, Sheerness during the day. The third vessel, the *Mytilus*, had been finished for service by Portsmouth Dockyard equally as hastily as the ill-fated *War Newab*, and, it soon transpired, with no more care. She commenced loading her cargo at Hamble in Southampton Water.

The whole force again sailed but the wind fell light from the south-west during passage which forced another postponement until the following night. The *Mytilus* had shown the same symptoms as her predecessor during her short journey out and back, developing a heavy list due to leaks between her internal bulkheads. On the night of the 4th/5th they tried again. This time the force was organised as follows:

Force A (Target-Calais): *War Nizam, Mytilus*; Destroyers *Campbell, Cottesmore, Mackay* and *Walpole*; Minesweepers *Salamander, Selkirk* and *Sutton*; MTB's *31* and *32*; M.L.'s *108* and *110*.

Force B (Target-Boulogne): *Oakfield*; Destroyers *Hambledon* (with Agar embarked), *Garth, Venetia* and *Witch*; Minesweepers *Elgin, Hussar* and *Speedwell*; MTB's *34* and Norwegian *5*; ML's *106* and *111*.

Force C (Covering Force): *Veteran, Venomous* and *Wild Swan*

Again the force sailed but the weather frustrated them. The wind stayed stubbornly south-west, or south-south-west and did not change after dusk as expected. The promised bomber support to cause a diversion was cancelled as well due to the weather and Lucid was postponed yet again. The crews of the fireships had a hazardous task ahead of them. They had to set fire to their ships close into enemy territory, get off their floating furnaces and make their escape in the escorting ships before the wall of flame cut them off. After three false starts not surprisingly they were highly tensed-up and it was decided to give them a rest before the next attempt, which was planned now for the night of the 7th/8th October.

Ill-luck continued to dog the whole operation. The *War Newab* unloaded her mixture at Port Victoria and her mixture was added to that of *Oakfield* and *War Nizam*. *Mytilus* was ruled out because of unseaworthiness. *War Newab* still had some 1,400 tons which was to be unloaded at Thames Haven but she was left behind at Sheerness with a reduced crew. For the night of 7th/8th, these two sailed with the escorts much as before, but the *Hambledon*, with Agar again embarked, struck a mine on the way out and was badly damaged. The Calais force, following some way behind, still had to cross the freshly mined area, and meanwhile the Boulogne force had now been reduced to two ships for escort purposes as *Vesper* had to tow *Hambledon* back to port. Again the wind failed to veer as had been hoped for and the operation was yet again postponed until 1st/2nd November.* *Wild Swan* took no further part in this abortive mission.

More mundane problems occupied the *Wild Swan* after her return to Harwich when she was sent to reinforce the escort of convoy FS6 for which the 4th Minesweeping Flotilla were busy sweeping a fresh path, after German ships had laid mines ahead of it. But this task was to be her last on the East Coast, fresh orders were to send her to a new theatre of war. The prospects looked bleak when this was announced; the North Atlantic, with winter fast approaching. . .

* As a point of interest 'Lucid' never did sail again. The idea was killed off due to a combination of badly-prepared fireships, lack of destroyers and doubts on its chances of success so late in the year with unpredictable stormy weather.

CHAPTER SIX

A Dour Struggle
October-December 1940

As the threat of invasion receded, the need for semi-permanent stationing of flotillas on the East and South-east coasts lessened. While the destroyers remained on station in readiness, however, and the heavy losses and damage sustained in the withdrawal from Europe had yet to be made good, the German submarines operating in the Atlantic had benefited.

The main convoy route was that of the HX (Halifax) convoys, OG (Gibraltar) convoys, SL (Sierra Leone) convoys and the slow SC (Sydney, Cape Breton, Canada) convoys. As U-boat strength increased, the great strategic advantage of having the French Atlantic ports at their disposal came into play. They could now range much further afield and made the South-Western Approaches virtually untenable. All convoys were diverted to route in and out of the North-Western Approaches instead, to the Mersey, the Clyde or Londonderry. In recognition of this fact HQ of Western Approaches Command moved from Plymouth to Liverpool in February 1941.

By the autumn of 1940 not only were the U-boats ranging ever further afield and in ever greater strength but their efforts were aided, and supplemented, by the use of very long-range aircraft of the Luftwaffe based in France, notably the Focke-Wulf FW200 Kondor aircraft of KG40 based on airfields near Bordeaux. Although these aircraft could only carry comparatively light bomb-loads they could seek out unescorted merchantmen far beyond the escorts' range for 1,375 miles from their bases and deliver their attacks with relative immunity, having little or nothing to fear from the pathetic AA weapons of the merchant ships themselves.

Equally as damaging was the fact that such aircraft could home U-boats onto convoys that they would otherwise never have found. The German tactics of attacking on the surface instead of submerged also found the defence unprepared, although such methods had been openly advocated by the head of the U-boat arm, Admiral Karl Dönitz, *before* the war started. At night on the surface, the conning-tower of a U-boat offered only a tiny target, whereas the bulks of the

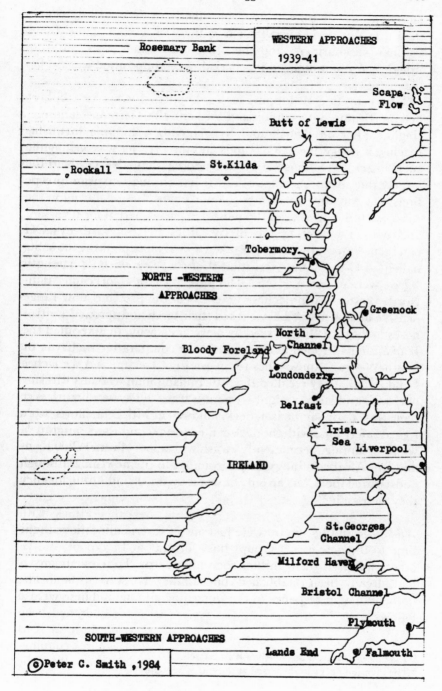

WESTERN APPROACHES
1939-41

Rosemary Bank

Scapa Flow

Butt of Lewis

Rockall   St.Kilda

Tobermory

NORTH -WESTERN
APPROACHES

Greenock

North
Channel

Bloody Foreland

Londonderry

Belfast

Irish
Sea   Liverpool

IRELAND

St.Georges
Channel

Milford Haven

Bristol Channel

Plymouth

SOUTH-WESTERN APPROACHES

Lands End   Falmouth

©Peter C. Smith ,1984

merchantmen in convoy stood out like barn-doors. Little wonder then that this period was known as the first 'Happy Time' by the German submariners, and their most successful 'Aces' all established their reputations in this period, when opposition was negligible.

The rising tide of shipping losses threatened to starve a hitherto defiant Britain into submission without the Germans landing a single soldier on British soil! By September shipping losses had reached a staggering 448,621 tons and the Premier was writing that such losses were 'most grievous', adding that, 'No doubt this is largely due to the shortage of destroyers through invasion precautions. . . . Anyhow, we cannot go on like this.'*

So, with the passing of the most dangerous period for invasion,† and with a mounting toll of casualties in the North Atlantic, emergency measures had to be taken. On 22nd September it was signalled to C-in-C, the Nore that *Malcolm, Veteran, Wild Swan* and *Wivern* were to be sailed ASAP for Liverpool for escort duties in the North-Western Approaches. Veterans of the previous year looked pensive at this news. They sucked their teeth and screwed up their noses in disgust. When asked by newcomers why, they recalled how *Wild Swan* had rolled and heaved in the comparative shelter of the South-Western Approaches to the south of Ireland and the west of Land's End. They recalled the little midshipman who just vanished one dark and stormy night without a trace. They recalled clawing their way aft down the iron deck, holding on with both hands to the rigged safety lines with the deck canted over at impossible angles, the wind screaming, permanently awash with a foot of water sluicing to-and-fro. All these things they recounted to the newcomers, smiled and assured them, 'It can only be worse up north, lad.' And, for once, they were right!

Wild Swan and her group were just one of several allocations at this time to the new escort groups busy forming at Liverpool, and yet others followed them thither soon afterwards. Four escort groups had already been established, but another five were to be formed immediately in response to the worsening situation. These were as follows:

---

* *Their Finest Hour, The Second World War,* Cassell.
† The invasion fleet was dispersed at the end of September.

5th Escort Group: *Walker, Wivern, Westcott, Vansittart* and *Caldwell.**
6th Escort Group: *Verity, Veteran, Watchman, Chelsea.**
7th Escort Group: *Wanderer, Warwick, Wild Swan, Clare.**
8th Escort Group: *Vanquisher, Viscount, Whitehall, Winchelsea, Castleton.**
9th Escort Group: *Harvester, Havelock, Hesperus, Highlander, Hurricane.*

By 30th September they were operational from their new base, *Wild Swan, Wanderer* sailing as the escort for the convoy OG45 of four eight-knot ships, with the Mersey slipping behind them at 1122 that morning and the 10,515-ton armed merchant cruiser *Salopian* which was due to take over as ocean escort before dusk on 30th October. Under the command of Commander A.F. St G. Orpen, SO 7th Escort Group in *Wanderer*, this duty was completed without incident. On 30th October two other events also took place. The German pocket battleship *Admiral Scheer* was passing, undetected, north of Iceland ready to descend upon the Atlantic convoy routes. Secondly, the submarine *U-99*, under command of one of the new-breed aces, Lieutenant-Commander Otto Kretschmer, sailed from her base at Lorient on her sixth war cruise. The paths of all these ships were to converge on the North Atlantic convoy route on 5th November.

Wild Swan and *Beagle* had been ordered to sail from Liverpool to rendezvous with the very important convoy HX83. Unlike the OG45 convoy of four ships plodding on at eight knots, this convoy was a ten-knot convoy consisting of thirty-three very valuable ships, so they were given a powerful destroyer escort for the last stage of their journey to the North Channel. Even so, at ten knots, an average HX convoy would have taken more than a fortnight to cross the Atlantic, even in good weather.

During the whole period she was working in the North Atlantic, *Wild Swan* only lost one ship from convoys she was escorting. HX83 proved to be the sad occasion. On 5th November, the following convoy, HX84, was set upon by the *Admiral Scheer*. Thanks to the gallant self-sacrifice of its only escort, the AMC *Jervis Bay* (Captain E.S.F. Fegen), which went down fighting, gaining vital time for her charges, only five on the convoy were sunk, the rest scattered.

On this same day, but much further east, HX83 also came under attack, but this time from *beneath* the waves. *U-99* had already added

* Ships marked with an asterisk were ex-US 'Four-Stackers' re-named after towns common to both Britain and the USA.

to Kretschmer's total of 'kills'. On the evening of 3rd November, at 2140, she had torpedoed the *Casanare* (5,376 tons) a lone merchantman discovered unescorted in position 53°58′ N, 14°13′ W.

Later the same evening Kretschmer stumbled on even bigger game: the 18,724-ton armed merchant cruiser *Laurentic* crossed his sights and he hit her with his first shot, bringing her to a standstill. She stayed afloat, however, and so, after circling and closing the range, *U-99* fired two more torpedoes into her wallowing bulk at 0453 on the 4th, which finally sank her. In between these attacks on *Laurentic* Kretschmer had even more good fortune when yet another AMC appeared, the *Patroclus* (11,314 tons), and, just after midnight, she too was hit by a single torpedo and crippled. On finishing off his first target Kretschmer had likewise to deal with his second victim, as she was proving even more stubborn and required a further five torpedoes to finish her off.

This left *U-99* with just one torpedo left, and Kretschmer steamed away towards the North Channel in search of a billet for this one. He was not long to be disappointed for, at 2000 that night, he located HX83. He sent a shadowing report and then closed in.

At the time of the attack HX83 had been steaming steadily in normal cruising dispositions at nine knots (see diagram) with the escorts disposed as illustrated. They consisted of the destroyers *Active, Achates, Beagle, Hesperus, Hurricane* and *Wild Swan* plus the corvette *Picotee*. Two Canadian destroyers, *Saguenay* and *Skeena*, had left the escort earlier on the arrival of *Beagle* and *Wild Swan*.*

The weather was fine, with a slight swell; the visibility two miles. Asdic conditions were logged as being 'OK' but not as good as would have been expected in such weather. The moon was not visible and only listening watch was being kept by the destroyers. It would have made little difference of course for *U-99* attacked on the surface as usual. Although the German logged an attack time at 0255, the times logged by the British destroyers all differ from this considerably.

It was at 0210 that the officer of the watch aboard *Beagle*, closest to the motor tanker Scottish Maiden, saw and heard an explosion which appeared to be in the starboard wing of the merchant ships. He roused his CO who at once turned *Beagle* out 90° and loaded starshell. He did not fire, however, because on observing that neither *Wild Swan* ahead nor *Hurricane* astern had taken any similar action at

---

* By co-incidence, in this, one of her first North Atlantic convoy operations, and, nineteen months later in her last, *Wild Swan* was in company with HMS *Beagle*.

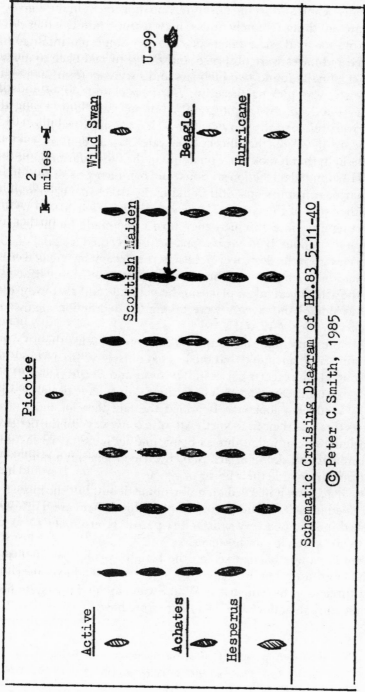

U-99

Wild Swan

Beagle

Hurricane

2

⊢ miles →⊣

Scottish Maiden

Picotee

Active

Achates

Hesperus

Schematic Cruising Diagram of HX.83 5-11-40

© Peter C. Smith, 1985

all on his beam, and seeing absolutely no movement in the convoy to indicate anything remotely amiss, he was uncertain whether or not an explosion had *really* taken place. After some ten minutes had elapsed red flares were observed and *Beagle* turned back to investigate; she finally found two lifeboats and survivors from the tanker. While she was picking these up, *Hurricane* closed with *Beagle* and swept round to give protection. Half-an-hour later these two destroyers rejoined the convoy after seeing yet more red flares.

Aboard *Wild Swan* the officer of the watch saw an explosion at 0205 but thought that it took place on a ship in the port quarter of the convoy. He sounded off 'action stations' and commenced full Asdic anti-submarine transmissions. Still thinking the attack had been made on the other side of the convoy, however, *Wild Swan* held her station, expecting any time an emergency turn to be made by the convoy. After half an hour *Wild Swan*'s 'Sparks' intercepted a signal of 1579 kilocycles from the destroyer *Achates* to the *Active* which stated that a ship had been torpedoed. This only served to confirm in *Wild Swan* that the attack had taken place on the port side and that the escorts on that side of the convoy were taking belated action against the attacker as per the WACI's.*

The summary of the meeting held later on to discuss this attack by Captain Lake concluded that the U-boat must have fired from a position outside the escorts between *Wild Swan* and *Beagle*; that the latter had a narrow escape and that both ships, 'must have been keeping a totally inefficient lookout'. It added the fact that for most of the escorts this was their first North Atlantic convoy. With the benefit of hindsight we can judge this as being unduly harsh as it was not a determined and skilful attack that thwarted them but a random firing from far outside their limits of vision.

For *Wild Swan* it marked an unfortunate debut, but she more than redeemed herself, she never lost another ship in her care. For *U-99* it marked the end of a very satisfactory patrol. Kretschmer's luck was not to last much longer however.

Wild Swan was back at sea on the 11th, escorting convoy OB242 with her group.† These dour convoy operations set the pattern of the next three months, which one Wild Swan summed up as; 'tedious, boring and uncomfortable.' Another wrote how:

---

* WACI = Western Approaches Convoy Instructions.

† *Wanderer* (SO), *Gardenia, Clare* and *Hibiscus* sailed at 1115.

At this stage early in the war, destroyers were not being refuelled out in the open sea; so they had to return to sheltered waters when fuel stocks became low. This requirement sometimes clashed with the pressing need to remain at sea until the last minute, perhaps to assist a convoy, or to locate and rescue the survivors from a ship which had gone down.

This was later illustrated in a most graphic manner. On 15th November they were ordered to transfer to convoy HG46 with *Wanderer*, *Warwick* and *Clare* leaving the corvette *Gardenia* to tend to the merchantman *Fishpool* (4,950 tons) which had been damaged in 55° N, 17°04′ W by an FW200 'Kondor' the day before. HG46 was not subjected to submarine attack and reached port in safety.

The weather now turned bad with the onset of winter, and in the North Atlantic in the old destroyers all their worst fears were realised. It was grim, the only consolation being that it reduced the numbers of U-boat attacks as the convoys were harder to find in such conditions. Patrick Satow describes one aspect of operating in 'Winter-North Atlantic'.

When the ship was steaming at a fairly high speed of more than about 22 knots, and going in the same direction as the ocean swell waves, it was sometimes quite difficult to keep her on course. Each successive swell wave would lift the stern and cause the bows to swerve up to 30 degrees on either side of the intended course.

The somewhat erratic track followed by a ship under these conditions out in the open sea could be controlled to some extent by frequent alterations of rudder to port or to starboard. However, this put an added strain on the veteran ship's steering gear, and along with other ships of similar age, there were occasional breakdowns.

Once the steering gear was out of service, it was necessary to keep one propeller shaft running at a constant speed, whilst attempts were made to keep roughly on course by varying the revolutions per minute on the other shaft. This was a wearisome and somewhat tricky undertaking. If the resulting ship's track remained too wildly erratic, it was necessary to reduce her speed through the water to regain an acceptable measure of control.

The reinforcing of the North Atlantic Escorts by the transfer of the old destroyers, by the addition of the new Flower Class corvettes and the passing into service of some of the refurbished Town class ships had the desired effect and soon the U-boats were finding it much more difficult to penetrate convoy screens. They turned away in their frustration to concentrate on easier pickings, and it was the stragglers or independently routed ships who suffered as a consequence. Air attacks, by contrast, increased.

On 26th November the C-in-C, Western Approaches, Admiral Sir Martin Dunbar-Nasmith, VC, still at this time operating from Plymouth while the bulk of his ships were working from Gladstone Dock in Liverpool,* sent a signal to the Group to 'Meet, convoy HX87. Ten hours late'. Sailing of both HX85 and HX86 had been delayed due to the *Admiral Scheer's* foray. HX87 was also held up but this delay was caused by bad weather. *Wanderer, Warwick, Wild Swan,* and the corvettes *Campanula, Clematis, Fleur-de-Lys* and *Periwinkle* sailed to comply with this order at 2100 that night. But there soon came a series of diversions.

During the afternoon of the 27th a series of signals reached *Wild Swan* concerning the loss of two merchant ships. The first:

> *C-in-C, WA to Wild Swan*: 1507. *Charles F. Meyer* tanker. Straggler from HX87, damaged. Detail one ship to investigate report of ship attacked by submarine 56° N, 13°52′ W at 1124 GMT.

Another was intercepted later: '*Malin Head Radio*: 2227. *Diplomat*, British, 8,240 tons, straggler from HX88, torpedoed.' And then a third: '*C-in-C, WA to Wild Swan, Campanula, Fleur-de-Lys*: 2325. Attack submarine in position 55°45′N, 11°57′ W.' And this was followed immediately by a further exhortation: '55°45′ N, 11°57′ W. *Wild Swan* and *Campanula* to attack.'

At the time these signals were received the ships concerned were plunging their way through one of the worst storms of that month, rolling, crashing down into the jet-black troughs and reeling, dizzy and breathless, into the next. They could barely make headway towards the given positions of the stricken ships let alone attack in such a swirling cauldron. Both *Diplomat* and *Charles F. Meyer* subsequently sank as a result of torpedo hits, but for many years their assailant was a mystery. No U-boats reported any attacks in this position of the Atlantic. The only submarine which had been in the area was the *U-104* (Lieutenant-Commander Herald Jürst) but she was

---

* The actual transfer of Western Approaches HQ to Liverpool took place ten days after Admiral Sir Percy Noble took over as C-in-C, on 7th February 1941.

claimed sunk by the corvette *Rhododendron* on 21st November. There can be little doubt, however, that this date is incorrect and *U-104* is the only boat that could have sunk these two ships. The last message received from her was on 19th November in position 60°30' N, 14°13' W. She had left Lorient on the 12th of the month and never returned.

The 28th saw a further exchange of signals which, in their brevity, sum up the situation better than any more detailed description could do:

C-in-C, WA to Wild Swan, Fleur-de-Lys and Campanula: 0144. Sunderland reports four lifeboats in position 56°02' N, 12°15' W at 0100 28th.

Fleur-de-Lys to C-in-C, WA: 0500. Your 0144. In view of distance neither *Campanula* or *Fleur-de-Lys* are participating – weather.

Wild Swan to C-in-C, WA: 1001. Am approaching positions, searching for survivors. Asdic installation out of action due to recent weather. Corvettes not due for several hours, intend to take survivors to Londonderry and refuel.

On 1st December, mercy-mission safely accomplished, weather-beaten and battered, *Wild Swan* and *Fleur-de-Lys* arrived at Liverpool with HX89 which they had joined for the last stages of the journey home. It had been a rough trip! Worse was to come. Kondor attacks in November had sunk eighteen merchant ships, and RAF attacks on their bases near Bordeaux were completely ineffective. Hasty work was put in hand in order to make up for lack of aircraft-carriers by embarking fighter aircraft aboard ships equipped with catapults. These were later to become the CAM ships (Catapult Armed Merchantmen) which had a slight impact until the advent of the escort carrier much later.

A development on the enemy side was the introduction of the Wolf Pack whereby one submarine found a convoy and shadowed it, homing in others for a concerted assault, against which the weak escorts stood little chance. One of the first of such attacks took place at this time, by four U-Boats against convoy HX90, and resulted in the loss of ten ships of the convoy and the escort, the AMC *Forfar*.

As the Official Historian was to note: ' . . . if the enemy adopted surface attacks the Asdic, which had an effective range of some 1,500 yards and could not detect a surfaced U-boat, immediately lost much of its value.'

Some postwar historians have claimed that sloops and other such escorts were the best anti-submarine ships (an analysis of the results shows otherwise) and that the destroyers' speed was of little value.

This is refuted if the facts are examined, for as Roskill later wrote: 'Our flotilla vessels had to fall back on the hope of visual sighting and, as many of our escorts were too slow to catch a surfaced U-boat, even if they sighted one, they were unlikely to achieve her destruction.'*

The Kondors were equally hard to combat at this stage of the war. The decision was taken at Portsmouth Dockyard to convert the seaplane carrier *Pegasus* (Captain P.G. Wodehouse) so that she could carry three Fairey Fulmar fighter aircraft of No 807 FAA Squadron. *Pegasus* was then escorted northward, through the Irish Sea to join the North Atlantic convoys in readiness for her first operation, Specimen I.

On 9th December *Wild Swan* and the corvette *Fleur-de-Lys* sailed to rendezvous with the seaplane-carrier, the destroyer *Highlander* and corvettes *Campanula* and *Periwinkle* eight miles north of Altcarry with convoy OG47 and the sloop *Leith* and corvettes *Primula* and *Gardenia*. The weather was wild and vile. On the 12th C-in-C, Western Approaches warned them to keep a lookout for convoy SC14 whose position, due to conditions was 'uncertain, may be met, during night passage, to the southward'. They pounded on. The original plan was to initiate Specimen, the detaching to a watching position of the *Pegasus* and her own escort, but bad weather made this deployment increasingly more academic. Patrick Satow recalls:

> Owing to the generally appalling mid-winter weather in the North Atlantic, I believe that Operation Specimen was of limited operational value. I can remember the extensive pitching of the ship (that is the bow and stern rising and falling) out in the Atlantic rollers, and wondering how any aircraft could be flown in such conditions without unduly risking their crews.

This is reflected in exchanges of signals on the 13th between the escorts of OG47 and C-in-C, Western Approaches. The *Fleur-de-Lys*, whose Asdic dome had been damaged, was detached to assist the *Campanula*, who suffered main engine defects, back to Londonderry. This left just *Leith* and *Periwinkle* to guard the convoy once *Pegasus* and *Wild Swan* had been detached. Despite the weather, intelligence on the gathering of a wolf-pack was obtained which led to an alteration in course to avoid them, which further delayed things.

Captain Wodehouse was later to report:

* Roskill, *War at Sea, Volume 1, HMSO.*

The average weather conditions during the operation were as follows:-
Clouds 7/10 to 10/10 at 1000-feet with occasional short bright intervals.
The wind was equally, averaging 35 knots but with gusts up to 58-65
knots, with intermittent rain storms. . . . Had an aircraft been
catapulted it is doubtful if a second aircraft could have been successfully
loaded to the catapult in less than two hours on account of the motion of
the ship. But that in itself is not important as only one aircraft is required
to be in the air on any one day. The ship, owing to her lack of speed, could
not have remained hove-to during the operation without losing touch
with the convoy.

On 13th December Western Approaches had ordered that *Pegasus*
and two corvettes were to remain with OG47 until the morning to
meet convoy SL57 in position 53°09′ N, 16°50′ W at 1004 on the
16th. The remainder of the escort was to remain with the convoy
until further orders. *Wild Swan* was to report after being detached,
when clear of the convoy.

By the 15th, however, it was clear that the first attempt at Specimen had not worked. Several further Specimen operations were
mounted during the winter using *Pegasus* which, if not rewarded with
spectacular 'kills', gave a working knowledge of the problems of
operating catapult-based fighters with convoys and enabled the
development of shipborne air-power that was later to do so much to
win the North Atlantic battle. But *Wild Swan* was not further
involved.

The battering that the old destroyers were receiving was bringing
out their age. Of even more limiting a factor was their lack of range;
they constantly needed to refuel which was not always easy. One sol-
ution was for many of the 'V' and 'W' classes to be converted in dockyards for long-range work. As mentioned earlier in the book, boilers
were taken out, resulting in loss of speed above 25 knots, but
increased bunkerage of oil fuel; they became known as 'Long-leggers', whereas the 'Modified W' class, which could not have this
done, were known as 'Short-leggers'. Churchill's outburst on the
lack of destroyers not only ignored the crippling cuts he imposed
before the war while at the Treasury, they also overlooked the fact
that in order to achieve this desirable feature of longer-ranged
destroyers, some had to be taken out of service to be so converted. It
was Admiralty policy, when enough of these ships had been so
readied, to send them to relieve the 'Short-leggers'. This was indicated in a signal of 18th December.

ACNS (H) to C-in-C, WA: 1543. *Wivern, Wild Swan, Vansittart* and *Witherington* are to be transferred to command of C-in-C, Portsmouth. *Witherington* now and the remainder on relief by *Vanoc, Witch* and *Volunteer*.

But that was not to be yet awhile, and nor were *Wild Swan*'s crew privy to such information. All they knew that one bleary and stomach-churning week at sea followed another. The weather continued to be vile and even when they reached the grubby haven of Gladstone Dock, they were to find no rest. After the beginning of the devastating 'Blitz' on London during October and November, the Luftwaffe was paying similar attention to the smaller cities up and down the country. Naturally their attentions turned to Liverpool, now the focus of the incoming convoys on which the very life of Britain depended. On the nights of 20th to 22nd December it became Liverpool's turn. The docks took the brunt of attacks by two hundred bombers and nineteen merchant ships were damaged in varying degrees and one was sunk.

The crew of the *Wild Swan* played a valiant part in this ordeal. Commander Sclater was to recall:

> Little rest was obtained in Liverpool, for frequent air attacks were experienced, and the watch onboard was often called to assist in fire-fighting in the docks. Among the reservists onboard were several members of various fire brigades, who did excellent work. Some of these were later allowed to return to their peacetime occupation, being considered more useful as firemen than seamen. One of them Able Seaman Patchett, the captain's coxswain, was promoted directly to boatswain (FF).

Patrick Satow has similar memories of this period:

> There were many important targets on Merseyside, and the area had its full share of air raids. These were particularly fierce in December of 1940. When in harbour, the destroyers were normally berthed in the Gladstone Dock at the western end of the city. One night a landmine fell on one of the warehouses nearby, and this caused a lot of damage on the dockside. One of the crew went to a callbox close to the ship next morning to ring up his home.
>
> The phone box had taken much of the blast from the land mine. In those days there was no Subscriber Trunk Dialling, and long-

distance calls were handled by an operator. The first coin was inserted, and then the full effect of the near miss became apparent. As the caller pressed Button 'A' to speak on the line, there was a tremendous crash and he got the jackpot. The entire contents of the coin box cascaded onto the floor, and the call continued for an unlimited period without further payment!

During these hazardous times, it became known onboard the ship that a room could be booked at Liverpool's Adelphi Hotel for only about ten shillings [50p] a night. But a room on the top floor could be secured for only half a crown [12½p], if an undertaking was given to get up during the night and put out any fire bombs if they came through the roof! There were few takers for *this* special offer.

There were times when the Fire Services on Merseyside were stretched beyond their limits, and some of the crew of *Wild Swan* agreed to lend a hand whenever possible. One night, during these winter air raids, there were fires ranging from one end of the city and docks to the other. A detachment from the ship joined a fire engine in Bootle which headed towards the city centre.

Suddenly, on turning a corner, there was a bombed public house open to the sky. No one could be seen; this was understandable as the raid was still in progress. But it was obvious that much of the bar stock would be missing by morning if left unattended. So a quick halt was made to take on liquid refreshments, before the assembled company continued on their way.

About two miles further on, the road was blocked by fallen telephone poles and broken wires. At the roadside was a locked warehouse, with a menacing glow inside which could be seen through the lower windows. A telegraph pole was used as a battering ram to break down the door, and the fire was tackled successfully before it got a hold on the premises.

As usual the Luftwaffe did not content itself with merely bombing the city; the seaward approaches to the docks were also vulnerable to mining. Not only were magnetic mines laid at this time, to which *Wild Swan* had some immunity, but also the acoustic mine. These, as their name implies, were detonated by the sound-waves of the ship's propellers passing overhead. The first were discovered in August 1940 off the south coast and by late 1940 the enemy was sowing them regularly. Once recovered the secret actuating mechanism, a simple carbon granule microphone, was quickly discovered, and remedies put in hand but, as always, such devices, fitting an electrically-driven hammer in the bows of ships, could only be introduced slowly. In the interim the acoustic mine scored some success, although nothing like as spectacular as had been achieved by the first magnetic mines.

One of the more immediate counters to the menace of the acoustic mine was the order that destroyers should only proceed at speeds of less than nine knots or more than 22 knots in waters where they were suspected, like Liverpool Bay. Whenever possible *Wild Swan* was driven at the higher speed, and, though a number of these weapons were detonated at a distance, no damage was incurred. This immunity only extended as far as *Wild Swan*'s special luck however; others were not so fortunate.

Late on the afternoon of 23rd December *Wild Swan* left Liverool astern of the destroyer *Warwick* (Lieutenant-Commander M.A.G. Child), to fuel at Londonderry before joining convoy OB263. At 1645, just as they were passing the Bar Light Vessel at a distance of some five cables, *Warwick* set off an acoustic mine and was badly holed in her engine room. The internal damage was severe. She was completely disabled and, as she settled low in the water, with her upper deck almost awash, *Wild Swan* was gently manoeuvred to secure the crippled ship alongside. Once secured in this position all surplus personnel and confidential books were transferred from the *Warwick* and the possibility of getting her back to port was discussed between their respective captains. Commander Sclater later wrote:

> It was found that there was a good chance of getting her into harbour, so we started to tow her back, still secured alongside. All went well, and speed was gradually increased to nine knots. Soon, it became dark, and, to add to our difficulty in navigating the narrow winding channel, a heavy air raid began.

Patrick Satow amplifes this:

> Then, under cover of darkness, but with many of the navigational aids blacked out for the duration of hostilities, *Wild Swan* proceeded up the twisting channel of the Mersey, until she reached the safety of Liverpool.

When an almost waterlogged ship is lashed alongside another in this way, there are considerable difficulties in steering. The whole operation could have ended so easily with both ships stranded on the mud banks which lie so close on either side of the safe channel. The crew of *Warwick* were able to climb across to the safe deck of *Wild Swan*, and men were kept on the alert to release the hawsers immediately in case the ship under tow had foundered.

As they reached Gladstone Docks, rescue tugs arrived and took over the tow, but not before the young midshipman of *Warwick*, John A.T. Sim, RNR had clambered aboard and gone up to *Wild Swan*'s bridge to thank them personally for a magnificent feat of seamanship.

It was 2111 by the time they reached dock and went alongside, with shrapnel raining down on them, and landed *Warwick*'s crew and CB's. The crippled destroyer herself was eased into Tranmere Bay and successfully beached. Later she was docked, rebuilt and served for several more years before being torpedoed and sunk off Land's End in 1944. Commander Sclater was particularly glad to be partly responsible for her salvage, 'as she was the first destroyer in which I had served.' They then sailed for Londonderry for the second time and arrived without further mishap.

On Christmas Eve she sailed from there to join the escort, at 2145 hours, of OB263 and later overtook them. This consisted of the sloop *Rochester* and the corvettes *Fleur-de-Lys*, *Gardenia* and *Periwinkle*. While taking them north in typical dirty North Atlantic weather Christmas Day 1940 was 'celebrated'. C-in-C, Western Approaches joined in the festivities by ordering them to join the escort of homeward-bound convoy HX96 later. In order to keep this convoy away from the hell of Liverpool, with its minefields, air raids and devastation, it was re-routed to the calmer waters of the anchorage by the Scottish island of Lismore, south of Port Appin. The routing instructions sent are typical of the period and are reproduced to show just what the decoders had to put up with.

C-in-C, WA to *Rochester*, *Wild Swan*, *Fleur-de-Lys*, *Venomous*: 2158. HX96, 30 unescorted ships. Steer course 100°; 27th, 60°12′ N, 15°00° W, 101° at 8 knots, then, through 60°12′ N, 13°00′ W; 58°00′ N, 09°30′ W: Split in 56°30′ N, 08°40′ W. Route, keeping north of QZK229(D), 56°05′ N, 06°38′ W; 56°16′ N, 05°48′ W; 56°22′ N, 05°39′ W, thence to anchorage in Lynn of Lorne, North of Black Island.

CHAPTER SEVEN

Rescues and Refits
December 1940-April 1941

By December 1940 there were new faces aboard the ship. First to arrive was the new ship's 'Doc', Temporary Surgeon-Lieutenant F.H.D. Hutter, appointed on 20th December. Now Air-Commodore Hutter, RAF, he recalls his first impressions of *Wild Swan*'s crew and the ship herself thus:

> When I first joined the Navy as a RNV (Special) R officer I was very young as a doctor and quite ignorant of the Navy. To say that I was 'all at sea' is an understatement. I suppose, in common with many like me I was self-opinionated and probably not a very good officer.
>
> I joined the ship in Liverpool in the winter of 1940-41 (after Xmas). I had arrived up from Portsmouth and found the ship had sailed some time before so I had to wait. It was a miserable, cold, cheerless Christmas as there were many air raids and the city had been largely destroyed.
>
> When she got back my first impression of her, apart from being relieved to see her, was how *small* she was and how crowded her decks were with guns and all manner of warlike fittings. As I approached a seaman ran down the gangway, took my bag and explained I was not allowed to carry my own bag on board (that's really all I had; all most of us had). It was my first meeting with a member of the ship's company. They were unfailing in their courtesy.
>
> The captain, Lieutenant-Commander C.E.L. Sclater, whom I met very quickly, was a small, slight man with a beard. Anxious, as he had good reason to be at the time, probably shy, certainly on the surface, reserved. On my first or second day I was invited to his cabin to play chess. This became a regular meeting whenever circumstances permitted at sea or in harbour. As for me I looked forward to these sessions more than I can say. At first we were pretty evenly matched. Later I built up an ascendency, probably due to the captain's natural preoccupation with his many and ever-growing tasks.

I also met Pat Satow, in those days a sub-lieutenant. He was the navigator. In the worst weather imaginable, no sun and no star sights possible, he always seemed spot-on. To me it seemed absolute magic. He was always cheerful and the ship's tensions seemed to bounce off him. Of all the ship's officers, I can see him now cheering the wardroom up simply by his presence.

My first trip to sea aboard her was to escort a ferryboat full of boy seamen from Fleetwood to Douglas, Isle of Man for training in HMS *St George*, the naval establishment there. A mild experience of rolling and pitching. I didn't like it! A short job and we soon returned for a few days in port. A rubber warehouse was burning steadily away nearby and going ashore was difficult.

Stoker Linford recalls this time thus:

Long hours and dreary work. We usually escorted convoys to around 14°-20° West and brought others back. Our accommodation was fair, but bathing and lavatory conditions primitive, with cold water only in mid-winter! The forces canteen in Gladstone Docks closed at 2000.

We formed fire-fighting parties when the docks burnt for days. I can recall we supplied the ship with fresh frozen beef from a bombed container ship one morning at 0200 when returning from a fire-fighting patrol; we sailed at 0600!

Newcomers or old-boys, however, the remorseless war in the North Atlantic carried on and they had to accept life as they found it.

They were off once more on 5th January to Londonderry for their regular refuelling stop, accompanied by the corvette *Gardenia*, and then to join their old companions *Fleur-de-Lys* and *Periwinkle* in escorting convoy OB270, six ships sailing from Greenock, in thick fog, westward. In the event one vessel, the *Surprise*, failed to sail and the convoy was diverted to keep it well clear of convoy SC17 escorted by *Witch* and the sloop *Aberdeen*. The thought of the close-packed ranks of merchantmen approaching each other on converging course in dense fog was enough to give everyone bad nerves, but in the event there was no untoward incident. On the 7th, ships from both groups were sent to meet another convoy.

C-in-C, WA to Witch, Wild Swan, Laburnam, Fleur-de-Lys, Gardenia, Campanula and Periwinkle: Meet SL.60,31 unescorted ships. 1000/9, 53°35′ N, 16°00′ W, steering 068° at 8 knots.

It seemed like another routine trip, but it turned out to be quite eventful.

Since the beginning of the war the ss *Clytoneus* (Captain S.G. Goffey), a 6,273-ton steamer, had made several journeys to and from the Dutch East Indies. On 8th January she was bound from Cape Town to Liverpool with a general cargo. She had a crew of sixty-two including a naval gunlayer and a seaman gunner in charge of the solitary 4-inch gun and the 12-pdr AA gun with which she was armed. She was also carrying a single passenger, a distressed British seaman. At 0900, in a position 56°23′ N, 15°28′ W they were attacked by an FW200 Kondor. Two bombs scored direct hits, but the Kondor came back a third time and flew right down the starboard side of the ship, machine-gunning the whole time, and when abreast of the engine room dropped two more bombs. They fired back at her.

Stung by this, the giant aircraft flew up the port side of the ship machine-gunning all the time, circled the bow and back down the starboard side, dropping yet another bomb. By 1100 the ship started to settle by the stern. The crew was mustered and the remaining boats on the starboard side were lowered. The captain toured the ship to see if everyone was off. He and the engineer reboarded and checked the engine room once more but it was clear the ship was beyond aid. By this time all the midships superstructure and bridge had gone. They had managed to transmit an SOS on their emergency aerial as the proper aerial had been blown away.

As night approached, Captain Goffey went back to the ship once more and found the after deck awash and that amidships she was still burning furiously. He returned to the boats and they set course for the north of Ireland. They were then some 280 miles north-west of Bloody Foreland. As they left they could see the flames in the night. There was a tank containing 680 tons of palm oil in the ship and this exploded with the heat, breaking the ship in half. The First Mate saw her go down at 1800. Then they were on their own.

The ss *Bassano* (Captain D. Casson) was a 4,843-ton steamer which had sailed from New York for Liverpool on 31st December, independently-routed, with a general cargo. She had a crew of 52 including one Royal Marine and one Canadian gunner for the 4-inch and the 12-pdr gun with which she was equipped. She also had five passengers. She was a fast vessel, hence she did not join a convoy, but her speed did not save her on this trip. At 1630 on the afternoon of 9th

January in position 57°57′ N, 17°42′ W, whilst she was steaming at thirteen knots and zig-zagging, she was struck by a torpedo on her port side, about 370 feet from her bows.

We had just altered course when we were struck, otherwise I think we should have been hit amidships. My galley-boy, who is a flying man and a racing motorist and was on my ship working his passage back to England to join up, reported seeing the submarine break surface. He said he saw an officer come out of the conning tower, take a photograph and go away again. I did not see any of this as I was superintending the lowering of the boats. This galley-boy also said he saw a 'U' painted on the side of the submarine with '3' after the letter, the last figure being a '7', but I would not vouch for any of these statements.

Thus wrote Captain Casson. The ship did not list after being hit but began to settle bodily in the water. They could see and taste acrid black smoke. The starboard boat was lowered and floated away empty, so they took to the two boats on the port side and later transferred some survivors to the starboard boat.

Eventually they got away and rigged sea anchors; there were thirteen in the captain's boat, twenty-five in another boat and eighteen in the third. 'The last I saw of the *Bassano* she was in a big cloud of smoke and flame with her bow right up and I could see right underneath the ship.' They had managed to get a wireless message away which was picked up by Valentia Radio. They could not pull against the sea as it was too strong and the wind was in the wrong direction for sailing. In the captain's boat they made a tent of the sail and all got underneath it. Night came on. They drifted steadily for 24 hours with no sign of rescue.

When the signal was received ashore from the Blue Funnel Liner, Western Approaches Command at once detailed *Wild Swan* to steam for the area of the reported sinking and search for *Clytoneus* survivors. When this order was received in the earlier minutes of 9th January, *Wild Swan* was already dangerously low on fuel. Nonetheless she swung away on the new bearing and headed out through the night. Also in the area was the armed merchant cruiser *Esperance Bay* (14,204 tons) and she was similarly searching.

Wild Swan to C-in-C, WA: 0049. Your 0005/9. Ship not located. Have searched 55°40′ N to 56°20′ N, 14° to 16° W. Am continuing search.

All through the day they quartered the vast ocean, looking for the veritable needle in the haystack but not until 1400 was their patience rewarded. As Commander Sclater remembered:

> After a lengthy search, boats were sighted about thirty miles from the expected position and all the crew were saved. We made the survivors comfortable and set course for the nearest base, Londonderry.

Captain Goffey recalled that:

> The destroyer HMS *Wild Swan* came over to us, first picked the Mate's boat and then came and picked us up. We were told that the second mate's boat had been picked up by another ship.

Wild Swan signalled to C-in-C, Western Approaches:

> Am in company with *Esperance Bay* in position 56°45′ N, 15°35′ W. She has just picked up one boatload of survivors from *Clytoneus* who was bombed 8th forenoon. Survivors state she has sunk. Am searching for three more boats.
>   *Wild Swan to C-in-C, WA*: 1243. My 1233. Have rescued remaining survivors. Incendiary injuries. Am proceeding to join SL 60.

While Doctor Hutter attended to the burns of the patients the other survivors were made as comfortable as they could be aboard the little ship. Course was set back to the convoy but, at 1723 that afternoon, a fresh signal was received. '1723. Investigate *Bassano*, torpedoed 1719 today in 57°58′ N, 17°38′ W.'
    As the captain later was to write:

> An hour or so later we were ordered to investigate a faint SOS which had been heard, emanating from a point about a hundred miles to the west of us. Fuel was running short and only a brief search could be made.

In fact they extended their search long beyond prudent limits, as Patrick Satow records: 'A considerable degree of risk was taken. Instead of abandoning the search in mid-afternoon, the ship continued combing the area until dusk.
    Commander Sclater again:

As we regretfully abandoned the operation, and headed for home, the masthead lookout thought he caught a glimpse of a distant object. We steamed in the direction indicated, but nothing further could be seen. Our hopes were unfulfilled.

A little while later, a boat's sail became visible just above the horizon. We picked up the occupants and they directed us to a second boat nearby.

There is no doubt in my mind that Providence intervened on behalf of these men. A gale sprang up the next day, and, if we had not found them, they would have had little hope of survival.

Their ship was sailing alone from New York to Liverpool with a cargo of valuable war stores and aircraft, when she was torpedoed without warning, and sank in a few minutes. Everyone was saved except the radio officer, who stayed behind to send the SOS.

Captain Casson wrote:

We were very pleased to see the smoke from the destroyer on the horizon, and after we had been picked up they treated us very well indeed, and everything possible was done for us, in spite of the fact that they had already picked up 62 of the crew of a ship belonging to the Blue Funnel Line, and their complement must have been almost double.

But they were not out of the wood yet, as Patrick Satow recalls:

. . . before land came into sight, a very worried engineering officer came onto the bridge. He duly saluted the captain, and told him that he expected to lose suction on his fuel line in the last of his available tanks at any time. The captain asked him to do his best and the engineer went below.

About an hour later, the north coast of Ireland was sighted on the starboard bow, but the engineer officer had returned to the bridge. He requested permission to break up the wardroom furniture to feed the boilers, and expressed his considered opinion that the ship was not going to make it. Happily, the chairs and tables from the officers' mess were not needed, but it had been a very close call.

As Commander Sclater recalled, it was all worthwhile in the end.

We had a slow and anxious return to Londonderry. Shortage of fuel limited our speed to ten knots, and we had insufficient in hand even to zigzag.

However nothing rejoices the heart more than saving human life, and we arrived at last, with that wonderful sense of achievement that even successful action cannot give.

There was one unexpected bonus, of a kind, from this remarkable operation, as Stoker Linford recalled: 'Among the many survivors we picked up from merchant ships I remember one in particular, a Chinaman, who manned the soup pot in the galley for three weeks and never left it, even after the ship had docked and his mates had disembarked!'

There were further changes in the wardroom around this time. A new Number One, Lieutenant Kenneth Talbot Holland, joined the ship as did a new sub, Sub-Lieutenant D.H. Revill, RNR. Both were very young officers, the first lieutenant disguising his very youthful appearance with a fair-haired and sharply-pointed beard. Telegraphist Lingard recalls that he kept the ship smart but appeared rather timid at times. As well as additions there were losses, some tragic. Convoy OB275 sailed on the late afternoon of 18th January, ten ships, three flying kite balloons as some form of aerial defence, steaming at a nominal nine knots. In fact the atrocious weather they met when they poked their noses outside the Bar made the description 'convoy' almost meaningless. For escort they had the sloop *Aberdeen* and corvettes *Fleur-de-Lys* and *Periwinkle*, but *Wild Swan, Witch* and the ex-US four-stacker *Montgomery*, were ordered to Londonderry from Gladstone to refuel and join on the same day. That short trip was a nightmare; both the motor boat on the starboard side of the ship and the whaler on the port side were smashed to bits by the giant seas. But worse followed: '*Wild Swan* to C-in-C, WA: 1850. Two ratings lost overboard in heavy weather.'

It was the tragedy of last winter all over again. Patrick Satow writes:

Lifelines were rigged along both sides of the ship as usual, but . . . in the dark in the North Atlantic, there was little chance of survival.

It is worth remembering that most of the crews serving in our little ships would have suffered even greater hardship than they did during heavy weather, if it had not been for the prodigious efforts of those at home who sent them additional clothing. Somehow, out of the very limited resources available, mothers, sisters, wives and grandparents performed near miracles by making thick seaboot stockings, gloves, Balaclava helmets, double knitted jerseys and other garments, which were all deeply appreciated.

Even so this particular trip was one of the worst ever. After clawing their way westward through this howling maelstrom they somehow rendezvoused with the scattered remnant of HX102 incoming from the States. *Wild Swan* managed to collect four of them and shepherd them eventually into the comparative tranquillity of Aultbea in Loch Ewe on the morning of 27th January. Others were not so lucky and the convoy was scattered all over the North Atlantic. Some ships never made it.

This nightmare voyage was not yet over for *Wild Swan* however, although events were now to take a better, if strange, turn for her and her crew. She was returning to Liverpool with the remnants of the convoy in misty weather on 29th January. Having seen the merchantmen safely into harbour *Wild Swan* was about to follow them in, when a large merchant vessel was sighted near the Bar Light Vessel, but about a mile outside the swept channel. As they approached to shepherd her into safe water it was observed that she was stopped and that all her boats were missing. A signal lamp was used to try and ascertain whether assistance was needed, but to no avail. It became evident that there was no one aboard.

The vessel was the ss *Westmorland* (Captain Henry A. Fryer) an 8,967-ton steamer which had sailed from Glasgow with stern instructions to keep strictly to the swept channel and to keep to nine knots speed when outside the Rock Light. The German aircraft had been assiduously sowing the shallow waters of Liverpool Bay with all types of mines and already two other ships had been lost on them through disregarding their routing instructions.

By 1150 visibility was one to two miles, with a fresh easterly wind when, some three miles from the Bar Light Vessel, 'a violent explosion occurred which was reported to the Chief Officer as the effect of two mines'. *Westmorland* immediately commenced to heel rapidly to port and settle by the stern and the engine room telegraphs were run to stop. The list was too great to use the starboard boats so the crew abandoned her in the port boats and drew off from the ship for about three quarters of a mile. Way was still on the ship.

This was the situation that *Wild Swan* found a little later. Commander Sclater recalled what happened next:

A quick inspection revealed that she had been mined and abandoned, but was in no danger of sinking. The next step seemed to be to find the crew and get them back onboard. A search was made and the boats were discovered about three miles to seaward. The entire crew were picked up and taken aboard *Wild Swan*, the boats being taken in tow. . .

[Later] I took *Wild Swan* alongside the damaged ship. A party of *Wild Swan*'s seamen clambered onboard to secure tow ropes, and then the merchant ship's crew went back onboard their ship. I noticed that we were drifting fast towards the Bar Light Vessel. Bearings showed that the damaged ship was bound to hit her, would probably sink her, and then drift ashore. We managed to tow her clear, still secured alongside, while a proper tow rope was being prepared.

A quick calculation revealed that her draught was too great to move her up harbour, so she was towed to a safe anchorage in the swept channel and instructed to let go her anchor. We stood by her until the arrival of the salvage tugs, whose despatch I had requested earlier. They pumped her out, and she was safely berthed the following day.

Eventually, with the supervision of Captain Hart RNR in charge of salvage operations the *Vigilant* supervised the rescue tugs *Alfred*, *Coburg*, *Slone* and *Wapping*, with the *Alexander* standing by, and she was taken into Gladstone Docks at 0312 next morning.* For *Wild Swan* the ending was a happy one, as her captain records: 'Permission was obtained to make a claim for Salvage Services, and, after lengthy proceedings (about a year) the sum of £600 was awarded and shared amongst *Wild Swan*'s crew.'

Surgeon-Lieutenant Hutter recalls the North Atlantic routine like this:

Of course the weather was vile and I noticed the roll and pitch of the ship. The captain invited me to the bridge on the first occasion

---

* *Westmorland* was saved and lived to sail again. On 1st June 1942 she was torpedoed in 35°55' N, 63°35' W by *U-566*, and sunk. *Wild Swan* outlasted her by sixteen days.

and told me to stand around and I'd feel better. In spite of the greater movement up there I was indeed better at once and even enjoyed the wild weather; in a way. Mr Derbyshire, the engineering officer, swore it was better down in the engine room as the keel moved least of all. I tried it but it was not so good, hot, oily and swamped.

For a while we had an army major aboard as a passenger, just for the ride as it were. He was a retired officer, medalled and wounded in World War I. There seemed to be a lot of officers taking trips in warships in lieu of leave and our major did well. But on a later trip we had aboard two young RNVR officers who had been on AMC's and who wanted to see what the real Navy was like. They quickly found out, spending the entire trip on their backs, groaning. They vanished ashore when we put into Loch Ewe on our way home!

I eventually became reasonably adjusted and ate well. Evening meal served up two soups. One was a greasy concoction, the other pea soup. The captain got tired of this and once remarked, 'Same soup, Guns?' (The warrant torpedo gunner was our catering officer). It was known as 'Same Soup' ever after! It often made me sick but I could reappear at once and eat the rest of the meal. Pea soup was marvellous. Any queasiness was instantly dispelled. . .

The weather seemed to get steadily worse with each week that passed, or perhaps their resistance to its constant clamour was lessening. On 1st February *Wild Swan* was the Senior Officer of the escorts for convoy OBC251 from the Clyde. The convoy consisted of twenty ships and they left at 2300 that night in the teeth of a storm. As they made their way slowly down the dark waters of the Firth of Clyde a signal came in from the Flag Officer, Greenock, warning of a new danger waiting for them off storm-lashed Ailsa Craig.

FOIC Greenock to Wild Swan: 2330. Keep sharp lookout for *Pallaeter*, Belgian coaster, reported abandoned in 55°15′ N, 5°18′ W at 2330/1.
    FOIC Greenock to Wild Swan: 2355. My 2330/1. Drifting south-east. Keep sharp lookout.

The convoy reached Loch Ewe safely despite this hazard and the weather. Almost at once, early on the 3rd, *Wild Swan* sailed again south to Londonderry with the corvette *Anemone* and the old minesweeper *Fitzroy* to refuel and join *Witch*, *Montgomery*, and corvettes

Campanula, Periwinkle and *Pimpernel* in locating and guarding the incoming convoy HX105. They staggered south, oiled and sailed but next day fresh orders came in for the three destroyers to rendezvous instead with convoy OB281 and remain with it until further orders.

By this time both the ship and the crew were feeling conditions of strain. That *Wild Swan* was due to be replaced by 'Long-leggers' was not generally known but what *was* clear that she was in bad need of a refit and her crew of some kind of rest. After the conditions on this trip these feelings boiled over on the lower deck.* Signalman Harrison recalls what happened next:

> This trip was so uncomfortable that it caused the major part of the ship's company to put in a request to state a complaint. From the bridge it almost resembled a minor mutiny with a large proportion of the seamen and stokers lined up all along the upper deck to see the captain. The captain did not speak to them all individually but did address the whole ship's company. He promised to speak to the C-in-C about it. The next day the C-in-C came aboard and promised that after one more trip the ship would go south for a refit.

Commander Sclater gives further information thus:

> *Wild Swan* had been driven hard for over a year and the Atlantic gales soon found her weaknesses. Leaks developed in her deck and hull, and in rough weather, her living quarters became flooded, making conditions onboard most unpleasant. Furthermore, her crew had undergone a year of considerable strain, without the relaxation of leave. Little rest was obtained in Liverpool.
>
> *Wild Swan* had splendid engines, and had been kept running by great exertions on the part of her engine room staff under Mr Derbyshire, commissioned engineer, RN.
>
> As long as she could steam, the question of her annual refit was constantly shelved by the harassed base staff, who had as many damaged destroyers on their hands as they could cope with. It was not until February 1941, when I raised the question with Admiral Sir Percy Noble, the new Commander-in-Chief, in person, that the long overdue refit was arranged, and *Wild Swan* was allowed to

---

* All the old destroyers were similarly affected, not just *Wild Swan*. As some form of compensation the Admiralty re-introduced 'Hard Lying' money for such ships.

sail to London. She had run continuously for fifteen months without a breakdown.

They sailed for one last convoy operation in the North Atlantic, then south. And so it was decided. Just how badly the ship needed the refit was emphasized *en route*. Again let her commanding officer recall the story:

> On returning to Gladstone Dock after leaving this convoy, 48 hours leave was given to each watch as usual, in the midst of which orders were received to proceed forthwith to London to refit at the yard of Green and Silley Weir. As many as possible of the Libertymen were recalled with the help of the local police, but we had to proceed northabout with little more than half the ship's company.
>
> The weather was bad and the ship received a battering in the Pentland Firth, but conditions improved when we were passing down the East Coast. Running down the narrow swept channel in darkness from buoy to buoy, with minefields on one side and the Yorkshire coast on the other, the officer of the watch informed me that the buoy he had just sighted ahead was showing the wrong flashing signal. A look at the magnetic compass showed that we were steaming north-west instead of south-east and it transpired that the gyro compass had veered exactly 180 degrees and the helmsman had, in following the gyro compass, unsuspectingly turned the ship onto the opposite course!
>
> We proceeded very carefully by magnetic compass after that; until the gyro was rectified, and reached London safely. If the gyro had veered any other amount we should have been in deadly trouble.

Once at the dockyard the whole ship's company went on leave for fourteen days with only a fire watch left on board. Signalman Harrison recalls:

> I was one of the watch for the first half of the refit which took about a month. I did not go home when I got leave as my home was in Dundee which was too far. Anyway I preferred to see a bit of the Capital.

It was unfortunate that *Wild Swan*'s arrival in London once again coincided exactly with the latest moves of the enemy. Having turned

from the Capital when *Wild Swan* was on the Mersey, the Luftwaffe
now followed her back south again. London had undergone the real
'Blitz' with the docks and East End and the City in particular suffering from weeks of continuous attacks. For a while they had started to
recover from the battering they had received while the bombers were
busy in the provinces. But Hitler had his attentions on his next prey.
No further attempts were to be made to revive the abandoned 'Sea
Lion'; instead his erstwhile ally Stalin was to be smashed in another
lightning campaign on land. He had little doubts about his chances
in this friendly element, and had no desire to trust his luck at sea.
While Panzer and Stuka units moved into their positions in occupied
Poland along the Vistula, attention was diverted from this build-up
by a renewal of the air attacks on London.

Wild Swan actually entered the dock to be taken in hand for her
refit on 20th March 1941, the same day as the Luftwaffe delivered the
largest of their raids directed against south-eastern London. It was a
Wednesday:

> The first of four massive spring raids on the capital which brought the
> long blitz to a close took place. In a six-hour bombardment from 2000 to
> 0200, 500 bombers dropped over 450 tons of high explosive and 3,400
> canisters of incendiaries on east and south-east London. Whatever may
> have been the experiences of other parts of the Metropolis, so far as
> Deptford, Greenwich, Lewisham and Woolwich were concerned this
> was the most intensive attack of all.*

The friendly and efficient firm of Green and Silley Weir (now alas no
more) was located at the Royal Albert Docks (North Woolwich).
There were three drydocks there and above a large crane capable of
lifting 100 tons. *Wild Swan* was not the only Royal Navy vessel there
at this time; also docked was the destroyer *Winchester*. Located as she
was in dry-dock *Wild Swan* was particularly vulnerable. With only
one young officer and a few crew aboard, the night of the 20th was an
impressive 'welcome' for them, as W.K. Harrison recalls:

> Whilst *Wild Swan* was propped up in drydock London had one of
> her many bombing raids and the dock area was getting a particu-
> larly heavy pasting. The poor old *Wild Swan* was creaking and
> groaning on her wooden chocks inside the dock.
>   The movement got so bad that the officer in charge, a young

* From the privately published book *Red Alert* by Lewis Blake, London.

midshipman, was frightened that the ship would fall off its blocks. He therefore ordered the quartermaster to pipe 'abandon ship'. To my knowledge this is the only time any of His Majesty's ships have been abandoned on dry land!

The work involved was quite large and the refit was not due to complete originally until 17th April. There was a major overhaul of the ship's engines, boilers, condensers, heavily worn steering gear, electrical circuits etc. There was no real action damage as such to repair, but her hull needed sealing and repairing in numerous places. Her armament remained the same, the only additions having been the twin Lewis gun put in earlier and the two Bren guns she had 'acquired' at the time of Boulogne.* According to the ship's navigation officer: 'Somebody in authority must have requisitioned supplies of ammo for these guns, because I don't think we were ever without adequate supplies onboard.'

However, opportunity was taken to fit the ship with radar. Lack of this device had been keenly felt during the first half of the wartime commission. Although the set fitted was of an early type, it was still a valued asset. It was a 286M type ASV set† the aerial, which resembled a wire mattress, was situated atop the foremast and linked to a specially constructed radar (or RDF Radio Direction Finding as it was at first code-named) office. The operator rotated this aerial until an echo was obtained. It was then stopped while the range and bearing were read off. Continuously rotating aerials giving all-round cover were still years away, and so the radar transmissions, of the wide-beam type, were sent out only ahead of the ship and on both bows. As a result, it was quite often necessary to swing the ship round to search in other directions. The display of echoes was also elementary, and a good deal of guesswork was needed to identify the returning echoes.

When the work was almost completed the Luftwaffe returned to this part of London with heavy raids on Wednesday, 16th April and Saturday, 19th April. In the latter the actual dockyard she was in was struck by several heavy bombs and both destroyers were slightly damaged.

The blast of near-miss bombs caused slight damage to *Wild Swan*, causing oil fuel tanks to become strained and leak. Her fighting effi-

* According to her commanding officer. Most destroyers supplemented their meagre AA defences in a similar way during the war.
† ASV = Air/Surface Vessel, i.e. could be used to detect both.

ciency, however, was only slightly impaired. *Winchester* was more seriously affected. Extra repair work to make good this damage was delayed by the damage done to the dock itself, and the *Wild Swan* was not ready for sea until 26th April. But a few yards either way with the bombs that hit the dock and it could have all been very different, as Patrick Satow, now back from leave, observed at close hand:

> During this night's blitz I was onboard, and I can remember that the offices of the dock company were badly damaged by fire. This destroyed some of the drawings and records of work relating to *Wild Swan* but as the refit was almost completed, the loss was not as serious as it might have been. Although damage to the two destroyers was only superficial, it brought home to everyone the appalling risks to which any ships in dry dock were exposed. If the dock gates had been breached the inrush of a wall of water did not bear thinking about.

But, yet again, her luck held. Another of her nine lives had been expended, and, posted to Portsmouth as part of the 1st Destroyer Flotilla, a whole new chapter of her life was now about to start.

CHAPTER EIGHT

Southern Climes
May 1941-August 1941

At Portsmouth as part of the 1st Flotilla *Wild Swan* found herself in the company of the destroyers *Vansittart* and *Wivern*, under overall command of Commander Michael Meyrick, the senior officer, in the latter ship. Stoker Linford was glad to be back at his home town, but not happy at what he found there. 'Back at Portsmouth, my parents had been bombed out and were in hospital at Alton and then they were put in accommodation there.'

There were several new additions to her crew at this time, one of them being Telegraphist D. Lingard:

I joined her in April 1941 at Portsmouth during heavy bombing of that port after finishing my telegraphists' course at Pompey Signals School – my first ship. The first three weeks we spent in escorting from Portsmouth. Apart from the captain and the first lieutenant I had little contact with the officers other than the signals officer. He was a rather dashing, efficient young man, both with signals and navigation and appeared satisfied with the way the W/T office was conducted. He was in his 20's and all visual signalling worked very efficiently under his direction, with the help of Yeoman Burton.

My superior was Petty Officer Telegraphist R.C. Clement, a time-served man who lived in Worcester Park, London. Like many in the *Swan* he had been recalled for the duration. He was aged about 35 and organised the W/T office, kept all the signal books etc., up to date and ensured all batteries, aerials and the office was ready for any emergency, including a jury-rigged aerial should it ever be needed, as it eventually *was*. I was happy working with both men.

The refit had been necessitated I was told not by enemy action damage but by bad weather damage in the North Atlantic. The new equipment that had been added just before I joined her was mainly anti-submarine gear and radar. The only addition to her W/T equipment had been a note-magnifier to the receiver, which was always manned at sea. The W/T office was very small and positioned at the break of the fo'c'sle and rather exposed. She was not dazzle-painted, just plain battleship grey.

Another newcomer was Engine Room Artificer A.H. Rippon:

I joined *Wild Swan* early in May. The ship was in Portsmouth Dockyard recovering from a refit and in the usual chaotic state. It seemed a relief, however, to escape the bombing of the city and the Royal Naval Barracks. I was a bit overwhelmed by shipboard life and regaled with tales of her earlier exploits. There was even an old messmate who remembered the ship on the China Station.

I was sent on a week's leave on 13th May and on my return found the ship in greater chaos; this was called 'Storing Ship'. Air-raids seemed frequent with bombs falling in the harbour and on the mudflats.

While he was away *Wild Swan* had not been idle. One of her first duties was to help escort the heavy cruiser *Berwick* from Spithead to Rosyth. She had been hit by 8-inch shells from both Italian and German cruisers and needed a lot of repairs. The first stage had been completed and she was due to sail to Rosyth for the rest.

At 2130 on 12th May *Berwick* was sailed, routed westabout via the Irish Sea with four ships of the 1st Flotilla as escorts, *Wivern*, *Wild Swan*, *Berkeley* and *Blencathra*, the latter pair until dark on the 13th. She was due to arrive Rosyth at 0800 on the 14th, via the Minches, and, had *Wild Swan* accompanied her all the way, she would have circumnavigated the British Isles since February, but she did not, being instructed only to accompany the cruiser as far as Smalls light vessel. *Wivern* and *Wild Swan* returned to Plymouth at 2200 on the 13th, and thence back to Portsmouth where another job awaited them.

Their responsibility was the big French submarine *Surcouf*, the largest submarine of the day. She had been one of the ships boarded at Portsmouth the previous year when the French surrendered, and her crew had killed one of the British officers. However she had joined the Free French and had been used to provide escort for the Halifax and other Atlantic convoys as a protection against surface raiders, without success. She had just completed a refit at Portsmouth and was bound for the more clement climes of Bermuda to work up. *Wild Swan* took her through 49°45′ N, 4°27′ W and thence returned to the Needles, and Portsmouth.

Meanwhile bad weather and increased resistance had seen a shift of U-boat operations south where they found little to stop them. In May thirty ships totalling 176,168 tons had been sunk within 600 miles of Freetown and Bathurst. Admiral Dönitz had despatched a group of submarines to those waters especially to catch some juicy targets and despatched supply ships thither to keep them operating at maximum strength.* Armed merchant raiders were also at large in these waters, but it was the submarine menace that caused the concern in May and the Admiralty cast around for ships to send out to Freetown quickly, in order to reinforce the division of 'B' class destroyers stationed there. On 17th May they signalled various commands to rustle up destroyers to escort a convoy from the Clyde south and then join Freetown Command. This prompted a response next day:

C-in-C, Portsmouth to Admiralty: 1317/18. Re Adm 2051B/17.† I have now *Wivern, Wild Swan* and *Vansittart* here and, in view of strain on Western Approaches destroyers, suggest all three should be detailed for this new commitment.

This was promptly taken up:

Admiralty to C-in-C, Portsmouth: 2236B/19. A small, fast convoy known as WS8X and consisting of *Waiwara* from Newport and *Port Wyndham* from Mersey will be ready to leave UK about 27 May. Speed of slowest ship 15½ knots. Ocean escort will be *Neptune* of Home Fleet. C-in-C, WA is

---

* U-boats operating at this phase were *UA, U-38, U-69, U-103, U-105, U-106, U-107* and the Italian *Calvi* and *Tazzoli*. Supply ships were *Egerland, Nordmark, Lothringen* and *Python*.

† A note on signals from *Wild Swan's* Navigating Officer is in order here: 'Naval Signals: Times of Origin. The letter 'B' indicates that it was originated at 2051 by Double Summer Time or two hours *ahead* of GMT. This was being kept in the United Kingdom at that time, principally as a means of saving fuel throughout the land. If a signal bore the suffix 'Z' it was based on GMT. If suffix 'A' was used, the time was one hour ahead of GMT. So 0536Z = 0636A = 0736B on the same day. When a ship was on passage, it was usual to change the clocks before reaching a port of call, so that they corresponded with those on shore. When crossing the Atlantic, or on other long passages, the change of time onboard was carried out as convenient to a ship's routine, watchkeeping, etc., when passing from one time zone to another. One hour is equivalent to 15 degrees of longitude, so three hours *behind* GMT would normally be centred on longitude 45° West. The time zone would extend from 37½° to 52½° West longitude. Some world maps or atlases print these standard time zones, where the system can be more easily seen. It will be noticed that, although a ship might be *west* of Greenwich, the time being kept was two hours *ahead* of GMT which is normal solar time for such places as Murmansk, Leningrad, Cairo or Durban.'

requested to supply A/S escort. *Wivern*, *Wild Swan* and *Vansittart* from
Portsmouth are all available as part of escort. These three ships should
be ordered to break-off and proceed to Gibraltar to refuel when fuel conditions so demand. *Wild Swan* to be taken in hand at Portsmouth for
repairs. To be completed 24th.

As for reinforcing Freetown:

Admiralty to General: 0900/20. Following destroyers have been selected,
Wivern, *Vansittart*, *Wild Swan* and *Vimy*. First three are sailing in concurr-
ence with 2236B/19. *Vimy* is expected to arrive Freetown at end of June.
On arrival of *Vimy* at Freetown *Highlander* is to be sailed for UK via Gibraltar.

Wild Swan was ready by 24th May, but, before these movements were
put into effect there were to be other, more dramatic, interventions in
their schedule.

The drama which took the headlines at this time was of course the
hunting down and eventual destruction of the battleship *Bismarck*.

After *Bismarck* had sunk the *Hood* with appalling loss of life, and
damaged *Prince of Wales*, for an agonising period she slipped her pur-
suers and it seemed for a while that she might yet make good her
escape. Even when she was finally re-located making for Brest lack of
fuel gave rise to a desperate situation whereby the British battleships
King George V and *Rodney* would have to call off the attack, or, at best,
be left with no destroyer escorts in an ocean filled with vengeful U-
boats. As a hedge against both of these possibilities many ships were
brought to a state of readiness, though not ultimately involved.
Three such ships were the *Wivern*, *Vansittart* and *Wild Swan*, and their
part is best illustrated by recording the signals concerning them at
this time:

ACNS(H) to C-in-C, Portsmouth: 1858B/26. *Wivern*, *Vansittart* and *Wild
Swan* are to proceed to Plymouth with all despatch.
    C-in-C, Plymouth to ACNS(H): 0046/27. Arrived, *Wivern*, *Vansittart* and
Wild Swan 0040.
    C-in-C, Plymouth to ACNS(H): *Wivern*, *Vansittart* and *Wild Swan* have
fuelled and are at one hour's notice.

The loss of the *Hood* was a bitter blow to many, Lieutenant-Commander Sclater for one had served aboard her, as had many of the

long-serving regulars. Even the newcomers felt something unique had passed as Duncan Hutter later recalled:

> I remember vividly a high speed run by night to Plymouth and the very deep gloom over the whole ship on the morning when the news of the *Hood* broke. Each man felt it personally and very deeply. We stayed at Plymouth near the breakwater with steam up in company with our flotilla mates, presumably in readiness to form an emergency torpedo striking force if necessary. There was much relief when *Bismarck* was sunk without our aid.

In the event, *Bismarck* had been despatched and other destroyers sailed to help escort the British victors safely back to port. At 2335 on the 27th, orders were received by the C-in-C, Plymouth, to proceed instead to the aid of the *Registan*, an armed boarding ship which had been bombed and set on fire. The flotilla increased speed to 26 knots and set course accordingly steering line ahead, in order *Wivern, Vansittart, Wild Swan*. Soon a glow could be seen on the horizon which changed as they drew nearer, into a fiercely burning ship. At 0220 they came up to her, reduced speed and *Wivern* ordered *Wild Swan* to investigate possible boats from the ship. The weather at this time was cloudy with a force 3 wind ESE, calm with a slight swell. A.H. Rippon recalls:

> After one day at sea I had lost all interest in everything, *Bismarck* and all, except my own misery! We were chasing at high speed to help a ship (it was rumoured to be a tanker hit from a shell from *Bismarck*!!) but I could not have cared less. I was gloriously seasick.
>
> At last we came up on this burning vessel in the middle of the night. The sea was still rough but we picked up quite a few burned and oil-covered survivors. Seasickness prevented me from having a very active part in this drama or indeed having very much sympathy for them at the time.

After a short while shouting was indeed heard in the water and the 10-inch signalling lamp was switched on revealing a Carley float with a number of men aboard, sixteen in all in charge of a paymaster sub-lieutenant. They were in an exhausted condition and took some time getting aboard the destroyer. While this was being done the ship's whaler was lowered and pulled in the direction of further faint cries heard from astern. Two further men were found floating in life jackets. They too were rescued and *Wild Swan* circled looking for more survivors, going slowly to windward with the searchlight directed at the black water just ahead of her bows. Two men clinging to a spar were soon sighted and the ship was taken alongside them. They proved too exhausted to help themselves and so Lieutenant Burnley and Leading Seaman Mitchell dived overboard and fastened lines around them so they could be hauled in. *Wild Swan* searched further until dawn at 0725 but no further survivors were found.

Meanwhile the St Ives lifeboat had arrived on the scene and later so did two motor launches and a tug sent out by C-in-C, Plymouth. *Registan* continued to burn fiercely amidships and was listing about 20° but, at 0725 *Wivern* ordered *Wild Swan* to break off the search and they set course for Milford Haven in line ahead in open order at 26 knots to land survivors. In Lieutenant-Commander Sclater's words:

> Everything possible was done to make the survivors as comfortable as possible as soon as they were got onboard. Four men never regained consciousness although artificial respiration was continued for about an hour. At 1100 these four men were buried at sea. I wish to commend the gallantry of Lieutenant Dudley Eric Burnley, RANVR and Acting Leading Seaman Gorden Sewell Mitchell, in risking their lives to save others.

Wivern reported that *Registan* was still afloat and burning at 0730 off Cape Cornwall and that they had picked up 36 survivors and eight dead. These survivors were landed at Milford Haven on the 28th. Soon afterwards the *Cleveland* landed ten survivors from the bombed merchantman *Royixon*. Many of *Wild Swan*'s crew were destined to see Milford Haven under similar circumstances and again in *Vansittart*'s company little over a year later.

Convoy WS8X bound for the Cape consisting of the merchantmen *Duchess of Bedford*, *Port Wyndham* and *Waiwara*, sailed at 2230 on the last day of May 1941 with the aircraft carrier *Victorious*, cruisers *Norfolk* and *Neptune*, AMC *Esperance Bay* and the Canadian destroyers *Assiniboine* and *Saguenay*. The heavy escort was due to the fact that the merchantman and the AMC were loaded with vital troop reinforcements for the Middle East. Crete had just fallen and things were looking blacker all the time in that theatre. Although *Bismarck* had gone, capital ships *Scharnhorst, Gneisenau* and *Prinz Eugen* were at Brest and could sail at any time.

The three destroyers rendezvoused some fourteen miles off Oversay with the convoy and powerful escort at 0700B on 1st June and commenced their journey southward. Later the escort was reinforced by the destroyers *Legion* and *Piorun*, with *Brighton*, *Sherwood* and *St Mary's* for part of the journey.

However important the need to protect the convoy from surface raiders, the main concern at Gibraltar was increased submarine activity. An Italian submarine group had been operating west of the Straits for some time and indications were that German U-boats also were moving into that region. Interlocking with the arrival of WS8X was a complex plan for flying off Hurricane fighter planes to reinforce Malta's defences, which involved transferring planes and men between the carriers *Furious*, *Argus* and *Victorious* west of the Straits. It was essential that they and the famous Force 'H' from Gibraltar had adequate anti-submarine protection while this was being carried out, as the following exchange of signals showed:

Admiralty to FOICNA*: 1341/2. In view of submarine activity it is important that *Wivern*, *Vansittart* and *Wild Swan* should, when detached, proceed with utmost despatch constant with fuel remaining.

FOIC NA to WS8X: 1308/2. Destroyers to report ETA when 100 miles from Gibraltar.

Admiralty to FOICNA: *Wivern*, *Vansittart* and *Wild Swan* were detached from convoy for Gibraltar at 0600 on 3rd in 48°40′ N, 20°59′ W.

FOICNA to Admiralty: My 1308/2 and 1020/1. *Wivern*, *Vansittart* and *Wild Swan* will be only V's available to meet *Victorious*.

On 6th June the three destroyers duly arrived at The Rock, hastily refuelled and that same morning sailed again escorting the carrier *Argus* and transport *Nea Hellas* bound for the UK. They joined *Victorious* in 34°03′ N, 14°36′ W at 1100 on the 8th as her anti-submarine screen. The *Neptune* was detached independently to Gibraltar, the *Norfolk* and other escorts had long since gone home, but *Victorious* remained in company with *Argus* during that day parting company at 2000 in 35°36′ N, 16°10′ W. Next morning Force H, led by Vice Admiral Sir James Somerville, hove into sight at 0700: *Renown*, *Ark Royal*, *Sheffield*, *Faulknor*, *Fearless*, *Foxhound*, *Forester* and *Fury*, a world-famous collection of fighting ships which had become a legend in

* FOIC, NA = Flag Officer in Charge, North Atlantic Station, i.e. Gibraltar.

both the Mediterranean and the Atlantic Ocean with their daring raids and efforts in outfacing the Italian Fleet on numerous convoy runs to Malta.

They had the old carrier *Furious* with them and during the day she and *Ark Royal* flew off six Swordfish to ferry the Hurricane party from that carrier to *Victorious* to ready the fighters which had still to be assembled. By midday 75 men had been transferred and *Furious* sailed for home escorted by *Sheffield*. Meanwhile the old destroyers, while happy to be in such distinguished company, could not hide their age. *Wivern*, short of fuel and with a leaking oil fuel tank, was sent into Gibraltar at 1030, and after *Furious* departed *Vansittart* and *Wild Swan*, the latter suffering from weather damage, were also detached, arriving on the 10th.

Lieutenant-Commander Sclater remembers being the early butt of Somerville's famous acid wit on this occasion:

> Force H had joined up with the squadron from the Home Fleet well to the west of Gibraltar steaming west with *Wild Swan* in the centre of the screen ahead. Suddenly the Flagship signalled to me. '*Wild Swan* return to Gibraltar forthwith.' With destroyers on either side and battle-cruiser and aircraft carriers astern I could not turn immediately and had to go ahead at full speed to give myself room to get clear. Very quickly Admiral Somerville signalled: 'Gibraltar the other way!'

On the 12th she was taken in hand for repairs at Gibraltar which were completed the next day. Force H and *Victorious* sailed from the Rock this day for the flying-off operation but the three destroyers were not required and were ordered to proceed to Freetown via Bathurst.

FOIC, NA to destroyers: *Wivern, Vansittart* and *Wild Swan* to sail for Bathurst then Freetown, ETA Bathurst 0800Z/18th.

Wild Swan to FOIC Freetown: ETA *Wild Swan* Freetown 0730/19th *Wivern, Vansittart* delayed Bathurst due fuelling problems.

FOIC, NA to FOIC Freetown: *Wivern, Vansittart* and *Wild Swan* informed imperative arrive Freetown by PM on 19th.

They were very much in demand at Freetown, and were to get little rest from the moment they arrived. The captain wrote:

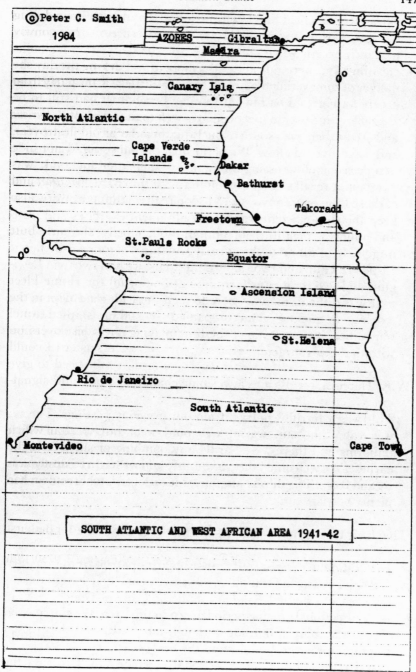

AZORES   Gibraltar

Madeira

Canary Isls

North Atlantic

Cape Verde
Islands

Dakar

Bathurst

Takoradi

Freetown

St.Pauls Rocks

Equator

Ascension Island

St.Helena

Rio de Janeiro

South Atlantic

Montevideo   Cape Town

SOUTH ATLANTIC AND WEST AFRICAN AREA 1941-42

We arrived safely at Freetown and found that there were no berths alongside for us and we had to anchor or secure to a buoy in the harbour, except when going alongisde the depot ship for boiler cleaning. We were not allowed ashore after dark because of the danger of contracting malaria. There was little to attract us ashore except for golf and bathing at Lumley Beach.

Our routine was to meet convoys well to the north of Freetown and escort them well south of the Equator as far as our limited fuel endurance would allow. We performed the full ceremonial on the first occasion of 'Crossing the Line' but thereafter ignored it.

I cannot recall a single encounter with the enemy in the course of those Freetown convoys and I soon realised that the only way to keep the ship efficient was by very frequent exercises and drills and much expenditure of ammunition, mostly at improvised targets. In addition to the normal armament of four 4.7-inch, one 12-pdr HA gun and two single pom-poms, we had two twin Lewis guns and two Bren guns (acquired at Boulogne).

It was difficult to avoid boredom on these long sea trips in the tropics, frequently unaccompanied by other ships, and I remember passing some of the time playing chess on the bridge with the ship's surgeon.

W.K. Harrison recalls it as a welcome change:

This was a terrific contrast from our previous postings. The sea was calm, the sun warm, we could wear our tropical white uniforms and there were hardly any bombing or shells flying in earnest. We welcomed the tranquillity and we had a leisurely time by and large. The ship's company was on four watches and we had plenty of spare time.

The navigation officer recollects the first crossing of the Equator:

In addition to carrying out anti-submarine patrols from Freetown *Wild Swan* escorted a number of convoys on their long passages between the United Kingdom and the Cape of Good Hope, in both directions. On one period at sea in this area, the ship passed through a point in latitude $0°$, longtitude $0°$. Indeed she crossed the Equator several times, and the first occasion of so doing was marked by holding the traditional ceremony of 'Crossing the Line'.

Shortly before reaching latitude 0°, some of the less widely travelled members of the ship's company asked what would happen when she actually crossed the Line. Various unlikely stories were circulated to add interest to life onboard in these tropical waters. One was that there was a steel band running right round the world to mark the Equator, and the ship would have to stop before making a gap to pass through. Another was that everyone onboard would feel a definite jolt; but they would be warned just before it happened and no damage would be sustained by the ship.

The ceremony itself was centred on a large temporary swimming pool made of canvas, erected on deck and filled with sea water from the fire hoses. As the sea had a temperature of 28°C (82°F), there was no need for the pool to be heated. The ceremony was presided over by the commanding officer, and those 'Crossing the Line' for the first time were put through a selection of rather undignified duckings, accompanied by liberal quantities of soap applied with a large paint brush.

The first of many such convoys took place when *Wild Swan* and *Brilliant* sailed from Freetown at 0600 on 27th June as anti-submarine escort for the ss *Cameronia* along with the corvette *Cilicia*. They remained with the liner until midday on the 30th then left and arrived at Bathurst to refuel, before sailing back to Freetown where they arrived on 2nd July.

At midday on 7th July she left Freetown with the destroyers *Brilliant* and *Wivern* and the corvette *Asphodel* to rendezvous with the cruiser *Galatea* and the AMC *Moreton Bay* escorting another fast troop convoy, WS9B and returned south with them, returning to Freetown with them at 0800 on the 10th. On 24th July *Wivern* and *Wild Swan* sailed at midday as anti-submarine escort for the giant liner *Empress of Australia* for as long as their fuel permitted and were later joined by the AMC *Canton* which was acting as ocean escort. They were again back at Freetown early on 30th July. Thus the routine established itself, Freetown, refuel, Bathurst-Freetown. Neither port call enchanted the lower-deck or the engine-room personnel very much, as Stoker Linford recalls:

Bathurst and Freetown were typical West African ports. We did not spend much time at Bathurst and very seldom went ashore there, but when we did we were always welcomed by the RAF who had a base there. Freetown was a stinking hole, inevitably short of beer in the canteen. It seemed that any convoy ship which had been sunk on its way there turned out to be the beer-boat and the only alternatives were local brewed beer and gin (ugh!) 'Long Tom Pier' was the landing spot and it could tell many tales of returning tipsy matelots, both old *and* young.

Conditions in an old V & W at Freetown were hell. It was the worst place I can remember for humidity, twenty minutes down below was plenty. We had local coloureds for boiler cleaners but they had to be supervised. Usually it was three or four weeks on convoy runs, and two or three days in harbour. Several times we were attacked in harbour by the French planes operating from further north, everyone taking part in the shoots at them but I never saw one hit or brought down.

The Captain (D) of the destroyer flotilla at Freetown was Captain R.St V. Sherbrooke, DSO. The Commander-in-Chief was Vice Admiral R.H.T. Raikes ashore. By the time the three V & W's had joined his command the worst of the submarine campaign was already over. It came as no great surprise, therefore when, on 2nd August, the Admiralty ordered three destroyers back to Gibraltar on a temporary basis to help deal with this new threat. Vice Admiral Raikes was continually to protest at their absence, but the FOIC, Gibraltar, Vice Admiral Sir Frederick Edward-Collins, retained them for as long as possible. So desperate was the need for fast anti-submarine ships that the three destroyers, two of which had been ready for the scrapyard a few years before, were subject to a war of signals between the two flag officers as to whom could grab them first!

Admiralty to C-in-C, SA: Owing to heavy U-boat concentrations near Gibraltar three South Atlantic destroyers have been ordered to North Atlantic Command temporarily. *Wivern, Wild Swan* and *Boreas* leave Freetown 0600/3.

C-in-C SA to C-in-C, NA: *Wild Swan, Wivern* and *Boreas* to sail at 0600/3 and refuel at Bathurst then to Gibraltar.

Wivern to C-in-C, SA: Your 2109/2. Intend sailing from Bathurst with *Boreas* and *Wild Swan* on completion oiling 1630. ETA 1700/9.

However C-in-C, SA was not likely to part with the ships that were in the most pristine condition. *En route* both *Wivern* and *Boreas* developed faults and, by the time they were met off Gibraltar by the flotilla leader *Duncan* on the 10th, *Wivern* had such bad condenser trouble that she had to be sent home right away for a full refit. So all Admiral Edward-Collins got in the end was *Boreas* and *Wild Swan*. They were both quickly pressed into service on the threatened HG convoy route. Together with the Force 'H' destroyers *Duncan, Forester* and, later, *Fury*, they sailed from Gibraltar at 1700 on 11th August at 1700 to carry out an anti-submarine sweep in the western approaches to the Straits. On completion of the sweep they were ordered to relieve the destroyers *Avonvale* and *Eridge* with HG70 and escort to the prudent limit of their fuel before returning to Gibraltar on the 16th. This became their new pattern of operations.

HG70's departure had been reported by Italian agents on the 9th and a wolf pack consisting of the *U-93, U-94, U-79, U-109, U-124, U-371, Finzi, Marconi* and *Vaniero* assembled between Gibraltar and the Azores to intercept. The Admiralty made the following assessment of this grim situation early on the 12th.

HG70. It is estimated that six or more submarines are near HG70 west of Cape St Vincent. Catalina reports U-boats shadowing at 1400 and two Focke-Wulf Kondor aircraft in sight 1630. *Boreas* and *Wild Swan* joined the convoy at 1415 from Gibraltar and FOCNA has asked C-in-C, WA to send destroyers to meet convoy on 15th when four destroyers now escorting must leave for Gibraltar to refuel.

FOCNA to destroyers: HG70. Vessels addressed are to remain with convoy until prudent limit of endurance then to Gibraltar. *Avonvale, Eridge, Boreas, Wild Swan*.

Among the other escorts was the flotilla leader *Faulknor*, returning home for a much-needed refit, the sloops and also several corvettes from WA. The escorts foiled several attempts by this strong force of submarines to get to grips and inflict a substantial defeat on the HG route. Time and time again the U-boats probed, but each time aggressive action by the escorts drove them off and held them at bay. It was a major victory for the escorting ships and the only loss was a solitary freighter bombed by Kondors on 11th August. On the 13th, for example, at sunrise *Faulknor* drove off one submarine that showed itself ahead of the convoy at 0630. I have described this attack in detail before but now Lieutenant-Commander Sclater tells it in his own words:

While escorting HG70 home in August *Wild Swan* was stationed on the beam and a flashing light was sighted on the horizon. The masthead lookout then reported that it was a surfaced U-boat signalling to a Focke-Wulf Kondor aircraft which had been circling the convoy. We and the *Faulknor* charged off at full speed to attack. The U-boat quickly submerged but we picked up an echo on our Asdic and both destroyers dropped several patterns of depth charges without any obvious signs of success until the Escort Commander ordered both ships to rejoin the convoy.

The Asdic had indicated that the U-boat was very deep and we set our depth charges to explode at 500 feet, the maximum depth setting. After our operational reports had been digested by the anti-submarine 'experts' a critical account of the action appeared in the next monthly *Anti-Submarine Digest* stating that U-boats *never* dived as deep as 500 feet and that that setting should not be used. However, a month later, an article in the same publication stated that it had now been learned that U-boats *did* dive to 500 feet, and beyond, so we felt vindicated. Later on intelligence reports confirmed that this U-boat had arrived at Brest badly damaged by our attacks.

Even if the satisfaction of a confirmed 'kill' was denied to *Wild Swan*, by keeping the enemy down or away from the merchantmen the object of their endeavours had, nonetheless, been attained: 'the safe and timely arrival' of yet another convoy of war goods in the UK and the thwarting of one of the biggest packs of U-boats so far assembled. A.H. Rippon recalls typical Gibraltar convoy work at this period as follows:

We now commenced long periods of weary, monotonous convoy work usually at about four to five knots chasing round the perimeter of the merchant ships, complaining about their black smoke and investigating all manner of sightings and Asdic alarms.

There was occasional excitement at depth charge attacks, and several times we obtained oil samples and debris and hoped for a 'probable' kill.

There were occasional gun duels at long range against the ever inquisitive Focke-Wulfs and once, tremendous excitement when a Sunderland flying boat reported a battleship some hours away. We steamed out to engage in a do-or-die attack and, after some hours steaming, we challenged this giant, expecting to be blown out of the water in reply. But, as usual the RAF got it wrong and our Nazi 'battleship' turned out to be an inoffensive Portuguese destroyer on exercises.

Wild Swan eventually arrived back at The Rock at 1610 on 18th August to refuel and make ready for her next voyage. At Gibraltar things were more pleasant than in West Africa of course, but they did not long savour Gibraltar's delights for later that day they sailed again with convoy HG71. This group had the sloop *Deptford*, corvettes *Auricula*, *Convolvulus*, *Marigold* and *Samphire* as close escorts, while *Wild Swan* was joined on the 23rd by *Vimy* from home and the tug *St Nectan*, operating to the prudent limit of her endurance as an additional escort. Again a pack of U-boats sought this convoy, but this time failed to find it. They returned to Gibraltar on the 24th but next day were sailed again to carry out an anti-submarine patrol to the west of the Straits. Although operating from Gibraltar, they were, of course, still only on loan, as a signal from that theatre of war confirmed.

> *C-in-C, SA to Admiralty*: 18th DF. Following destroyers nominally based at Freetown will form 18th Destroyer Flotilla: *Boreas, Brilliant, Vansittart* (Divisional Leader), *Velox, Vimy, Wild Swan, Wivern* (Divisional Leader), *Wrestler*.

Patrick Satow recalls this particular patrol as follows:

> The ship was lying alongside in harbour at short notice for putting to sea. She was ordered to proceed out into the Atlantic to search. . . On that day, it so happened that the commanding officer was in the local hospital for a short time, and the first lieutenant, always known as 'Number One', took command. The officer so doing was Lieutenant Kenneth Talbot Holland, and other officers had to undertake some additional duties.

The German and Italian submarines were still lurking west of the Straits in considerable numbers at this time and *Wild Swan* soon flushed one of these worthies from where she had been skulking, off Cape St Vincent.

> *Wild Swan to FOCNA*: 0158/25. One enemy submarine on surface bearing 330°, distance one mile, course 290°. My position 37°N, 9°W, based on a fix at 0100.

The first sighting of the U-boat was on the radar screen plot by a very alert radar rating and this was followed up by a visual sighting by the officer of the watch. If they were lucky in picking up the tiny silhouette of the U-boat's conning-tower, then their own bulk was easier to spot and the submarine crash-dived almost at once. A 'doubtful' Asdic contact was obtained, but she searched in vain firing off starshell from time to time in the hope of sighting her should she have again surfaced, but to no avail. After three hours fuel was running low and she had to return to Gibraltar.

Next night she was sent back to the same area with the corvette *Spiraea* but they were back at the Rock on the 27th unrewarded. The passage of submarines through the Straits was causing alarm at this time and strong patrols were mounted to try and prevent it. In fact the bulk of the Italian movements had taken place earlier, but the Germans were contemplating reinforcing their own war effort in the Mediterranean where their Luftwaffe and Army units had been operating with success since January. On the night of 29th/30th August *Wild Swan* was part of a strong force sweeping the Straits on this work; the destroyers *Vimy* and *Vidette*, corvettes *Campanula, Campion, Hydrangea* and *Wallflower* and Motor Launches *ML170* and *ML171*. The acute shortage of destroyers at Gibraltar was causing concern as FOCNA reported at the time. With *Boreas* also needing refitting he complained that two of the three destroyers sent as 'reinforcements' from Freetown were ' . . . lame ducks . . . ' and no use. *Frantic* ducks however *were* useful and the Admiralty agreed that *Wild Swan* could be retained on loan to the 13th Flotilla until its *Vidette* had been refitted, although officially *Wild Swan* should have reverted to the 18th Flotilla at Freetown. *Boreas* herself needed to sail for a home docking and when convoy HG72 sailed with seventeen merchantmen on 2nd September, she was included as part of the escort along with the sloop *Leith*, catapult ship *Maplin* and corvettes *Campion, Campanula, Bluebell, Hyacinth* and *Wallflower*. *Wild Swan* and *Farndale* provided the close escort until dusk on 7th September when they were to leave, refuel at Ponta Delgada on the island of São Miguel on the Portuguese-owned Azores group.

They were to be relieved by *Vimy* and *Croome* from Gibraltar, and then they were to sail to join convoy OG73 and escort it back to Gibraltar. Meanwhile *Boreas* was also to refuel in the Azores, rejoin the convoy HG72 and thence go to Londonderry. All these complex movements revolved around the short range of the destroyers and the need to have maximum numbers of escorts with the convoys as they passed through the danger areas. It was fortunate indeed that we were able to take advantage of Portuguese neutrality and the fact she was 'our oldest ally' to use her ports in this manner. But of course that neutrality could be used, and was, by the enemy for similar purposes. On this occasion all went well and there were no actual U-boat attacks on HG72, but they were in contact all right. On 4th September *Wild Swan* sighted one at 1748 some seven miles, bearing 243°. As Patrick Satow recalls:

It was usual in such cases for the escort to be sent out on the reported bearing, to force the U-boat to submerge and so make it lose touch with the convoy it was hunting. Depth charges would probably not be dropped unless a firm contact had been obtained with the Asdic equipment. By the time the escort had covered the seven miles, in about 20 minutes, the U-boat could well have gone deep in the Atlantic waters, and then be difficult to find.

We now know that *U-98* had first reported HG72 on the 3rd, but evidently Lieutenant-Commander Robert Gysae, her commander, did not relish *Wild Swan*'s attentions. Although there was a large wolf-pack in the area, with up to fifteen German boats and four Italians, no ships were lost from this convoy. On the 7th *Wild Swan* and *Farndale* refuelled at Ponta Delgada as planned. The navigation officer was to recall how:

Some of the convoys on passage, heading either to the north or south, were routed a considerable distance out in the Atlantic to the west of Portugal and north-west Africa. One result of this was that their naval escorts sometimes had insufficient fuel to get back to Gibraltar. In spite of the fact that our escorts were on war service, an arrangement had been made for them to refuel when necessary in the Azores.

This group of attractive islands situated about 1,300 English statute miles west of Gibraltar, belonged to Portugal which was a neutral country. There was therefore no black-out on land at night, and such visits were much appreciated by the fortunate few who made them.

Unless there was some kind of emergency, with the ship in real difficulties, these visits to ports of call in the Azores were strictly limited in duration. However, there was time to savour the delights of a pleasant environment, with a peaceful and friendly community. Also long remembered were some of the fresh provisions taken onboard, including such luxuries as pineapples which were virtually unknown in Britain in 1941-2. Having taken

onboard all that was needed, and having allowed part of the crew
a few hours onshore, the ship would leave harbour, and set her
course to join the escorts of yet another precious convoy.

A.H. Rippon also has memories of these neutral havens:

> Several times, having been active, either sub-hunting or inves-
> tigating sinkings and picking up survivors, we found it necessary
> to go into the Canaries, Azores or Cape Verdes to top up fuel
> tanks. Like all 'V' & 'W's' *Wild Swan* did not have great endurance
> at high speed.
>
> On one occasion at Ponta Delgada we were amazed to see a U-
> boat secured alongside the oiling jetty. We moored on the seaward
> side of her, took on a minimal amount of fuel then slipped out to
> the three-mile limit and began a 48 hour Asdic watch outside the
> harbour.
>
> There was no trace of the submarine and we had to return to
> harbour to complete oiling and get back to our convoy.

Wild Swan finally arrived back at Gibraltar on 13th September with
convoy OG73 and the destroyers *Duncan* and *Farndale*, sloop *Fowey*
and corvettes *Begonia*, *Hibiscus*, *Larkspur*, *Myosotis*, *Periwinkle*,
Springbok and *Stonecrop*. Again they were not attacked but they
learned that the destroyer *Croome* had sunk the Italian submarine
Baracca off Gibraltar on the 8th while they were away. They were still
needed there:

> *C-in-C, SA to Admiralty*: 1806/11. With movements of fast convoys and
> commitments such as *Eagle* and *Revenge* lack of the four destroyers to Gib-
> raltar is felt and it is difficult to maintain groups as demanded. Extra
> requirements to sail for Takoradi and to south are also heavy. Though
> requirements elsewhere are appreciated it is requested that *Wild Swan*
> and *Vimy* may be sent to Freetown the moment time allows. Concur
> *Wivern* and *Boreas* should refit UK.

Vice Admiral Raikes got short shrift from the Admiralty, beset on all
sides with similar demands for destroyers from all the other areas of
the war.

> *Admiralty to C-in-C, SA*: 1545/13. With very limited availability of
> destroyers at our disposal their allocation between Gibraltar and

Freetown must always be regarded as adaptable to meet emergency requirements. For that reason decision must stand on four destroyers.

There was no doubt that the need for them was at Gibraltar, the large concentrations of German and Italian submarines remained to the west, and plans were being laid to send through two groups of U-boats into the Mediterranean Sea within a short period. By contrast, sinkings had declined to almost nothing in the Freetown area.

The task of protecting the HG and OG convoys was not made easier by the knowledge that there were active bands of agents in Spain and Tangier who plotted the sailings of every ship with great care and passed on their sightings to the U-boats and the Kondor squadrons. Although Spain always evaded the issue when challenged, it was also known that some of her own fishermen and the like were acting in a similar capacity. In particular spy ships, disguised as innocent trawlers but equipped with sophisticated radio equipment and signal books, lingered in the known convoy routes and transmitted courses and speeds to Berlin and Rome. Gradually counter-intelligence in Britain identified these vessels and warnings were passed on to be on the alert for them and to arrest them if possible.

SOWP to WP: 1130A/19. Friday. *Primier Enrique* and *Segundo Enrique*. Suspected of reporting and other activities for the enemy, Spanish steam fishing vessels *Segundo Enrique* (113 tons) believed painted white with number 5300 on bows, and *Primier Enrique* (101 tons), are probably operating off Straits of Gibraltar, Canary Islands and southwards. If sighted they are to be brought in for examination.

This was further amplified soon afterwards:

FOCNA to Gibraltar forces: 1155/21. *Primier Enrique* believed to be transmitting intelligence useful to enemy on short wave set. Likely to be met in Cadiz, Gibraltar or Canary Island area. If encountered prompt action must be taken to prevent destruction of incriminating documents or other evidence and ships to be sent in under armed guard.

Like other ships to whom these signals were addressed *Wild Swan* drew up her plans to deal with this situation and an armed boarding party was on stand-by. We shall be meeting these and other Spanish trawlers later in our story. For the time being the two *Enriques* remained elusive.

CHAPTER NINE

Needles in the Haystacks
September 1941-April 1942

Another HG convoy now followed between 19th and 24th September, with *Wild Swan* again sailing as local escort for HG73 which had left two days earlier with 25 merchantmen escorted by the catapult ship *Springbank*, two sloops and eight corvettes. *Wild Swan* and *Vimy* provided additional escort between the 20th and 23rd and fully paid their way when the Italian submarine *Torelli* was attacked and damaged on the night of the 21st/22nd. The *Springbank*'s Fulmar was also successful in driving off a FW200 Kondor on the 24th. Thus far the convoy's luck had held, but two signals received on the 21st gave due warning of what they were in for.

> *FOICNA to Vimy, Wild Swan, Begonia & Jasmine*: 1712Z/21. HG73 was probably sighted by Italian U-boat 1712Z/21.
> *FOICNA to Vimy, Wild Swan, Begonia & Jasmine*: 1920/21. Italian submarine made enemy sighting report of HG73 at 1811A/21. This has been reported to other U-boats possibly within 60 miles north to north-east of convoy.

Vimy and *Wild Swan* had to leave them on the 23rd but they still had ten escorts. It was not enough. On the night of the 26th/27th the wolf packs homed in the middle of the Bay of Biscay. In continual attacks nine of the 25 merchant ships were sunk, totalling 25,818 tons, and the *Springbank* herself. Radar breakdowns in the escorts contributed to their defeat: one of the worst enemies, over-use and abuse of W/T traffic could help the enemy home in on it and indeed, while on passage back to Gibraltar early on the 24th, *Wild Swan* herself picked up what Vice Admiral Edward-Collins was later to describe as 'meaningless chatter' at a range of 1,250 miles, from convoy SL87. This convoy was of eleven merchant ships with four escorts and was also intercepted and heavily hit, losing seven of the merchantmen.

Nor was this traffic intercepted by any specialised equipment, W/T or otherwise. *Wild Swan* was never fitted with HF/DF.* As her navigation officer states:

* HF/DF = 'HuffDuff' = High Frequency/Direction Finding. She would have been fitted in the summer of 1942, had she survived.

There was probably a watch being kept on the ship on one of the frequencies in use by the Atlantic convoys. It would most likely be associated with exceptional radio propagation conditions, under which transmissions could be bent round to follow the curvature of the earth, instead of being lost out into space.

There is certainly no recollection of our having specialised radio gear, because most of the 'fixing' of the positions of U-boats out at sea was done by more fully equipped shore stations. The results were passed as quickly as possible to ships which had the need to know.

On her return to Gibraltar *Wild Swan* conducted a series of runs over the local degaussing range on 26th September to carry out a check on the lasting effectiveness of the earlier trials carried out off the south coast of England at the beginning of her commission, combined with a further check on the ship's change of location to a lower latitude, where the earth's standing magnetic field is differently aligned in the horizontal and vertical planes.

On conclusion of these tests she and *Vimy* sailed to Bathurst to take part in one of the movements mentioned in Vice-Admiral Raikes' earlier signal, namely to meet and escort the aircraft carrier *Eagle* which was on her way home to refit at Cammell Laird's yard at Liverpool. She had sailed from Freetown escorted by the light cruiser *Dunedin*, the sloop *Bridgewater* and two corvettes. *Vimy* and *Wild Swan* were to take over escort off Bathurst on the morning of 6th October. *Eagle* was to be routed east of the Canary Islands and *Vimy* was to be detached in about 26°N to return to Bathurst while *Wild Swan* continued the escort to Gibraltar. The two destroyers remained at Bathurst from 2nd to 5th October and then sailed to comply with these movements, but they soon ran into heavy storms which severely hampered the attempts at a rendezvous, as the series of signals indicates.

Vimy to C-in-C, SA: 0300/6. Your 1321/4th. Not met: My position course and speed are 14°41′ N, 19°06′ W, 001°, 18 knots. *Wild Swan* in company. Weather.

Vimy to C-in-C, SA, *Wild Swan*: 1300Z/6. Pending further instructions at 1600 *Vimy* turns back at 18 knots; *Wild Swan* continues on route as your 1321/4th at 14 knots.

Eagle to FOCNA: 1245Z/7. ETA 1800A/8th. *Vimy* not met. *Wild Swan* requires fuel, proposed to detach her 9th/10th to proceed to Funchal, Madeira. Passed to *Dunedin*.

FOCNA to Eagle: Your 1245Z/7. Owing to lack of fuel at Funchal *Wild Swan* is to fuel at Las Palmas. Permission is being obtained for *Wild Swan* to fuel there on 9th. *Vimy* to proceed to R/V with *Wild Swan* at 0600.

Wild Swan to FOCNA: 1922A/9. *Wild Swan* left Las Palmas 1800/9 to rejoin *Eagle*.

After battling through further big seas the carrier and the destroyer eventually arrived safely at Gibraltar, being met by the destroyer *Croome* and the French minesweeper *Commandant Duboc* on 11th October. In the interim Vice Admiral Raikes had been trying once more to get her back under his wing.

C-in-C, SA to FOCNA: Propose *Wild Swan* returns to Freetown to enable my other destroyers to dock.

FOCNA to C-in-C, SA: 1844/10. Intend sailing *Wild Swan* for Freetown on 16th October.

FOCNA to C-in-C, SA: My 1844/10. *Wild Swan* now six months out of dock. Do you want me to keep her until I can dock her, probable date 18th October?

C-in-C, SA to FOCNA: Your 1744/11th. Yes please.

Now the long-awaited transfer of the German U-boats from the Atlantic to the Mediterranean had begun, six U-boats passing successfully through the Straits during the latter part of September despite the special patrols. On 4th November a second group was to be sailed from their base in the Bay of Biscay. By the end of the month therefore a further exchange of signals was deciding *Wild Swan*'s immediate future.

Admiralty to FOCNA: In view of present situation submarines retain *Wild Swan* until arrival of *Wishart*.

C-in-C, SA to Admiralty: FOCNA. I hope that will not be necessary.

But it was. Prior to her refit at Gibraltar *Wild Swan* underwent trials at the Rock during the second and third weeks of the month and Vice Admiral Edward-Collins had good use for her where she was.

FOCNA to Admiralty: 2222/24. Subject to satisfactory trial intend sailing *Wild Swan* PM/24th to reinforce escort convoy OS9G.

FOCNA to OS9G, Wild Swan: *Wild Swan* sailed 0001/25th to pass through 37°22′ N, 19°00′ W at 0600/27th, steaming along approach route, speed 14 knots at R/V with OS9G.

FOCNA to C-in-C, SA: As next WS convoy will not leave UK till about

Wild Swan in storm-force winds, North Atlantic, 1940.

(Above) Coming on for a 'dusting'.
Looking astern from *Wild Swan's*
bridge with a gale blowing from
port to starboard. Notice the angle
at which the White Ensign is being
held by the strength of the wind.
On such days as this disaster
struck *Wild Swan* twice, and on
two separate occasions men were
swept overboard and never seen
again. There was little or no hope
of being found in such conditions.

(Right) High seas running in
winter. It was in such weather that
Wild Swan lost her Midshipman on
one of her first voyages. She
herself was to be lost in these self-
same waters a few years later.

10th/11th and in view of scale of attack near Gibraltar area it is considered desirable for *Wild Swan* to remain at Gibraltar until arrival of *Wishart* which should be about 30th October.

And so it was. *Wild Swan* sailed from the Rock to meet the special fast convoy of three troop ships reinforcing the escort which consisted of the Dutch destroyer *Isaac Sweers*, the sloops *Fowey* and *Leith* and the corvette *Stonecrop*. They arrived safely at Gibraltar on 1st November. On the 10th of that month *Wild Swan* entered the drydock at Gibraltar to undergo her much needed refit, due to complete on the 14th. Meanwhile, four more U-boats had passed through the Straits into the Mediterranean. *Wild Swan*'s refit had almost been completed with good effect when startling news was received during the afternoon of 13th November; the aircraft carrier *Ark Royal* had been torpedoed.

Several German U-boats were lying in wait for Force H off Alboran Island. Some evasive routing was carried out, but not enough and two of these submarines made attacks on the carrier. *U-205* (Lieutenant-Commander Franz-Georg Reschke) fired a three-torpedo spread at *Ark Royal* and claimed one hit on a destroyer and two on the carrier. *U-81* (Lieutenant-Commander Friedrich Guggenberger) fired four torpedoes at the battleship *Malaya* claiming two hits on her. In reality, although one of the escorting destroyers, *Legion*, had a torpedo explode in her wake, only one missile struck home, and this, from *U-81*, hit *Ark Royal*. Despite intensive destroyer hunts and searches by radar-equipped Swordfish from the carrier the two U-boats escaped unscathed. Now began the long fight to save *Ark Royal*. Stoker Rippon remembers it thus:

It was during a boiler clean in Gibraltar dockyard in mid-November that we were informed that *Ark Royal* had been torpedoed about 30 miles out from Gibraltar and we were required at maximum speed.

One boiler was in use, one boiler was cleaned but not closed up and No 3 Boiler was in the middle of the cleaning drill. We thus left harbour on one boiler whilst making the others ready. By the time we reached *Ark Royal* we were making about 25 knots on two boilers and joined the other units providing a screen around the carrier.

At 1549 Vice Admiral Somerville aboard *Malaya* signalled the Vice

Admiral at the Rock to send tugs to assist *Ark Royal* and for the
immediate despatch of anti-submarine vessels and aircraft from the
North Front airstrip, to provide a strong patrol around the crippled
ship. At 1710, when *Malaya* was some eight miles east of Europa
Point she passed a whole flotilla of craft on their way to help, the *Wild
Swan*, tugs *St Omar* and *Thames*, and motor launches *ML121, 130, 132,
135, 170, 172* and *176*. While *Wild Swan* joined the *Laforey, Legion* and
Lightning in an outer screen the motor launches maintained an inner
screen.

> Depth charges were dropped in sequence almost continually. Our
> ERA staff prepared portable pumps and hoses and there was talk
> of boarding parties to help with the salvage work. The carrier was
> listing badly and one of the sea-going tugs from Gibraltar was sec-
> ured alongside and found herself being gradually lifted out of the
> water so was forced to slip her ropes. Soon afterwards the crew of
> the carrier abandoned ship.

Patrick Satow recalls that:

> Despite a high speed dash from The Rock, we arrived well after
> dark and virtually never saw the crippled ship. Strenuous efforts
> were made by others present to tow the stricken carrier back to
> harbour, but the elements were not on our side, largely due to the
> adverse current of surface water in that area. . . It was the east-
> going surface current which hampered efforts to tow the *Ark Royal*
> to safety, and in the small hours of the morning the aircraft carrier
> went down. Her crew were taken aboard by escorting destroyers
> and only one man was lost, but *Wild Swan* was not instructed to
> take any of these survivors.

On completion of this sad episode it was back to routine convoy
duties once more for *Wild Swan*. During the period she was based at
Gibraltar, the crew enjoyed generally better weather and sea conditions than had been experienced during her service in the North
Atlantic in higher latitudes, but from time to time they caught a
'dusting', as with the *Eagle* trip. Again ERA Rippon:

> We returned to convoy duties and again endured long, slow trips
> in sometimes atrocious weather. *Wild Swan* was a very wet ship,
> most messdecks being awash and the small freeboard making
> movements on deck very difficult. She was also very poorly equip-

ped in the way of forced ventilation and in the tropics most people found space to sleep on deck.

In the engine-room canvas windcatchers were rigged to form a chute leading to the upper deck to divert air from our passage below. Naturally there were a continuous list of minor mechanical problems in a ship so old which required our attention, leaking steam joints, valves and the main shaft and stern glands were the most persistent 'leakers'.

I recall a Med convoy, Malta-bound. We were not called upon to go all the way through (probably due to our restricted range) and most on board were a bit disappointed at missing a run-ashore in the 'Gut' at Valletta. I also have a recollection of air raids at Gibraltar by Vichy French bombers from bases in North Africa.

The Malta convoy in question was not, in fact, a real convoy but a dummy, or diversion convoy, under the codename of Operation Chieftain. The object was to occupy the attentions of the Italian air force in Sicily and the Luftwaffe from their bases in Greece and Crete so that they would not unduly interfere with the Army offensive in the Western Desert, Operation Crusader. This convoy sailed at 1830 on 16th November with the merchant ships *Blair Atholl, Baron Newlands, Shona, Cisneros* and *Ottinge* and the Royal Fleet Oiler *Brown Ranger* posing as a merchant tanker.

These ships were escorted by *Wild Swan* with the sloop *Deptford* and corvettes *Convolvulus, Rhododendron* and *Marigold*. The convoy headed eastward into the Mediterranean hoping for once, to be reported and shadowed for a time, long enough to pull Axis bombers westward away from Auchinleck's troops on the 18th. At nightfall the merchant ships one-by-one began to break off from the convoy and return westward independently while the escorts were to carry out an anti-submarine sweep between Gibraltar and $1°30'$ E, returning to the Rock the night of the 19th/20th.

They stumbled on some of the wolf-pack that had recently passed through the Straits, which were still lurking to the eastward. It was in position $36°29'$ N, $2°17'$ W at 1140 on the 17th that *Wild Swan* got the first contact and carried out an initial attack. She was joined by the corvette *Samphire* and further searching was carried out and contacts attacked with no visible result. There were a number of 'non-sub' echoes and it was at first put down to yet another one of these. As her navigating officer stated:

There were always a good many 'non-sub' contacts and not many
confirmed U-boats. It was very much the luck of the draw as to
which escorts got the real thing, and therefore the chance to hunt
an enemy submarine to destruction.

As with the Italian submarine in the Bay earlier, this chance was
denied *Wild Swan*, but she must have caused some damage because
no submarine attacks were made on any of the merchantmen. The
day before the corvette *Marigold*, which had been delayed with
engine defects and was hastening to join up with the Chieftain escort,
surprised another submarine, the *U-433* (Lieutenant-Commander
Hans Ey), and sank her outright.

Their next job was to act as escort to the P & O Liner *Rangitata*,
loaded with service personnel on their way to the Middle East, via
the Cape. With *Wishart* she was to meet the liner and take her down
as far as Bathurst before handing over to other escorts, refuelling at
Bathurst and returning to Gibraltar. Two new members of her company were assigned to *Wild Swan* at this time, but did not actually
join her for a few weeks. They were Lieutenant R. Lockwood, RANVR
and Temporary Sub-Lieutenant Owen Pugh, RNVR. But *Wild Swan*'s
days at Gibraltar were now numbered and they had a longer voyage
than thought to join their new ship.

Surgeon-Lieutenant Hutter recalls:

We stayed in Gibraltar for a bit and did some convoy work in and
out of the Med as well as some mainly uneventful sweeps. In Gib
my duties as wine caterer began to be taken up and buying sherry
from Saccone and Speed, assisted by tasting sermons directed by
some of the more experienced officers. I bought a lot of 2/6d (12p)
with 3/6d (17p) for guests. Otherwise it was easy to get ashore and
everyone enjoyed the change.

Our midshipman at this time was from the Royal Indian Navy,
though a European. He demonstrated an ability to play the organ
and I used to listen to him playing in the Cathedral ashore. He
was given permission to play provided the music was suitable.
Other officers from the 'colonies' were our Australians, Lieutenant Burnley and later, Lieutenant Lockwood. They warned the
men in their forthright way against 'Penny Piss-ups'. Certainly
drunkenness was much increased possibly because the backstreet
wine shops sold evil mixtures very cheaply.

By contrast my memories of Freetown are of heat. How anyone

could stand it in a small ship with no air conditioning and very little ability to carry fresh food, I still don't know.

I managed to run quite a good cricket team when we were in but the main preoccupation of the men was drink. Palm wine (forbidden) and local beer, the result was an aggressive inclination I had not seen before and a tendency to accidents. Malaria took its toll, but not very heavily with us anchored far out from land. And the everlasting VD, which had not been a problem in the UK. . . Skin diseases due to sweat and heat; ringworm, prickly heat and septic conditions. At about this time, as a result of some hard quarrels with authorities, topees were abolished for general use. Mine got thrown overboard in a drunken spree on the quarter deck. The men were encouraged to get acclimatised and to get the sun and get themselves brown. Those who did were 100 per cent better. Sunstroke and sunburn did not occur except in new arrivals and they had mostly got it in the troopships on the way out.

Another condition that I have never seen mentioned was men coming from the troopers with swollen ankles. I assumed this was due to standing day after day on hot decks. However no matter what the tropical nastiness the ship's company coped. We did have cases that were moved to the hospital ship *Oxfordshire* but none of the mortality that affected previous naval appearances off that notorious coastline, the 'White Man's Grave'.

The change back to Freetown was initiated with another somewhat acrimonious exchange of signals between Their Lordships and Vice Admiral Edward-Collins at Gibraltar.

Admiralty to FOCNA: 1729A/18. It is not understood why *Wild Swan* is being held at Gibraltar for *Rangitata* when Admiralty 1055/5 approved your retaining *Wild Swan* for Operation Chieftain *only* if OG76 did not arrive on time.

FOCNA to Admiralty: Your 1729A/18. In order to effect economy in escorts; my earlier signal *Wild Swan*, 1210/2nd, and no comment was made. Used *Wild Swan* for Chieftain as *Bradford*, ex-OG76, was defective.

Wild Swan was back at Gibraltar on the 20th, having carried out further anti-submarine operations with *Vidette* on 18th and 19th November. She also carried out a gunnery shoot, as her captain recalls:

Lieutenant Revill was our gunnery control officer, a Scot, very

competent and cheerful. I remember our carrying out a very good
full-calibre practice shoot when at Gibraltar which earned the
congratulations from Captain (D) there, Herbert Williams. Soon
afterwards we returned to Freetown and I sent Captain (D) there,
Rupert Sherbrooke, the analysis for information.

Alas, pride came before a fall, for he sent us out to see if we could
repeat it and unfortunately some circuit was affected by the
humidity at Freetown and the shoot was not successful.

There was nothing wrong with *Wild Swan*'s gunnery when it was
really needed a few months later however, and that is what *really*
counted. At 0840 they sailed once more from Gibraltar and steered
south on 21st November. Their orders were to return to Freetown,
fuelling at Bathurst and keeping some sixty miles from the hostile
Vichy forces at Dakar, at a speed of 14 knots, to refuel at Bathurst at
midday on the 26th. This they duly complied with and arrived back
on station at Freetown at 0355 on the 27th.

Much had happened in the South Atlantic Commands area since
they had left it. On 1st December *Wild Swan* had received a signal
from Raikes: 'Proceed at 1730/1st to patrol area 20 miles square
about centre 8°30′ N, 14°30′ W.' But next day she was recalled to
Freetown again: 'Leave patrol so as to arrive Freetown 0800/3rd.'

Here they found a ST* convoy awaiting them, ST10 and they were
instructed to join its escort, the sloop *Bridgewater* and corvettes *Clover,
Freesia* and *Nigella*, early next day and return to Freetown later,
which they did on 8th December. Here the hunt for a U-boat group,
which was making north with over 400 survivors from their milch
cows *Atlantis* and *Python* to join four Italian submarines, caught up
with them as they lay alongside their depot ship, *Edinburgh Castle*.
Accurate D/F bearings had been received on 12th December, which
indicated a good chance of the northward-bound U-boats being on
about 150 miles south of the Cape Verde Islands on 14th December;
it was thought possible that they might make use of Tarrafal Bay,
San Antonio Island, to replenish their water supplies. These areas
were to be searched by *Vansittart* and *Wild Swan*, aided by Sunderlands from Bathurst, southward of the Cape Verde Islands during
daylight on the 14th and in the likely bays of those islands on the
15th. Permission was also sought for both ships to refuel at St Vin-

* ST = South to Takoradi, Gold Coast, an important aerial staging post and troop
convoy terminal in what is now called Ghana.

cent on the afternoon of the second day. If nothing was found another search was initiated for 16th December. All this was embodied in a series of signals sent to the destroyers concerned. There was, however a snag. If we could read the German traffic they were also reading ours. Moreover we were no longer able to read *all* their signals.

From September onward the German decoders of naval signals repeated their success story of the early part of the war and the *B-Dienst* cracked British Naval Cypher No 2 and could read it almost instantly. By December they could also read Cypher No 3. In direct contrast during December the British could no longer decipher the 'Enigma' instructions sent to the U-boats due to new codings. These had been initiated as there were grave suspicions on the German side after so many of their supply ships had been destroyed following the *Bismarck* incident the previous May. Carelessness on the part of subordinate commands in the way they used 'Ultra' information was also revealed when the British monitored their own radio traffic, one case cited being that of the C-in-C, South Atlantic who repeated to one of his destroyers the three U-boat positions which had been sent to him in an 'Ultra' signal.*

In this instance there was a lot of material for the German de-coders to get their teeth into:

> *C-in-C, SA to Wild Swan, Vansittart*: 1915Z/12. Prospects of finding four U-boats in company homeward-bound on 14th December are centred 150 miles due south St Jago Island. Leave as soon as ready on 12th and proceed to arrive 12°22′ N, 10°W at 0730Z. Instructions for search will follow.
>
> *C-in-C, SA to Admiralty*: Vansittart and *Wild Swan* plus flying boats will carry out search for U-boats on 14/12 in area south of Verdes.
>
> *C-in-C, SA to Vansittart, Wild Swan*: (1) My 1951Z. Proceed to arrive 11°45′ N, 22°15′ W 0630/14, then steer following course: 305° at 20 knots till 1030Z, 298° at 20 knots till 1500Z (2) From point at 1500Z/14 then 055° until 0130Z/15, then as necessary to arrive off Bravo Island at dawn 15th December. Sunderland aircraft will carry out crossover patrol arriving daylight 14th December.
>
> *C-in-C, SA to Consul, St Vincent, Cape Verde Islands*: Request you will obtain permission for *Vansittart* and *Wild Swan* obtain 100 tons fuel oil at St Vincent on 15th and 16th December.

Meanwhile subsequent D/F information indicated that the U-boats were again further on than had been thought and possibly to the eastward, and the search on 16th December was therefore amended,

* *British Intelligence in the Second World War*, Vol II. HMSO.

one destroyer searching in the islands and one to the north-eastward.

Sunderland to C-in-C, SA: 1855Z/13. Green. Nothing to report.

C-in-C, SA to Vansittart, Wild Swan: 1921Z/13. My 1207Z/13. Subject to permission to fuel at St Vincent carry out December 15th (b) *Wild Swan* only; to pass east of Fogo Island and arrive off Jalunga Point, Bravo Island at first light and carry out recce of coast of Bravo, passing west-about.

Consul to C-in-C, SA: 2010/14. Permission has been obtained.

Wild Swan to C-in-C, SA: 0836Z/15th. Nothing sighted. ETA 1500/15th 60 tons fuel left.

Patrick Satow remembers all these comings and going as follows:

Around this time *Wild Swan* went on her own to sheltered bays in the Cape Verde Islands, out in the Atlantic, to try and catch German submarines taking on fuel and supplies. The ship would steam quietly round and round each island's coastline, with her guns ready-manned. No submarines were actually sighted close to the islands.

Fixes obtained on U-boats in this ocean area were not often of any great accuracy, because the direction finding stations were quite a long distance away.*

The detailed signals continued to permeate the atmosphere:

C-in-C, SA to Vansittart, Wild Swan: 1339Z/15th. My 1923Z/13. If no result today 15th December, recce is to be repeated tomorrow 16th. (b) *Wild Swan* from St Vincent proceed to arrive off Bravo Island at first light 16th, carry out recce of Bravo Fogo and west coast of St. Jago in that order then west coast of Bonavista at dusk and then at Bathurst to refuel. Sunderland aircraft co-operating.

C-in-C, SA to Vansittart, Wild Swan: 2331Z/15th. Cancel my 1855/15th 1947/16 and para (b) of my 1339/15th. *Wild Swan* to search an area between 17° and 18°N, and 21° and 22°W, thence to Bathurst to fuel. Sunderland will search in vicinity of *Wild Swan*.

Recces on the 15th and 16th found nothing and *Wild Swan* arrived back at Bathurst on the evening of the 16th. By now the attack on

_____

* According to official sources, the Admiralty in fact took over direction of control of Ultra distribution to try and allay German suspicions, 'issuing instructions of which the origin in the Enigma intelligence was concealed by reference to . . . a D/F fix on a U-boat's transmissions. . . . '

Pearl Harbor had brought America and Japan into the conflict along with Great Britain and Soviet Russia on one side and Germany and Italy on the other. It made little difference to *Wild Swan*'s war but to the endless succession of defeats in Europe and the Mediterranean was now added an equally long list of disasters in the Far East, the loss of the *Prince of Wales* and *Repulse*, and the fall of Hong Kong on Christmas Day, just being the first of many tragedies. The already busy Cape route to the Middle East became even more vital as convoys of troops and aircraft spares were rushed thither into the cauldron of South-East Asia and swallowed up in that catastrophe. They saw nothing of the Americans.

After refuelling at Bathurst *Wild Swan* sailed to rendezvous with convoy WS14 and escorted it to Freetown arriving there with the aircraft transport *Athene* and relieving the destroyers *Croome* and *Exmoor*.

Christmas 1941 was spent at Freetown. It was not a joyous Christmas with the news coming out of the Pacific, but some of *Wild Swan*'s crew managed to to make it memorable, as W.K. Harrison recalls:

I remember going ashore on Christmas Day. We had some drinks and soon the whole ship's company were in high spirits. One of the Asdic ratings cut a carley float adrift and, with one or two other bodies, was sailing around the harbour in it. Our First Lieutenant, Kenneth Holland, got quite agitated about this and was shouting for them to return aboard.

He told the petty officer of the day that when they were back onboard he wanted them brought in front of him as defaulters. It was then that the Captain intervened and told the First Lieutenant to let them enjoy themselves because it was Christmas Day. They carried on singing and paddling their carley float.

Whilst ashore John Slowly bought himself half-a-dozen live chickens for 10d (about 2p) each. He carried them back aboard in a bag somehow but once aboard he decided the young chickens needed a mother and so he smeared treacle all over his body, split open his pillow and covered himself with the feathers!

At this time the ship's officers were sitting in the Wardroom having their Christmas dinner. The hatch directly above the Wardroom table was always kept open whilst in Freetown and John Slowly took his chickens along and emptied them down the hatch onto the officers below. They were naturally squawking and flying in all directions. . .

But the routine continued. On 15th January they were escorting SL98 with the corvettes *Auricula, Fritillary, Nigella* and *Orchis* in a seemingly endless plod at seven knots. On the 27th they sailed from Bathurst south again with another fast convoy, WS15, along with the battleship *Resolution*, destroyers *Vimy, Boreas, Milford*, the Canadian *Colombia* and another of the British-manned Turkish ships, *Demir Hissar*. The destroyers and the sloop, *Milford*, carried out an anti-submarine sweep before the convoy sailed then returned to meet it.

Boreas, Vimy and *Wild Swan* of course were only the local escorts and were due to leave the convoy at dusk on 31st January and return to Freetown, but instead they were sent to close the merchant ship *Salland* at 1800 that day, after she had reported herself chased by a submarine in 1°12' N, 50°40' W. This report was received via Ascension Island and was thought to be 'of doubtful validity'; certainly no contact resulted from their sweep. They were back at Freetown on 3rd February.

Between the 9th and 16th they escorted another SL convoy, SL100 at 7½ knots and off Cape Verde Islands transferred to the escort of OS18, with destroyers *Boreas, Vidette, Wishart, Wivern* (back after her refit), *Rochester, Scarborough* and *Bradford, Folkestone, Weston* and *Wellington*, all sloops.

Convoy OS18 consisted of the personnel carriers *Ulster Monarch, Sennen, Totland* and *Royal Ulsterman*, with the sloop *Gorleston* and five corvettes and they took them to 11°32' N, 20°42' W at a steady 8 knots. They were told by Freetown on Sunday 22nd to leave their charges in 9°10' N, 15°10' W and proceed to Bathurst at ten knots with *Brilliant* and *Boreas*, arriving on the 23rd along with the *New Northland*. Another quick refuelling and the three destroyers sailed at 0700 on the 25th to meet convoy WS16 on the 26th. This troop convoy had left the Clyde with 26 troopships on 16th February and had been escorted by Force H as it contained 40,000 soldiers. The three Freetown destroyers joined its powerful escort at 0905 on the 26th and escorted it south. It was a long journey as Commander Sclater was to recall:

One large troop-carrying convoy which we escorted into Freetown contained, I suspected, my brother-in-law, a brigadier. I asked the Commodore's ship by loud-hailer if he was on board. The reply was 'Yes', and, after the ship had anchored, I took *Wild Swan* alongside and brought him on board for lunch, returning him before the convoy went on its way.

On one convoy trip I took as my guest a District Officer of the Colonial Service with whom I had made friends. As usual the passage was uneventful but somehow the news got out and both he and I were severely reprimanded by our superiors!

After fuelling at Freetown *Boreas, Brilliant, Wivern, Wild Swan* and the sloop *Bridgewater*, with the corvettes *Jasmine* and *Nigella* sailed again on the next leg of the convoy's voyage south on 6th March at 0700. Included in the escort was the cruiser *Newcastle* on her way out to the East Indies. They arrived back at Freetown on 9th March. Next day they sailed escorting the Polish liner *Batory* at 13½ knots with AMC's *Bulolo* (6,500 tons) and *California* (16,792 tons) acting as troop ships and with *Brilliant* as the other local destroyer escort. They left them in 19°25′ N, 20°00′ W and returned to harbour once more on the 12th.

On the 23rd of the month she sailed with the 27 ships of convoy SL104 on a northerly course as Senior Officer of the escort, the corvettes *Bergamot, Snowdrop, Violet* and Free-French *Commandant Détroyer* (ex *Coriander*). On the 25th she rendezvoused at point 'P' to meet OS22 with four tankers included in its ranks in 10°15′ N, 20°10′ W and proceeded at 7½ knots, leaving them next day to refuel at Bathurst. She had embarked several passengers for this trip, two civilians from the *Stentor* and one Army hospital case from the *Nyanza*. This latter was in a bad way and Lieutenant-Commander Sclater signalled to the NOIC Bathurst to have transport and ambulance waiting for them on arrival which he estimated at 1000Z on 30th March. Patrick Satow remembers Surgeon-Lieutenant Hutter carrying out an emergency appendix operation aboard *en route*.

The medical officer onboard was always known as 'Doc', who cheerfully put up with the vagaries of weather, oppressive heat or storm and cold, and very restricted working conditions in a small destroyer. I can recall having to put *Wild Swan* on a very steady course, and to set the engine revolutions so that there was virtually no vibration, whilst he worked below on the patient who had been brought across by boat from the merchant ship (*Nyanza*).

Another new crew member was appointed at this time and joined the ship soon after along with Lieutenant Lockwood and Sub-Lieutenant Pugh – the new Gunner (T) Mr A.J.H. Timpson. Albert Timpson was a Hampshire man who had joined the Royal Navy as a boy in 1918 and served subsequently in eleven ships and shore establishments. His naval career matched *Wild Swan*'s, but he did not finally join her until 20th May. Owen Pugh however, was already aboard:

That winter was probably the nadir of the Second World War, and I remember only too well receiving the awful news of the loss of the *Prince of Wales* and *Repulse* after Pearl Harbor, whilst we were escorting a fast troop carrying convoy south over the equator *en route* for Cape Town. Our base, with normally three or four other destroyers, was Freetown, and our prime purpose was to either go north and meet the troop convoys, destined for the African campaign, or take them south from Freetown. These convoys were comprised of fast ocean liners, P & O's, Cunarders or Union Castle ships. They went into Freetown for water, fuel and fresh provisions, tho' the troops were not allowed ashore. We took them south over the line, and left them when they were clear of the known U-boat area. More often than not a Capital ship proceeding east would be left to take them on. The Med and Suez route was, of course, closed at that time.

We visited all the usual West African ports, Lagos, Accra, Takoradi, the Azores, Cape Verde Islands and Bathurst.

Another newcomer was F.R. Burrett, later to become a lieutenant, but at that time very much a 'new boy':

I joined the ship at Freetown in April, 1942, having taken passage in the liner *Alcantara*, taking three weeks from Greenock. I was a newly-qualified torpedo gunner's mate, aged 24, responsible for the one triple torpedo tube mounting with its Mk IV torpedoes and associated equipment and the depth charges. In those days torpedo personnel also looked after the domestic electrics, including the output end of the two 24½ kw reciprocator driven generators.

There was one depth-charge rack with six charges, at the stern and four of the older-type throwers, not those that retained the cradle. Sixty was the normal number of charges carried, both on deck and in a magazine aft.

The ship, commanded then by Lieutenant-Commander C.E.L. Sclater, was employed mainly as an escort for ships in convoy between the West African coast and the Azores, north of Bathurst and south to Lagos. I recall Lieutenant Satow, who lived in a cabin down a hole in the iron deck amidships; Commander Derbyshire and Mr

Timpson whom I remember as being constantly cheerful, while Satow was a carefree young man.

Patrick Satow himself recalls this period of endless convoy work thus:

Whilst operating in tropical waters off the west coast of Africa, *Wild Swan* was frequently joined by shoals of dolphins which seemed to enjoy romping around in the heavily aerated zone on both sides of our ship, caused by her movement through the water. Even at speeds of more than 20 knots, they would show their paces by keeping up with the ship, and every now and then leaping clear of the sea surface.

However, in some areas of great phosphoresence, these friends of the deep caused false alarms onboard, because their track and speed through the water looked exactly like a torpedo which had been aimed straight at the ship.

At other times, the remarkable little flying fish, no doubt through some error of judgement, landed on the ship's deck, and finished up as an extra item for someone's next meal. There was not much on them, but it was certainly a tasty morsel.

During the brief stops in harbour at Freetown, members of the ship's company went ashore whenever possible during the day, to escape from the gruelling heat onboard. One day after bathing, a small party came upon some natives in a settlement near the beach. A coloured lady asked whether those who had been swimming would like a cooked meal. The wooden homes were built clear of the ground, to keep out vermin, and the chickens ran freely over adjacent ground.

The idea was that one selected a nice specimen of the poultry, and then looked the other way whilst it became deceased and went straight into the pot to be cooked. In spite of the primitive surroundings, the meals were well prepared, and much enjoyed by those who sampled them.

It was now April and it seemed as if these days of tropical convoying would go on for ever. But changes were in the wind.

CHAPTER TEN

The Last Convoy
April-June, 1942

By the beginning of April to seize control of the important Vichy-controlled island of Madagascar an invasion force was assembled in Britain, and, on 23rd March, sailed from the Clyde to carry out Operation Ironclad, lest the Japanese, now pushing forward through Burma, forestall them and cut the last link to the Far East.

To give heavy naval support the main units of the Gibraltar-based Force H had been earmarked. Other ships from that force were to help escort the troopships carrying the 5th Infantry Division down to the Cape, while for air support the carrier *Illustrious* from home would join the *Indomitable* from the Indian Ocean. The passage of these forces through the West African area naturally placed a big strain on C-in-C, South Atlantic's meagre forces and *Wild Swan* was busy as never before slotting in to the various complex movements.

Naturally there were grave fears, and many rumours, that the Vichy would make a pre-emptive strike at this vulnerable convoy as it passed their main base at Dakar where the giant battleship *Richelieu* lurked. There were even stories that part of their massive fleet in Toulon would sail to help her.

On the last day of March therefore, *Wild Swan* and *Wivern* sailed to rendezvous with this convoy, codenamed WS17. The destroyers *Aldenham, Grove, Volunteer* and *Leamington* had already beaten off one attempt to attack it by sinking the *U-587* on the 27th further north but no attacks were made in southern waters. Other portents were stirring in the ether, however, and the Admiralty warned them all that:

> Information (Graded A2) received that French battleship *Richelieu* with three 6-inch cruisers *Georges Leygues, Gloire* and *Montcalm* may leave Dakar on 3rd and that battle-cruiser *Strasbourg* arriving there on the 5th.
> *Wild Swan to NOIC Bathurst*: 2021Z/2nd. *Illustrious* and *Devonshire* to refuel Freetown to be ready. Transfer Martlets* from *Archer*. ETA 0600/

---

* Martlets were Grumman Wildcat naval fighter aircraft supplied to the RN under Lease-Lend and renamed for some obscure reason. HMS *Archer* was an escort carrier which brought them over to join *Illustrious* for the operation.

3rd. Acknowledge.

Wild Swan to NOIC Bathurst: 2032/2nd. Information received from *Illustrious* that convoy is 22 hours late. Have insufficient fuel to meet and escort to Freetown. Am proceeding Bathurst to fuel then join convoy PM 3rd.

But bad weather intervened.

Wild Swan to NOIC Bathurst: 0900/3rd. Missing rendezvous. From *Illustrious* via aircraft, reports WS17 22 hours late.

Wild Swan to Shropshire. Alcantara: 1015Z/3rd. Will endeavour to meet you in 12°10′ N, 19°43′ W at 1930Z today, Friday.

The whole massive assembly finally arrived at Freetown on 6th April. As well as thirteen troopships and five motor transport vessels there was the submarine depot ship *Adamant* and ten other big ships escorted by the heavy cruiser *Shropshire*, the AMC *Alcantara*, and destroyers *Aldenham, Grove, Lookout* and *Wild Swan*, the corvettes *Commandant Detroyer* and *Hydrangea*. Included in the convoy were the landing ships, infantry, *Karanja* and *Keren* with their landing craft hanging business-like from davits along each side. Aslo present from Force 'H' were the battleship *Malaya*, cruiser *Hermione* and destroyers *Active, Anthony, Duncan, Laforey* and *Lightning. It was the biggest concentration of fighting strenght Wild Swan* had ever been in company with, and over the horizon were yet more ships, including *Illustrious*, and *Devonshire*. For the first time in this war, or so it seemed to most of her crew, the strenght was on our side and going *our* way, instead of forever coming *at* us.

The convoy replenished and sailed on the next leg of its long journey on the 11th at 1100, still with the codename WS17B, and was escorted by *Shropshire, Croome, Exmoor, Commandant Détroyer, Commandant Drogou, Hydrangea, Adamant* as well as *Wild Swan*, who stayed with it until the 14th when she returned to her humdrum duties at Freetown. After yet another convoy escort task, *Wild Swan* sailed with *Boreas* to rendezvous with the battleship *Malaya* returning from the south. They escorted her back to Freetown with the *Hydrangea*.

Donald Lingard remembers the tension well:

We and *Boreas* joined up with the battleship *Malaya* and were told that the French battleship *Richelieu* was leaving Dakar. We did not however, make contact.

There was every reason to suppose the Vichy Government would react violently to the invasion of Diego Suarez and attack British ships as they had in Syria the year before. Fortunately it did not come to that, and, as Patrick Satow recalls, the only contact between the British and the French on this patrol ended in complete harmony of thought and deed!

> Obviously this patrol resulted from intelligence reports that the Vichy ships might leave their port of Dakar; but, in the event, they did not. But *Wild Swan* did intercept a lone merchant ship off the western tip of Africa, suspected of carrying munitions for the Vichy French. A boarding party was sent across; but, after spending some time onboard examining the ship and her cargo documents, they returned to the destroyer, satisfied that the merchantman need not be detained. As a gesture of appreciation for the courtesy shown by the Royal Navy boarding party, the French Master gave them a huge cask of wine, which was gratefully received onboard *Wild Swan*. The contents of the cask were disposed of without difficulty at the appropriate time.

Before they parted Malaya said her 'thank you's' as Commander Sclater recalls:

> When we left her to refuel in Gambia the captain of *Malaya* made me a signal: 'Many thanks for your help. A pity *Boreas* was so rude.' It took me a little while to realise that he was referring to the North Wind which had created a very rough sea.*

After a slow speed in heavy weather to conserve what little fuel remained the two destroyers reached Bathurst on the 16th. Here they had a short interval ashore.

Wild Swan was now long overdue for a proper refit which neither Freetown nor Gibraltar could give. There was therefore every prospect that they would be sailed for home before much longer and much speculation aboard as to when. But for the immediate future there was still much for her to do. Nonethe less plans were being laid as witness a signal about her condition from Raikes to the Admiralty on 20th May which evoked the following response: '*DOD(H) to RAWA*: 1916/22. Your 1111/20. *Wild Swan* can be taken in hand for refit at Portsmouth on arrival in UK.'

* Boreas – god of the North Wind.

(Above) The W/T staff of *Wild Swan*, October 1941, at Gibraltar in front of one of her 4.7-inch guns. Telegraphist Donald Lingard, in the dark shorts on the far left, has just been up the mainmast cleaning the aerial insulators, the task usually assigned the most junior member of the team! Leading Telegraphist Anstey, Coder A. Leverton are next to him, while Petty Officer Telegraphist Robert C. E. Clement is on the left. *Wild Swan* may have been an old lady but she had a young crew.

(Right) The two single 2-pdr Pom-poms carried by *Wild Swan* throughout her long life were never the most efficient weapons. John Goulder (right) remembers the weapon thus: 'At times our antics to keep 'em firing would have made 'Dads Army' appear to be the acme of perfection. When I joined virtually none of them would fire more than 8 to 10 rounds and sometimes only 2 before they jammed.' During *Wild Swan's* last battle however, her tracer ammunition jammed true to form, but when it was changed for standard ammunition it gave a virtuoso *finale*!

(Left) Lieutenant-Commander C. E. L. Sclater, last captain of *Wi. Swan*. A portrait by Peter Scott when both were young officers aboard the Flotilla Leader HMS *Broke* in 1940. Bearded throughout most of his time as CC of *Wild Swan*, Lieutenant-Commander Sclater became clean-shaven just before she sailed on her last convoy.

(Below) HMS *Wild Swan* at speed A fine aerial study taken off West Africa in 1942 showing her appearance when she was sunk. Notice the typical dark hull and light upperworks of a destroyer working out of Gibraltar and Freetown at this stage of the war. Radar at the masthead, single 12 pdr in place of after tubes and other business-like modifications in contrast to the illustration facing page 48.

TS. 1940.

Meanwhile *Wild Swan* left Bathurst with *Boreas*on the 19th and joined the escort of convoy WS19. They duly arrived without incident at Freetown on the 22nd. More signals concercing her futue were exchanged:

> *RA,WA to FOCNA, Rpt Malaya, Colombo*: Intend to sail *Wild Swan* as additional escort to *Empress of Russia* sailing on 22nd May. Then she is to proceed to UK for refit. To screen *Empress of Russia* while *Colombo* is refuelling Ponta Delgada, *Wild Swan* will then proceed to Gibraltar with stores and ratings for *Malaya*.

At 0700 on the 25th *Wild Swan* sailed with the liner *Empress of Russia* as specified along with the Ocean Boarding Vessel *Largs*. *Wild Swan* was to refuel at Bathurst and then rendezvous with the liner once more while the light cruiser *Colombo* fuelled as indicated on 28th May. All was proceeding to plan and at first light on the 26th *Wild Swan* and *Largs* were in 9°55' N, 16°01' W and heading towards Bathurst at 14½ knots, when another change of plan was announced via signal:

> *DOD(H) to RA, WA, FOCNA*: 1937Z/26. Anticipated *Argus* will leave UK with WS en route for Gibraltar. She will require to part company in position 'XX' 44°10' N, 23°30' W at daylight on 5th June. *Wild Swan* will be required to R/V *Argus* in this position having fuelled Ponta Delgada and then escort *Argus* to Gibraltar. Timing of *Wild Swan*'s visit to Ponta Delgada should be arranged so that maximum fuel will remain on arrival at rendezvous point.
>
> *RA, WA to FOCNA, Admiralty*: *Wild Swan*, after refuelling at Ponta Delgada will R/V with *Argus* in position 'XX' at daylight on 5th or as otherwise dictated by SO Escort of WS19P and provide onward escort to Gibraltar.

Wild Swan was to rendezvous with the aircraft carrier *Argus*, who was carrying out another aircraft transport and ferry run from the UK to Malta, along with the *Beagle* which had been with WS19P, and all three ships arrived at Gibraltar on 7th June.

Tropical days and hot, clammy nights ashore in West African ports; long humid days crawling down to Takoradi or the equator; visions of peaceful neutral ports with lights and laughter; long, lazy days with little to occupy them save keeping station on giant liner or battleship; all had passed. Looking back the whole period was like a dream where the war was almost, but not quite, something remote and apart. All those golden days were gone. It was now official, they were going home!

No warship sailed anywhere without performing a useful function, fully fit or not. *Wild Swan* might be going home for a refit but she was to be gainfully employed. Their old companions at Freetown and Bathurst had long said their farewells. The medical officer of *Boreas*, then Sub-Lieutenant R. Russell Dickson, RNVR, recalls:

> We had spent a good deal of time in company with *Wild Swan* and she was our particular 'chummy ship' in West Africa and I had a good friendship with her MO, Dr Hutter.
>
> I recall our envy when she sailed for home at the end of her commission. A large parcel of 'rabbits'* for my fiancée left with her. We celebrated our Ruby Wedding a little earlier this year and it all seems a very long time ago!

Patrick Satow remembers their last voyage up from the tropics to Gibraltar thus:

> The ship was ordered home for a refit, and to give the crew some foreign service leave. By this time, her boilers and machinery in general were not functioning at their best, and instead of steaming directly northwards to Gibraltar, a call had to be made at Las Palmas to refuel.
>
> As with the Azores, the Canary Islands being Spanish were neutral in World War II, and they were suffering greatly from loss of trade, notably with their main crop of bananas.
>
> Arriving alongside the quay, a connection was made from shore to the ship's fuel tanks and the pumps were started. The local engineer in charge of the fuel depot came onboard, and he was offered some duty-free hospitality. Mysteriously, the pumps started to run ever more slowly, until it was advised that refuelling would take all night. It was explained to us that bananas must not be allowed to rot on the trees, so much of the valuable crop was being picked and dumped in the sea.
>
> Most of those serving in *Wild Swan* were invited to help themselves, and they took a complete branch home. After purchasing other fresh provisions, the ship continued her passage to Gibraltar. From there, she was to proceed up the coast of Portugal, and across the Bay of Biscay to Portsmouth.

---

* 'Rabbits', sailors slang for gifts and presents, not necessarily those intended to be declared at Customs!

At Gibraltar they found a HG convoy in the process of assembling. Ships were gathering in the bay in readiness, twenty merchantmen in all it transpired, with the Commodore embarked in the *Pelayo*. This was the main section of convoy HG84, but three more vessels, *City of Oxford*, *Empire Conrad* and *Slemdal* (a Norwegian vessel), were to sail from Lisbon and join the main section later. One of the vessels, the *Copeland*, was fitted out with special equipment and was to serve as both HF/DF Guard, tracking and monitor signals and 'fixes' and as a rescue ship to pick up survivors from her torpedoed comrades, leaving the escorts free to hunt. The escort itself consisted of the 36th Escort Group, whose commander, embarked in the sloop *Stork*, was the already-famous Commander Frederic John Walker. His personality and very own way of conducting things was far from conventional, but seemed to get results. However he was a great risk-taker in some respects. Nonetheless he had the reputation as a 'fighter' and, better-still, a 'hater' of U-boats, and was to be proved the right man in the right job.

His group was reduced by breakdowns and at this time consisted of three corvettes, *Convolvulus*, *Gardenia* and *Marigold*. The more powerful frigate *Rother*, the corvette *Jonquil*, were to escort the Lisbon section to the rendezvous point. For the first part of their journey home across the Bay of Biscay the two destroyers sailing home for refits, *Wild Swan* and *Beagle*, were to join them as temporary reinforcements.

The convoy sailed from Gibraltar at 1930 on 9th June. Not until 0800 on the 11th did the other three merchantmen sail from Lisbon. *Wild Swan* and *Beagle* were not due to sail until the evening of the 10th to overtake the main section and escort it for a while. There was still time for their crews to obtain last-minute 'rabbits' of their own, as A.H. Rippon recalls:

> Rumour had it earlier that our next convoy would be our last as it would be homeward-bound and this proved correct in more ways than one! We entered Gibraltar to refuel and the ship's company managed to stock-up with presents and items we were told were in short-supply in the UK.

Some remarkable passengers seeking a quick trip home also joined the ship, as Owen Pugh recalls:

> There were two British Army officers, ex-prisoners of war, who had escaped from a German POW camp, and made their way

with the help of the underground to Gibraltar via Switzerland, France and Spain. One was actually the cousin of our Number One, Lieutenant Holland, who had no idea he was coming aboard, or indeed, had even escaped!

A remarkable co-incidence. Donald Lingard confirms that the ship was very crowded. 'We had approximately 150 ship's company and about eight officers making our old boat very overcrowded and conditions extremely difficult in hot climates, but the cockroaches enjoyed it!'

At last everyone was safely aboard and dreaming of home. As dusk approached they cast off from the Rock for the very last time and headed out through the darkening Straits to the westward. From the Tower, FONC's HQ, a signal was duly despatched to Whitehall: '1800B/10. *Beagle, Wild Swan* sailed to overtake HG84.'

They may have sailed in darkness but they did not sail in secrecy. Almost as soon as their twin wakes had cut a frothy passage cleanly through the black waters off La Linea busy agents ashore and afloat were transmitting signals back to Berlin and Lorient, and on large scale maps in underground bunkers two more pieces of the HG84 jigsaw were being plotted into place. They had already reported the departure of the main convoy on the 9th and the Lisbon portion was similarly plotted as soon as it left harbour. Grand-Admiral Karl Dönitz now had ample time to draw up his plans for HG84's annihilation.

He planned a combined attack with U-boats, long-range bombers and constant surveillance by the Focke-Wulf FW200 Kondor aircraft from KG40 to keep them always in touch no matter what evasions the British might try. He had at his disposal at this time no less than eight U-boats ready to sail to their attack positions in the Atlantic. These he ordered to concentrate in the Bay area and attempt to make a co-ordinate assault as the 'Endrass' Wolf Pack, all boats to be in position by 14th June. Others joined in later.

It was not only German submarines that were operational in the Bay area of course; a few of the Italian boats were still based at Bordeaux, but they were not to be relied on and the Germans sarcastically commented that their plans were best made without them.

Naturally in the air it was an entirely German effort. For once Admiral Dönitz was able to call on practically every aircraft in the area to mount a heavy strike. Unfortunately his material was not of such a good standard as it used to be. For a start the long-range reconnaissance units, the Focke-Wulf FW200 aircraft of KG40.

By early summer of 1942 Luftwaffe strength had declined in the Bay of Biscay area, with only about forty fully operational Junkers Ju88 A-4 bombers available for offensive operations, together with a few *Staffeln* of the Kondors, complemented by a few long-range Junkers Ju88 A-5's. Continual squabbles with *Reichsmarshall* Göring, who resented *any* separate existence for flying units outside his control, had meant that many units had been wasted in orthodox bombing raids over England, where their special anti-shipping skills and training were negated. Conversion from obsolete types of aircraft to modern bombers had merely meant that this legalised 'poaching' had increased, Göring using the argument that modern aircraft should not be 'wasted' attacking merchant ships.

For long-range reconnaissance the Germans had for long relied on the Focke-Wulf FW200 Kondor. It had a range of 1,375 miles maximum for an outward leg and, as we have already seen, these planes scored many successes in the SW and NW approaches. However their bomb load was weak and reconnaissance was now their principal role. But, this force never exceeding forty aircraft, was much reduced and had only six planes avilable to it at this time. Only one weak *Staffel* from KG40 now remained in France. Nevertheless it was one of these aircraft that made the first sighting of the convoy on 11th June, and others which continued to shadow it subsequently, supplying both U-boats and bomber groups with precise location details of the convoy throughout most of its journey.

Of the bomber units available the most specialised had been the former KFlGr106. Under the 'modernisation' programme these *Staffeln* had been progressively re-equipped with the Junkers Ju88 A-4 bomber and had become conventional bomber squadrons, KG106, with *Staffeln* based at Lannion and Dinard. By May 1942, it had a paper strength of nineteen aircraft, which increased to twenty-seven with nineteen operational by early July, despite heavy losses.

One *Staffel* was detached and being used as part of a new unit being formed by merging into II/KG6, based at Beauvais. Similarly I/KG77 and III/LG1 were combining to form III/KG6 by the end of July. IV/KG6 had already been established with a *Stab* unit (Staff Unit) by June, and there was therefore quite a mixture of crews and aircraft during this transition period which meant that many units, in particular KG106 and KG77, were called upon to operate in tandem against convoy HG84. The other two *Staffeln* of KG77 were still mainly orthodox bomber units with no special skills over the water or in ship recognition, and this was to show up very shortly. II/KG77 was based at Creil/Rennes and III/KG77 at Beauvais/Vannes.

The first action of the battle for HG84 was an attack by a Sunderland on the Italian submarine *Luigi Torelli*, far to the north of the convoy, off Cape Finisterre at 0945 on the 11th. She was not involved in the attack on HG84 but her subsequent destruction occupied the time of several of its escorts, for good or ill. With her batteries damaged and on fire she was unable to dive for a time and was in a perilous position. After high-speed steaming throughout the night *Wild Swan* and *Beagle* had joined the convoy at 1100 that morning but, when word filtered through from the Sunderland about her attack, the Commander-in-Chief, Western Approaches, Admiral Sir Percy Noble, intervened and sent a signal to Walker at 1218 ordering him to detach two of the escorts to hunt for her and finish her off even though she was nowhere near the convoy itself. The *Beagle* was therefore detached at 1318 for this job. When news came in that German aircraft were in the offing it was thought desirable to provide AA support and, eventually, *Rother* was also detached to go to her aid as the Lisbon portion of the convoy was closer to her reported position. It was assumed that she would be trying to reach her base at Bordeaux, as eventually she did.

FOCNA to Rother, Jonquil: 1216. At 1005B/11 enemy a/c was operating in your vicinity and probably sighted *Rother* and *Jonquil*.

Stork to Beagle, Rother: 1318/11. *Beagle* is to comply with C-in-C WA's 1216B/11. *Rother* to remain in company.

C-in-C, WA to FOCNA: 1354/11. Your 1318/11. Request you consider detailing *Wild Swan* to support *Beagle* in view of probability of air attack.

Stork to FOCNA: Your 1216 and my 1318. Have ordered *Rother* to remain with her section of convoy HG84 as they are being shadowed by a/c.

Rother to Beagle, Stork: 1402/11. Parted company with *Jonquil* at 1354B/11.

Rother to Beagle, Stork, Jonquil: Am complying with your 1318/11.

Stork to Rother: In view of your 1402 cancel my 1318. *Beagle* will join you in search.

Beagle to FOCNA, Stork, Rother: 1701B/11. *Beagle*'s present position, course and speed is 37°50′ N, 10°50′ W, 001°, 26 knots.

Beagle and *Rother* searched from the 11th to the 13th, gaining an Asdic contact much closer to the convoy than the crippled Italian and carrying out prolonged attacks on it.

During *Wild Swan*'s stay with the convoy from 1100/11th to 2000/12th there was considerable enemy air activity and numerous reports and contacts indicating a wolf-pack was closing in, with alarming signals from the Tracking Room at Liverpool.

At dawn on the 12th one of Walker's ships, *Marigold*, was detached to meet the three merchantmen from Lisbon and to send *Jonquil* back to Gibraltar. Unfortunately the FW200 shadowing this section remained with them and was duly led back to the main convoy itself when they all joined up at 1300 on the 12th. The Kondor duly sent sighting reports back to Lorient. '*DDIC to Stork*: You were probably reported today by enemy a/c before 1150.' Of that there was little doubt. The convoy's course was therefore altered as soon as their unwelcome guest returned to his base. At 1500 they changed from course 320° to 350°. At 2000 that same evening *Wild Swan* was detached to proceed to Portsmouth and her refit. Mr Rippon recalls that:

> Some time after leaving the convoy we investigated a radar contact which proved to be a Merchant Navy type liferaft which we hauled on board for examination. In the event this proved to be a great piece of good fortune.

Owen Pugh also remembers this incident:

> It was a merchant ship's raft, constructed of wood and empty barrels, which Number 1 and I had seen floating. . . He must have had a premonition of impending disaster, for he decided to haul it aboard via the torpedo davits. This action was, without doubt, to save my life and about a dozen others.

During their run north there were other diversions. Mr Harrison recalls the next:

> On the way back home we contacted the *Beagle* once more as she had a hot scent and was carrying out a depth-charge attack on a suspected contact. We offered to help but her reply was to the effect that, 'No thanks, we can cope', or 'No thanks, we are just about giving up ourselves' or something similar. Anyway our fuel situation was that we could not tarry long.

Wild Swan continued on her way but her fuel situation after this diversion was such that she headed for Plymouth first, while *Beagle* proceeded directly for Greenock.

No matter what the condition of her bunkers an Asdic alarm would usually mean that an attack was made if possible and *Wild Swan* was so diverted on the 13th, as Donald Lingard remembers: 'We had suspected U-boat contact and spent considerable time and fuel searching, but later were forced to abandon the hunt and because of our lack of fuel were compelled to head for Plymouth direct.'

Petty Officer Linford has similar recollections:

During this final operation we contacted a U-boat, duly depth-charged it and sat on it until the Walker pack arrived. We then carried on back to Plymouth. Afterwards we heard that the pack had claimed that one as one of their exclusive sinkings!

During the evening of the 13th yet another signal arrived which caused further changes of plan: '*Admiral Superintendeant Portsmouth*: 2000/13. Your 1916/22. In view of Yard Message 1200 of 13/5 *Wild Swan* cannot be taken for refit before end of July without delaying work of equal importance priority.' Instead it was decided to refit her at Southampton, and thither she was to sail once she had landed her passengers and re-fuelled at Plymouth. She sailed steadily north at economical speed during the night and throughout the forenoon of the 14th. But there were yet more diversions in store.

The two Spanish spy-ships, the *Enriques*, which all ships had been warned about, were still at large at this time, some nine months later. They were still active from their home port of Cadiz and still sending back invaluable reports which were then sent to the submarines. Numerous Spanish fishing boats, and not a few Portuguese also, were plying their honest trade in these waters, despite the fact that several of them had come to violent ends at the hands of either Axis or Allied submarines over the years, but the Spanish Navy's Minister of Marine, Admiral D. Salvador Moreno Fernandez, had issued strict instructions for the fishing vessels to keep clear of this region. These instructions, however, were ignored. It was the fishermen's livelihoods and they ignored the risks and accepted the tragedies as part of the chance they took. *Wild Swan* sighted two ships that seemed to fit the detailed descriptions supplied earlier around early morning on the 14th.

Wild Swan to C-in-C, Plymouth: 0736B/14. Two enemy auxiliary vessels, bearing 050°, 8 miles, on course 100°. My course and position, 187°, 5 miles from 47°N, based on a fix obtained within half an hour of 0600.

Wild Swan to C-in-C, WA: 0813B/14. My 0736. Vessels are Spanish trawlers. Am boarding.

Wally Harrison was one of the boarding party and he recalls it consisted of an officer, himself as Signalman T/O, Leading Seaman Alison in charge of the boat's crew, the ship's whaler, and about eight crew members. A.G. Linford also recalls this incident:

On the last convoy, we inspected some Spanish trawlers and took off a skipper. If my memory serves me right we were actually in towards the middle of a fleet of Spanish fishing trawlers. I saw this on a quick visit up top but was kept informed of subsequent events by members of my 'gang'. I cannot remember which officer was in charge but I believe someone was brought back to the ship.

Owen Pugh thinks the probable course of events was as follows:

When the ships were sighted and near enough, they would have been visually challenged by Aldis lamp. The challenge and reply were changed daily, and known only to HM ships.

Patrick Satow adds:

The Admiralty might have supplied HM ships with silhouettes of these and other wanted vessels, and those sighted probably tallied with these. It is also possible that the previous warning to ships at sea had been supplemented by the Intelligence Branch at the Admiralty stating that suspect transmissions had been detected coming from that position at sea. The decision to classify them as 'enemy auxiliary vessels' would be taken by Commander Sclater, as commanding officer at the time.

Finally Commander Sclater himself confirms that the officer would have been the First Lieutenant, Kenneth Holland, in cases like this. In the event the ships were not arrested on the spot, possibly because *Wild Swan* had insufficient fuel to dally, nor were any signals sent asking that other ships be sent to take them in, so the probability is that although they resembled the *Enriques*, they were not spy ships themselves and were allowed to continue their work.

There were no other delays to their homeward journey and, at 0745 on the 15th, they finally arrived alongside at Plymouth. They were home and safe . . . or were they?

CHAPTER ELEVEN

To The Death!
17th June 1942

Once ashore they found that Plymouth was in a scurry and orders and signals were flying to-and-fro. They had first to land their several passengers and had already sent a list of names to C-in-C, Plymouth so that transport could be arranged. Commander Sclater recalls that the first lieutenant had asked whether his cousin could accompany them on their final lap to the refit dockyard, now known to be Southampton, as Portsmouth could not cope, and Sclater agreed to this. Subsequently that army officer's name was omitted from the list to be disembarked. This caused a flurry later, because they were almost immediately ordered to refuel quickly and sail to rejoin the convoy again.

They could not believe their ears when they heard this order. After a year overseas they had finally reached the safety of a home port and now they were to turn round and sail back again instead of the leave and refit they had been promised. The captain went ashore to visit the C-in-C, Admiral of the Fleet Sir Charles M. Forbes. But 'Wrong-way Charlie, as he was known in the fleet, was adamant. He only had one flotilla of Hunt class destroyers of his own and their endurance was not sufficient to do the job. Lieutenant-Commander Sclater pointed out that with a full bunker *Wild Swan* would herself only have sufficient fuel to meet the convoy, stay one day and then have to leave again, but the order stood.

The reasons were obvious. After *Wild Swan* had left HG84 the U-boat pack had closed in and subsequent alterations in course and counter-attacks had not thwarted it. On the night of the 14th/15th one submarine, *U-552* (Lieutenant-Commander Erich Topp) had made two deliberate attacks, at 0058 and at 0433, and had claimed six ships destroyed.

The Walker Group was clearly unable to cope and the Admiralty rushed reinforcements back to HG84 from wherever it could. The frigate *Rother* was sent back, along with her sister ship, *Spey*. The Polish destroyer *Krakowiak* was sailed from Falmouth at 0038 on the 16th and joined the convoy at 2045, and Catalina, Whitley and Sunderland aircraft were also sent out from England.

Wild Swan herself sailed at 1444 on the 15th. They sailed – but with reservations. The torpedo gunner's mate recalls:

> While at Plymouth we were alerted that our convoy had come under attack, and we were rapidly re-ammunitioned and stored and sailed at once to rejoin. Extra depth charges were stacked three deep across the after and iron decks; an extra 70 to our normal outfit were loaded, all lashed on deck. All these had to be primed and fitted with pistols during our high-speed dash back through the night.

The first lieutenant approached the captain and asked whether his cousin could be put ashore after all, but Lieutenant-Commander Sclater had to tell him it was too late now for that, which delighted the army officer himself who was keen to see some action, despite his previous adventures! He stayed. This move was far from popular with some of the lower deck however, as Wally Harrison remembers:

> We arrived at Plymouth and went alongside a tanker. We refuelled, re-provisioned and replenished our depth charges. We had some civilian and army passengers aboard from Gibraltar. One of them was a padre who I recall had a naval uniform on. The clergyman decided to stay aboard for the next trip. Being somewhat superstitious the crew felt this was a bad omen. Clergymen who are not part of the crew are always considered to be bad luck if carried as passengers.

But if one or two passengers decided to stay as extras, another decided to 'jump ship', and this did not improve the lower deck's morale either. Wally Harrison recalls this strange event:

> The incident occurred as we let go from the oiler. The ship's cat, called Whisky, suddenly ran across the deck and jumped onto the oiler. She was immediately retrieved by the Asdic rating who took care of her. (She had been rescued from the *Clytoneus* and brought up from a kitten by feeding her with milk from a fountain-pen filler.) However, as soon as the cat was released it again jumped across to the oiler. He only just managed to retrieve it a second time as the ships moved apart. He did not let go of her the second time but took her below. This had never happened before at any time during the commission and we also saw this as a bad omen.

The two incidents together made the ship's company restless. There was much moaning and groaning about these incidents and some quite openly stated that they doubted if the ship would ever reach its destination.

And so they sailed back to war. They were now a tight-knit, close and professional team. The commission had lasted two-and-a-half years and in that time there had been many new faces but they had blended well on the whole. With so many men in such a confined space there was the normal friction, heightened by the hardships, and some normal idiosyncrasies grated in such conditions. But, over-all, *Wild Swan* contained a well-disciplined, tough and loyal crew, probably at a peak of efficiency. The mix of former regulars and pro-fessionals, like Lieutenant-Commander Sclater himself, quiet and thoughtful; Mr Derbyshire, another quiet and totally dedicated officer, a complete professional, loyal and hard-working who kept *Wild Swan* out of dockyard hands far longer than most ships of her vintage; Albert Timpson, the TG, a regular for as long as *Wild Swan* had existed. Then there were the reserve officers themselves, both RNR and RNVR. They brought a leavening of youth and humour combined with efficiency to the team. The ship's surgeon, Duncan Hutter, described by his captain as, 'Tall, thin, red-haired and very professional'. One famous tale attributed to the Doc concerned the time they were at Gibraltar. The Doc conscious, as always, of his duty, cleared the lower deck and addressed the crew about the dan-gers of a particular drink (known as 'Merry-Merry' to sailors), a par-ticularly potent form of Jungle Juice. The effects were perhaps not as desired, for, naturally, having been warned how potent it was, the 'drinkers' went out looking for it. As Lieutenant-Commander Sclater recalled, most of them found it. 'They all got back aboard all right; nobody actually missed our sailing, but they were not fit for much for a while.' Duncan Hutter recalls another incident when he first joined the ship and was very green.

One of my earliest duties was to examine a seaman who was being sent to jail for desertion. My job was to see he was free from lice! My sick bay had no light in harbour and it was freezing cold. With the aid of a dim hand torch the lice were missed. He went off to jail where the lice were found. The controversy fizzled on for months till I eventually received a communication from London to say that my conduct in this respect was unsatisfactory. How I was to see in the dark, or what I could have done if I *had* found the lice, I still don't know. It took a long time for me to shake off a sense of unreality when dealing with Whitehall.

We had no casualties beyond two men swept overboard. They vanished over the side one dark night; but otherwise the health of the crew was incredibly good. Colds etc did not exist. Minor injuries were the main problems and toothache. The seamen were always wet and cold in the North Atlantic, usually the galley fires had been put out and food was also cold. My memory is of storms when it was impossible to venture on the upper deck. The watches changed when the ship adjusted course and speed.

Duncan Hutter also gives portraits of other officers aboard *Wild Swan* as she sailed on her last voyage:

The first lieutenant, Kenneth T. Holland, was a very efficient officer, as he needed to be in his responsible job and held everything together. He was slightly stocky and had a blond beard. Our engineer, Mr Derbyshire, one- or two-striper up from the lower deck. He took everything in his stride. He was one of our greatest assets and by his very presence gave me a lot of unconscious help when I was feeling low. As an engineer he must have been first class. We never had any troubles affecting our seagoing efficiency; more than can be said for other 'V' and 'W's'. . . . Sub-Lieutenant David Revill RNR was our gunnery control officer; small and fair, he was very good at his job. He came from the Shaw Saville Line. Our warrant gunner, Albert Timpson, helped make the wardroom mix and taught me much about the real Navy.

I seem to remember that in the wardroom towards the end of a day, Drambuie was a favourite drink. For some reason we had a lot of it! I can also recall that for some reason, I, the ship's doctor, took a delight in pouring it on someone's head and setting fire to it! It now seems a very dangerous thing to have done but, apart from singed hair, no harm ever resulted.

Patrick Satow remembers his captain thus:

A quiet and pensive commanding officer, who must have spent many of the long hours at sea turning over in his mind what events could occur, and the action to be taken. By so doing, he always seemed to be ready with a sound decision, thus saving valuable time when dealing with emergencies.

One of these thoughtful decisions had been to exercise the ship's full armament time and time again when on the West African station. This was to reap dividends. The policy was written later thus:

The pom-poms had been fired almost daily at sea and the crews were very well trained. On the South Atlantic station where the prospects of action were not very bright, I was convinced that the only way to keep efficient was by very frequent practices. As regards extra weapons we had two twin Lewis guns, one each side of the Flag Deck and a Bren on each side of the bridge (acquired at Boulogne). As regards control of these close-range weapons I had a simple private arrangement which worked satisfactorily. This consisted of loud rattlers at the 12-pdr and pom-poms, controlled by a push on the bridge which I worked myself. Short rings meant 'hostile aircraft starboard', and groups of two short rings 'hostile aircraft port', these signals gave the guns concerned permission to open fire. In addition, bearings and angles of sight were passed down by 'phone.*

On the lower deck they were veterans too. In the engine rooms they had kept the ship going in the tropics in relays, almost suffocating as they were at times. Chief ERA Pullen, Chief ERA Ted Gosling as his number 2 ERA 2nd Class, Bill Marsh, another survivor from *Royal Oak*, ERA 3rd Class Ron Coates, young ERA Young!-Andrew Rippon remembers them all. They all sailed for the last time as *Wild Swan* steamed south into the night.

At 1500 on the afternoon of 16th June, *Wild Swan* rejoined the escort of HG84, the first reinforcement to arrive. They found Walker's Group hard-pressed. Focke-Wulfs were in attendance and the rescue ship-cum-D/F-Ship *Copeland*, reported U-boat signals throughout

* Extract from a letter from Lieutenant-Commander C.E.L. Sclater, dated 6th July 1942, to Captain G.V.M. McLaughlin of the Naval Ordnance Dept, Spa Hotel, Bath. The NOD had written to congratulate him and ask how he did it, 'with everyone under the impression that the Oerlikon is a cure for all ills, any evidence as to what you were able to do with your somewhat more ancient weapons (which, we believe if well handled are still effective) would be of considerable interest.' They added that *Wild Swan*, 'certainly appears to have achieved a far better average than some of our best equipped ships', despite the fact that she had 'not very modern armament'. They also added, 'Our records show you to have two 2-pdr II*C's and a 12-pdr. If you have scrounged any extra weapons we should be glad to know if they were used, and this will not be held in evidence against you!'

the day. The Kondors finally had departed at 1300 having done their job to satisfaction. After *U-552*'s work of the 15th, which had sunk the *Etrib* (1,943 tons), *Pelayo* (1,346 tons) *City of Oxford* (2,759 tons), *Thurso* (2,436 tons) and the Norwegian *Slemdal* (7,374 tons), there had not been any other losses. Early on the morning of the 16th, at 0158, the *U-575* (Lieutenant-Commander Günther Heydemann) had fired a four-torpedo spread and reported one hit, but this was false and no other ship was hit. Much counter-attack work had left the CO's ship, *Stork*, low on depth charges, she only had eight remaining.

Thus, when *Wild Swan* arrived, Walker took the risk of re-stocking and, while the destroyer screened them, the corvette *Convolvulus* transferred another twelve depth charges by way of *Stork*'s motor boat. This was a slow process, but attempts to hold the two ships alongside each other proved impossible in the swell. Later the *Spey* and then the *Krakowiak* arrived, with some Catalina flying boats. At dusk Walker took the decision that further attempts at evasion were futile. The position, course, speed and escort of HG84 were known to the enemy by FW200 reports at 1300 and there were indications that at least five U-boats remained in the area of the convoy. The large alterations of course earlier had not thrown the submarines off, merely delayed the convoy. So Walker decided to go 'straight for home' and this decision was justified by the fact that the night of the 16th/17th was undisturbed.

Next morning all was well except that *Stork* now chose to develop condenseritis which further reduced the convoy's overall speed. *Rother* arrived at 0600 on this morning. However this increase in strength was only temporary, for, with the feeling that the convoy was now safe and others in greater need, the *Rother* and *Spey* were sent to join the escort of convoy SL112 at 1400.

The Focke-Wulfs had re-appeared at 1050 that morning and they remained in sight for about an hour, but the convoy itself enjoyed continuous air cover from 1436 to 2228 which kept the U-boats at bay. By 1600, as Lieutenant-Commander Sclater had predicted, *Wild Swan* was forced to leave again due to lack of fuel. The time was 1600 and the convoy was left in position 49°55′ N, 13°00′ W. Course was set by *Wild Swan* 090° at 15 knots for Plymouth. As Owen Pugh remembers: 'Running back to the convoy at near maximum speed to comply with our orders, used up a good deal of the fuel that we had just taken aboard so we could not stay any longer.'

'Six out of Twelve'. How *War Illustrated* saw *Wild Swan*'s last fight in the Bay of Biscay. For once the war artist did not need to exaggerate the scene.

A Junkers Ju88 A-4 bomber (M2+AK) of II/KG106 is revved onto the compass-checking platform on her home base at Lannion, France in 1942. This was one of the units which attacked *Wild Swan* on 17th June, 1942 and suffered heavy losses.

The ill-fated *Neuvo Con*. One of a fleet of innocent Spanish trawlers mistaken by the German bombers for convoy HG84. Three of her sisters were blasted by bombs but *Nuevo Con* was accidently rammed and sunk by *Wild Swan* in her death agony. Her crew reached safety along with the British survivors.

In France Dönitz had called off his U-boats, but, from the reports received from his Kondors, he knew where the convoy was. He had one last shot in his locker. A mass bombing attack was decided upon, using every available bomber at Dönitz's disposal. It was to be a dusk attack for maximum surprise and another FW200 duly despatched to home in on the convoy and guide the inexperienced bombers in to it. On runways in Brittany in the late summer after-noon the snarl of aero engines warming up disturbed the silence. Beneath the hunched shapes of Junkers Ju88's the armourers were fitting the 550-lb bombs with delayed-action fuses to detonate after they had punched through the steel decks of the ships. Only minimum delay was specified as their targets were not thick-skinned battleships but merchantmen. The big four-engined reconnaissance from KG40 passed over *Wild Swan* at 1952 on its way to HG84, as Lieutenant-Commander Sclater's report noted: 'One Focke-Wulf was sighted in a break in passing clouds overhead, height 2,000 feet, approximate course 320° flying towards HG84. It was engaged with-out apparent result.'

Owen Pugh: 'An hour or so after leaving the convoy we were spot-ted by a Focke-Wulf reconnaissance plane, which no doubt reported our position.'

The position where the Kondor was sighted was about 49°53′ N, 12°00′ W. Soon afterwards this aircraft arrived over HG84.

A Focke-Wulf appeared at the unprecedented time of 2220. This aircraft came closer than usual to the convoy and *Stork* was able to seize the opportunity to carry out a long-range HA full-calibre shoot. The Liberator escort kept watch above the clouds for the approach of hostile bombers or torpedo aircraft. The next few hours were spent at A/A action stations, but no attack developed.

The RAF had a go at this plane also:

Liberator *T/120* was escorting when, at 2220 a Focke-Wulf 200 closed the convoy and the Liberator got in a few bursts of fire to which the enemy made no reply. The Focke-Wulf continued on its course and was engaged by *Stork*. The Liberator did not pursue the enemy owing to lack of speed and forward armament, but remained above the clouds on the look out for the approach of enemy bombers, which, contrary to expectation, failed to appear.

Quite why they failed to appear soon became obvious some seventy miles to the west. The Focke-Wulf, unperturbed by all the attention it had received from naval guns and aerial machine-guns, reported back to base with precise details of all the British forces, as the Naval War Diary records:

> At 300 nautical miles west of Brest (Quadrant 25W4074) a convoy of 21 cargo ships and three to six escorts reported steering north-east. 20 nautical miles north-north-east of the convoy two further escorts were reported steering 050°.

On maps back at Lorient the convoy was placed firmly in square BE 3628, and the escorts to the north-east in square BF1418. But in the Junkers Ju88's, now winging their way through the darkening sky above a low cloud base, such precise plotting did not exist. They were looking for a convoy, an assembly of ships with warship escorts. They had little idea of what the ships would look like other than there would be a lot of them. They were on the correct route; it was merely a matter of spotting them and delivering their bomb loads. At 2100 they caught a glimpse of just such a target through the clouds and deployed to attack.

At just this time *Wild Swan* was starting to pass a large number of Spanish trawlers engaged in fishing on the Gran Sol Bank. The trawlers had firm orders not to do so, but ignored them. They were mainly of the small 100-175-ton *Pareja* type, single-funnelled, with one mast well forard and one aft, a small square wooden bridge and high bow with a straight stem. The flush deck swept down from this to an overhanging counter astern and a solitary lifeboat on the superstructure aft. On their bows, close to the stem, was painted the Spanish flag, each side, as well as their recognition numbers and port of registration. Normally this would be easily read and identified; in the dusk of that June evening, from the air, it was no protection at all. One such vessel was the 161-ton *Nuevo Con*. Like all the *Parejas* she was of wooden construction and had been built in 1941 by Hijos de J Barreras, S.A. of Vigo. Her dimensions were 88.3 metres by 20.6 metres by 12.1 metres. Her registration numbers were T.3cY, VIGO. She carried a crew of twelve, including her captain. There were about twelve similar vessels, all of them coal burners and working dutifully under a haze of smoke. Wally Harrison recalls:

We were on our own except for a fleet of fishing smacks (at the time I was led to believe they were Portuguese). We were passing right through the middle of this fleet when aircraft were sighted.

A.G. Linford:

We had been detached to proceed eastwards (afterwards we thought we might have been used as expendable bait) and we were jumped by Nazi planes when we were near to some Spanish trawlers.

Andrew Rippon:

Somewhere south of Ireland and prior to steering easterly for the Channel, we encountered this group of Spanish fishing vessels making lots of smoke. From the air I could imagine it might look like a convoy and escort.

Owen Pugh wrote in his report that:

On the evening of Wednesday, 17th June 1942, the first lieutenant and I were keeping the first watch, when, at about 2145 a number of aircraft were reported bearing Red 50, our course being 090°. At the time there were upwards of 20 Spanish fishing trawlers in the vicinity and apparently the enemy mistook these for the convoy which we had left some hours previously and which was some 80 miles to the west of our position. A FW Kondor had previously been sighted and fired upon and there was no doubt from the first of the aircraft's identity and intentions.

F.R. Burrett:

. . . we were passing through a fleet of Spanish fishing boats in fine, clear weather, when the action alarm sounded. Twelve Ju88s approached from the south-east and circled at low altitude (about 200 ft) at a range of about two miles, seemingly mistaking the Spanish boats for our convoy.

On his BBC broadcast, the navigation officer described the moment thus:

At 9.15 at night we heard the drumming of aircraft engines which grew louder and gradually passed right overhead. At the time we were arranging our zig-zag to avoid twelve Spanish fishing vessels which lay in our track, scattered over an area of about five miles across. The sky was covered with a thick sheet of low cloud.

He added to the author later:

It seems probable that the German airmen had been sent out from a base in occupied north-west France, and, in the gradually failing light of a summer evening, they mistook the fishing boats of a neutral nation for a convoy.

Some time earlier, at 2000, Lieutenant-Commander Sclater had initiated a signal giving *Wild Swan*'s position, course and speed, and that of the convoy, but it was never sent. The signals staff were still busy encyphering it when other, more urgent, signals, became necessary.

Wild Swan's last fight had now begun.

2116: Twelve Ju88's were sighted bearing 070°, at a range of four miles and a height of 1,500 feet just below the cloud base flying in loose formation. Owen Pugh:

Twelve Junkers 88's were reported on the port beam, and almost before I had time to ring for action stations, they were breaking formation to attack. On being relieved I proceeded to my action station* which was either at the 12-pdr or on the pom-pom deck. I chose the 12-pdr as dive-bombing had not then started, and at once identified the attacking aircraft as Ju88's; there being ten or twelve in all.

Donald Lingard:

I had the first watch and was on duty in the W/T office at the time, and whilst I heard plenty, I saw very little. The PO Tel and the Leading Tel were making signals to the Admiralty, mainly in plain language.

My opinion was that the Germans thought the trawlers were in company with us and attacked them as well as us. The aircraft

---

* Although Sub-Lieutenant Pugh was signals officer, his action station was with the close-range AA guns.

attacking us were obviously looking for the convoy that we had left and suspected that we and the trawlers were part of it.

The first intimation we had in the W/T Office was from the bridge and a stream of signals followed, which we transmitted to the Admiralty. I myself was manning the receiver hoping to record confirmation signals coming in from that source and Gibraltar.

Patrick Satow:

At the time the sky was covered with an almost unbroken sheet of cloud, having its base at about 2,500 feet (750 metres) above the sea. The surface visibility was good, but the enemy never seemed to realise that the poor defenceless fishing vessels were not involved in hostilities.

Wally Harrison:

I believe the dive bombers were looking for our convoy and thought they had found it when they saw the fishing smacks. With the very small size of these vessels the pilots would have got the impression they were viewing the scene from a greater altitude than they actually were.

*

2128: At this time *Wild Swan* opened fire with all her guns at individual aircraft in various sectors. The main guns, four 4.7-inch, were controlled by the GCO via the director with barrage fire initially, with fuses set to 5,000 yards. Lieutenant-Commander Sclater's report read: 'Sub-Lieutenant D.H. Revill, the GCO, is worthy of special mention for his coolness and skill in controlling the guns at this time.'

The German Naval Diary records that the attack was launched by two *Gruppen*, mainly from KG77, who attacked first, and then by KG106, who attacked next. The location was Quadrant 25W2044.

*

2129: '*Wild Swan to Admiralty*: 2129/17. Twelve aircraft bearing 070°. Distance 4 miles, course 189°. Am engaging.'

*

2131: Two of the German bombers suddenly appeared out of the
cloud base in a concerted attack from two directions, but were too
close and collided. One crashed into the sea, the other into a Spanish
trawler, blowing it up. These unfortunates were a Junkers Ju88 A-4
of KG106, and a Junkers Ju88 A-5 of KG77. The latter had joined
KG106's mission both to help and observe but had merely got in the
way when the attack commenced with tragic consequences for both
aircrew and the unfortunate Spanish trawler. The captain later
wrote that:

> The formation split up and, at 2131, two aircraft crashed into the
> sea. I thought at first they had been attacked by fighters but heard
> afterwards that many people saw them collide in the cloud base.

He also was to tell how:

> Suddenly I saw an aircraft dive vertically, release its bombs and
> crash into the sea after them. Another one dived onto a trawler, hit
> it, its bombs exploding and all that was left was a little brown
> smoke on the water. This was very heartening, for I thought that
> they had been attacked by fighters, but several people said they
> saw the two planes crash head-on in a gap in the clouds.

Owen Pugh:

> As I made my way from the bridge aft to the 12-pdr gun platform,
> I was surprised to see two of the planes plunge into the sea, before
> a shot had been fired almost, and I can only presume that they col-
> lided when breaking formation.

In his report he had written:

> I was surprised to see two of these (aircraft) dive seawards, and
> fail to pull out of their dives. At the time I thought the trawlers
> must have opened machine-gun fire at them, but since I am of the
> opinion that the two collided early on, and crashed . . .

Andrew Rippon:

Soon after passing the fishing vessels the 'action stations' alarm sounded and I moved to my action station, which was the magazine flood and damage control position in the WR flat below 'X' gun. A phone call informed us that aircraft were attacking from various sectors. The ship's speed increased and the guns opened fire.

Before finally closing the upperdeck doors I spotted one aircraft diving towards the ship with what appeared to be guns firing.

Patrick Satow:

Within a minute or two, of course, we were at full action stations and then the twelve Huns slowly dropped out from the cloud base. As they crossed ahead of us we opened up with our two foremost 4.7s. The first few rounds burst remarkably close, and at least two of the raiders appeared to be hit, and climbed back into the clouds. A minute or two later these two dropped out of the clouds again steering wildly. We held our breath as they collided head-on, each doing about 300 miles an hour. One caught fire and dived vertically on to a Spanish trawler. The whole lot blew up and a shower of pieces went flying through the air. The other dived headlong into the sea, quite close to the burning wreckage of his opposite number. He released his bombs about a hundred feet up – too late – they fell only a few yards away, and he also was blown to pieces.

During the early part of this fierce engagement, *Wild Swan* was steaming at nearly 25 knots, and altering course continuously to try and avoid the bombs which were falling alarmingly close. She had no time to go and look for German airmen in the sea who might have escaped.

*

2136: One of the bombers dived out of the clouds broad on the starboard bow. *Wild Swan* went to full speed ahead and her captain put the wheel hard a starboard. Four bombs were dropped and they straddled the ship, exploding under water abreast the after boiler room, flooding the after boiler room and engine room, breaking the ship's back and bringing down the mast. The engines stopped and the wheel jammed hard a-starboard. The ship rammed a Spanish trawler; it was the *Nuevo Con*, which sank while her crew climbed aboard the destroyer.

Lieutenant-Commander Sclater:

At 2136 one aircraft dived out of the clouds about Green 45°. This aircraft was engaged by the 12-pdr and starboard pom-pom without apparent result. The wheel was jammed and the ship circled to starboard finally hitting a Spanish trawler with about 5 knots headway. The crew of twelve climbed aboard as their vessel sank.

Patrick Satow:

Some of the Junkers 88's attacked the unfortunate fishing boats, and two planes were hit in their efforts to avoid the barrage of shells being sent up at them, weaving in and out of the cloud base; and whilst so doing, two of them collided and came down in the sea.

About this time *Wild Swan* experienced a very near miss which severely shook her entire hull, and caused extensive damage. As she lost speed, the rudder also jammed and the crippled destroyer was out of control.

Her speed through the water had dropped to only walking pace, when *Wild Swan* collided with a trawler which became impaled on her bows. The ship soon stopped, and the Spanish crew were hauled onboard. . .

Wally Harrison:

The bombs from the first aircraft missed the ship but were sufficiently close for the force of the explosions to de-mast the ship. I am not an expert on bombs or ammunition but I did get the impression that these bombs were more like mines – possibly meant to explode once they had sunk to a certain depth. It was this cluster of bombs that blew up below *Wild Swan* and broke her back. After the *Wild Swan* was damaged the PO Tel came up on the bridge and reported that we had no aerial for sending further signals but that he was going to rig up an emergency aerial.

The ship was slowly breaking her back and the midships was sinking deeper in the water as the stem and stern were rising. All this time other planes were coming in and all our guns were banging away. The fact that all the planes flew in from the same direction made it easier for our gunners. There were stripped Lewis guns going off from either side of the bridge as well as Brens, pompoms and the 4.7s. Everything was firing.

A.G. Linford:

We were almost hit in the first attack. My watchkeeping mate was 'Cock' Clayton and we were off watch at the time. The first bombs near-missed amidships. We split but held. The engine room was damaged and the steam pipes parted. The boiler was eventually shut down and we started to sink. We cleared all hands from forward and below brought them upon deck and gave help to the starboard AA guns, pom-poms etc. Able Seaman David Scott, who manned the starboard pom-pom, got a decoration. He earned it.

Andrew Rippon:

A salvo of bombs seemed to heel the ship to port and the propeller noises reduced quickly. I later learnt that the steering had been damaged and we had rammed a fishing vessel.

Owen Pugh:

It was not long before we were subject to intense bombing, and I well remember looking up to see four bombs descending, and feeling they were so close I could catch them in my tin hat. At one time during the action I looked forward and was surprised to see that we had been dismasted, and again later, that we were moving round in circles as our steering had apparently been damaged. In doing so we rammed one of the trawlers, which I think must have been impaled on our bows for a short time.

I opened fire immediately with long fused shells, on several aircraft on our port quarter, and from then until the end the gun was firing almost continuously. In the dive bombing attacks which followed, medium- and short-fused shells were used, and, I believe, with good effect. I myself saw no actual plane hit or damaged, indeed we were all far too fully occupied – but Able Seaman Clark, trainer of the gun, told me afterwards that he saw a shell explode on contact. This I cannot confirm.

F.R. Burrett:

A low-level attack was launched at us from astern, four bombs straddling the ship and exploding under the keel, breaking her

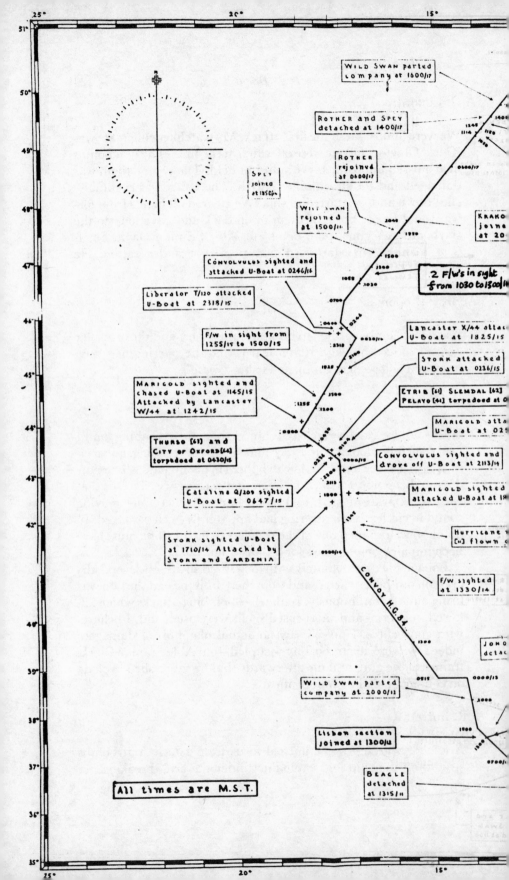

WILD SWAN parted
company at 1600/17

ROTHER and SPEY
detached at 1400/17

ROTHER
rejoined
at 0600/17

SPEY
joined
at 1850/11

WILD SWAN
rejoined
at 1500/11

KRAKO
joined
at 20

2 F/w's in sight
from 1030 to 1300/1

CONVOLVULUS sighted and
attacked U-Boat at 0246/16

Liberator T/120 attacked
U-Boat at 2318/15

Lancaster X/44 attac
U-Boat at 1825/15

F/w in sight from
1255/15 to 1500/15

STORK attacked
U-Boat at 0236/15

MARIGOLD sighted and
chased U-Boat at 1145/15
Attacked by Lancaster
W/44 at 1242/15

ETRIB [61] SLEMDAL [62]
PELAYO [41] torpedoed at 0

MARIGOLD atta
U-Boat at 025

THURSO [63] and
CITY OF OXFORD [64]
torpedoed at 0430/15

CONVOLVULUS sighted and
drove off U-Boat at 2113/14

Catalina Q/209 sighted
U-Boat at 0647/15

MARIGOLD sighted
attacked U-Boat at 18

STORK sighted U-Boat
at 1710/14 Attacked by
STORK and GARDENIA

Hurricane
[H] flown s

F/w sighted
at 1330/14

CONVOY H.G.84

JONO
detac

WILD SWAN parted
company at 2000/12

Lisbon section
joined at 1300/11

BEAGLE
detached
at 1315/11

All times are M.S.T.

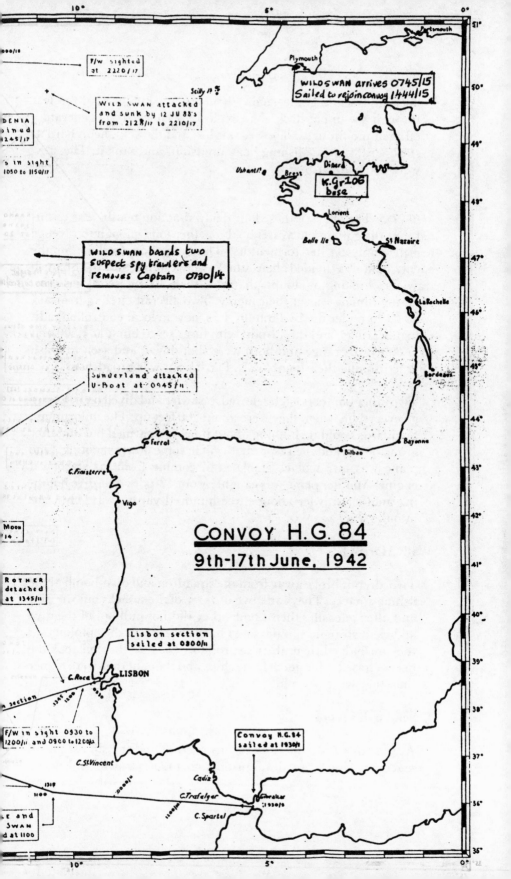

F/W sighted
at 2220/17

DENIA
oined
245/17

's in sight
1050 to 1150/17

WILD SWAN attacked
and sunk by 12 JU 88's
from 2128/17 to 2210/17

Scilly Is.

Plymouth

Portsmouth

WILD SWAN arrives 0745/15
Sailed to rejoin convoy 1444/15

Ushant I.

Brest

Dinard

K.Gr.106
base

Lorient

Belle Ile

St Nazaire

WILD SWAN boards two
suspect spy trawlers and
removes Captain 0730/14

La Rochelle

Bordeaux

Sunderland attacked
U-Boat at 0945/11

Ferrol

Bilbao

Bayonne

C.Finisterre

Vigo

CONVOY H.G. 84
9th-17th June, 1942

Moon
'14

ROTHER
detached
at 1345/11

Lisbon section
sailed at 0800/11

C.Roca

LISBON

1345 1200 0800

section

F/W in sight 0930 to
1200/11 and 0900 to 1200/11

C.St.Vincent

Cadiz

Convoy H.G.84
sailed at 1930/9

1319

1100

C.Trafalgar

C.Spartel

Gibraltar
1930/9

E and
SWAN
at 1100

back and sending the engine/boiler room bulkhead three feet through the upper deck. The explosions knocked the generators off their mountings, all power was lost and the ship, helm hard a-starboard, struck a fishing boat amidships and sank it. The crew were taken aboard.

*

2140-2145: The effect of these four delayed-action bombs was terminal, but the gallant old vessel held together long enough to revenge herself amply on her tormentors. Thinking she was done for the enemy bombers divided their attacks between her and the Spanish trawlers, thinking no doubt, that now the solitary escort was crippled, the convoy was at their mercy. Two aircraft circling to attack were taken under fire by both the 4.7s, now in local control on individual bearings, and the 12-pdr, with fuses set to burst at 1,500 and then 850 yards range and both were shot down, and seen to crash after jettisoning their bombloads. Patrick Satow's broadcast:

> Two other bombers each selected a trawler and dived on it, letting go everything when they were about 200 feet up. The unfortunate Spaniards could do nothing about it being unarmed but our after group of 4.7s and the 12-pdr both got in some pretty shooting. One plane was hit, a black smoke trail coming from his starboard engine. Another plane was caught by our 12-pdr while dive bombing another trawler about three hundred yards away. He went into the sea.

Wally Harrison:

> Two aircraft broke away from the squadron and dive-bombed the fishing smacks. They sank two or three of the smacks but were hit and after releasing their bombs they did not pull out of the dive and went straight into the sea. I have always had the opinion that they misjudged their altitude probably because they mistook the fleet of trawlers for much large ships and thought they were higher than they were when hit.

Owen Pugh's report:

> At this time I was more than surprised to find the ship stopped, and on looking forward was just in time to see a trawler sink under

our bows, and to notice that our own mast was down. We were quickly taking a heavy list to port, and I had to keep the gun trained to starboard, as I found we could quickly train to port, but that to starboard or upwards was extremely slow. I was also obliged to detail one hand to clear the gun deck of empty cordite cases which were fast becoming so numerous as seriously to impede the loading numbers.

I cannot praise the gun's crew too highly; the layer and the trainer did all that was asked of them, getting on the target quickly and holding it coolly and efficiently right to the end of the dives, despite heavy machine-gun fire from the planes. Especially I would mention Able Seaman Fisher, as captain of the gun. He worked heroically throughout and it was mainly due to him that such a high rate of fire was maintained.

Ready-use ammunition was plentiful and easily accessible. No misfires were encountered, and, broadly speaking, everything went much as in a 'dummy run'.

*

2149: Another Junkers came boring in towards the crippled destroyer, having witnessed the fate of its comrades, determined to finish her off once and for good. Lieutenant-Commander Sclater's report:

At 2149 an aircraft approached from Red 150°, angle of sight 10°. It came straight in almost as though it was going to make a torpedo attack and was hit by the port pom-pom. It came within 500 yards and then turned away to port and crashed bearing Red 60°, 3 miles.

The starboard pom-pom was captained by Able Seaman Harold R. Pearce and his shots all counted. Patrick Satow's broadcast describes the effect:

The machine was pouring black smoke and circled round with the rest at a respectable distance, keeping out of range of our long barrage. He slowly lost height, and finally hit the sea three miles off our port bow.

Bill Harrison:

The attacks were fast and furious. It seemed to me that the planes were being knocked out and were going down into the water as fast they came in to bomb. The whole attack seemed to me to last for about twenty minutes. There is no doubt that the gunners did a superb job and saved the day even though we lost the ship. As far as I know there were no casualties from the bombing.

The Yeoman was informing the captain that the PO Tel had rigged up a jury aerial and was transmitting. We did not know if the set-up was actually working. I grabbed a ten-inch lamp and started signalling SOS to the fishing smacks but of course I got no reply and after about five to ten minutes I took a group from the International Code of Signals which meant, 'Come alongside and take us off'. There was still no reply from them. During all this commotion I cannot recall us ramming the trawler. Nor do I have any memory of their crew coming aboard.

But come aboard they had! F.R. Burrett recalls:

I remember that there was no panic among the Spanish crew when they first came aboard. They seemed to regard the whole episode as a great lark!

That attitude quickly changed as attack after attack came in and *Wild Swan* sank lower in the water, as Owen Pugh records:

I was too busy fighting the ship to really know what was going on elsewhere, but I do recall the gunner running forward with a loaded .45 revolver, and ordering the trawler's crew out of our whaler, which they were endeavouring to lower, even while we were still firing and otherwise occupied!

*

2156: Another bomber made an individual and determined attack at this time, coming down to 500 feet in a shallow dive and dropped six bombs which burst underwater close to the starboard quarter. This aircraft was hit by the 12-pdr starboard, pom-pom and starboard Lewis gun and crashed near the port quarter. These bombs lifted the 12-pdr off its mounting but by then only six rounds of 12-pdr ammunition were left unused. Lieutenant-Commander Sclater:

The starboard Lewis gunner assisted in bringing down the aircraft that carried out the second serious attack on us. At least, his tracer bullets appeared to be hitting.

Between 2145 and 2155 two Spanish trawlers were deliberately bombed and sunk and this aircraft was continuously hit and crashed about 50 yards from another Spanish trawler.

Owen Pugh:

I witnessed one aircraft come down astern, and another some way off on the starboard beam. The other I believe crashed somewhere ahead and consequently on an obscured bearing from the gun deck.

The pom-poms I think did quite good work, though apparently belts loaded with tracer were continuously jamming and in the end guns had to be unloaded completely and reloaded with ordinary non-tracer ammunition.

F.R. Burrett:

Further attacks then developed from the starboard side, the 88s coming in at almost sea-level firing cannon and machine guns as they approached, so that the superstructure, funnels etc. were completely peppered. Incredibly no one was hit. As far as I remember, the only casualty during the action was a stoker with a grazed shin. He fell into the boiler room bilges when a deck-plate became displaced by the explosions.

During the action the 12-pdr aft of the funnels scored a number of hits, and at least two planes crashed to port after dropping their loads. No direct bomb hits were scored on us, most of them detonating alongside or under the ship. One enormous explosion sent all the upperd deck depth charges high into the air, crashing down among us. We had been defusing them. Again, incredibly no one was hit by them. Standing under the barrel of the 12-pdr to carry out this defusing, some of us were rendered partially deaf for life. To reduce the weight on deck I was ordered to discharge the torpedoes, but by this time the ship was beginning to break up and the order was given to abandon her.

All the extra depth charges had to be unprimed when it became clear the ship was sinking. I suppose a great number were simply set to 'safe' to prevent their exploding while men were in the water. None did.

Owen Pugh:

The two pom-poms jammed continually during the action, until
the tracer belts were replaced with standard ammunition. These
two guns and the 12-pdr were our main AA weapons. After the
first barrage Number One took charge of the after 4.7s, but unfortunately he could not get sufficient elevation against dive bombing
attacks, but I believe did well as they pulled away at low level.

Andrew Rippon:

After a while our guns seemed to be firing continuously and then
came the second blast of bombs bursting very close on our starboard quarter. Either these explosions, or the heel of the ship,
hurled me through the open hatch into the shellroom and I was
then occupied in climbing out of a ladderless compartment,
together with, I think, two ammunition supply ratings.

I was aware of the props stopping and shouts of 'Abandon
Ship'. On gaining the upper deck I could see that the HA gun was
askew on its mounting and crew members were trying to clear
Carley floats and the wooden raft we'd recovered earlier, and
launch them into the sea. Steam was escaping from the safety
valve exhausts and I realised that the main deck at the funnel area
was under water and the mainmast was bent or broken into an
unnatural angle.

Patrick Satow:

The sixth bomber caught us. He dived down out of the sun at an
angle of 50 degrees and, although the starboard pom-pom and
Lewis gunner fired through his wings, five bombs hit the water 15
feet from the ship's side and went off immediately under the keel.

All the guns were firing individually as the electrical circuits
and supplies were shattered. This quarter of an hour gave us time
to rig a jury wireless aerial. One aircraft came in and machine-
gunned us. Unfortunately for him the 12-pdr crew – by now all
stripped to the waist, scored a direct hit on one of his engines. As
he turned away, the forward guns engaged him and he slowly lost
height, hitting the water in a sheet of spray.

Before the aerial was finished somebody yelled, 'Look out, here
he comes.' High up above a machine was coming down at full

Wild Swan's survivors in the water just prior their rescue on 18th June. A rather shaky photograph taken from Sunderland *Y/10* which led HMS *Vansittart* to the scene. A few days later she herself was destroyed on another rescue mission.

How the wives and sweethearts heard the news. Telegram sent to the wife of one of the survivors.

rges to pay   P/JX 246924 D 9 PFT ++++

ECEIVED

TELEGRAM

| Prefix. | Time handed in. | Office of Origin and Service Instructions. | Words. |

8

10.35 PFT OHMS 38

OFFICE STAMP

No. _____

To_____

MRS AGNES LINGARD 5 DELAMERE DRIVE MACCLESFIELD

CHESHIRE

= REGRET TO REPORT THAT YOUR HUSBAND DONALD

LINGARD TELEGRAPHIST P/JX 246924 HAS BEEN

TEMPORARILY DETAINED IN ROYAL NAVAL SICK QUARTER

MILFORDHAVEN SUFFERING FROM EFFECTS OF EXPOSURE

at office = COMMODORE NAVAL BARRACKS PORTSMOUTH D 9

SHIP WITH 6 OUT OF 12 NAZI 'PLANES TO HER CREDIT

These photographs, exclusive to The Daily Telegraph, show the 1,120-ton British destroyer Wild Swan (left) and her gun crew (above), who, as reported in this paper last Saturday, destroyed six of 12 Ju.88 bombers which attacked the ship 100 miles west of the French coast.

The ship, damaged by bombs, could not avoid a collision with a Spanish trawler disabled by the raiders. The fishing vessel sank and three other Spanish trawlers were victims of the Nazis. The Wild Swan later sank. Her crew were picked up by another destroyer.

How the Press saw the story. Front Page of The Daily Telegraph with photographs of Wild Swan and her 12-pdr gun and crew.

throttle. He was about 2,000 feet up and had a long way to go. All the guns' crews spotted him simultaneously and I don't think I've ever seen so much stuff going up into one machine. He turned his cannons on us and let go four 500-lb bombs.

They fell a few feet from our starboard quarter. Although the Lewis and Bren gunners could see this lot coming straight for us, they kept a hail of fire right till the bombs exploded. The effect of this attack was positively devastating. There was a rending of steel plates as the old ship broke her back. The flooding of the engine room was completed, depth charges thrown into the air and the 12 pounder lifted clean off its mounting. The remaining machines were still circling us at a range of five miles. I rather suspect they were strafing the remaining Spaniards who were all heading for home.

*

Firing was continued with the 4.7-inch barrage at any aircraft that came within range. The jury rigged aerial was put to use soon afterwards: '*Wild Swan to Admiralty*: 2205B/17. Am in danger of sinking due to bombing.' Then came one final drama, as the navigator's broadcast revealed:

The petty officer telegraphist came up with the shattered remains of the code-book and a good deal of grime on his face and hands. He had been working like a Trojan for half an hour. Anyone who saw the shambles would have doubted his word that the emergency wireless worked. But it was put to the test and within three minutes a last SOS was passed through to Gibraltar – a thousand miles away – on ten feet of aerial.

Our last attacker, badly injured, came towards us. He was barely 200 feet up and I think his object was to bale out close enough to be picked up by one of our boats. The forward group distrusting him as much as any of us, continued firing star shells at him. There was nothing else left to fire. Two burst very close and he made a steep banking turn to get away. He appeared to stall, black smoke streamed out of his tail and he dived towards the water. Several times he just cleared the wave tops. He wasn't hit again but he never regained height and after a number of desperate attempts to escape that bomber joined the other five at the bottom of the Atlantic. The remaining aircraft disappeared to the south-east, evidently having had quite enough for one day.

CHAPTER TWELVE

Homecoming
17th June 1942 and after

By 2210 there were no aircraft left in sight, the iron deck was level with the water and the ship slowly breaking in half. The boats and rafts were all got away and abandon ship was ordered at 2220. All secret and confidential matter was placed in the steel chests. Service certificates were placed in the ship's whaler. Attempts to attract Spanish trawlers were made but they all disappeared. In the words of the Admiralty Weekly Summary:

> By then the surviving Spanish trawlers had very intelligently made off, so the crew of the destroyer and the twelve survivors from the rammed trawler had to rely on the whaler, which held forty-one, and the motor-boat, which held thirty-one, while the others were on Carley floats and a large Merchant Service pattern raft which had been recovered at sea.

Before they left one last signal was got away: '*Wild Swan to Admiralty, Gibraltar en clair*: 2226B/17. Am abandoning ship.'
Patrick Satow:

> The remaining aircraft had probably released all their bombs and soon withdrew towards the French coast. It was as well that this happened at about the time that *Wild Swan* stopped; because if the attacks had continued, the ship, so aptly nicknamed 'The Frantic Duck', would have been 'The Sitting Duck'.

Indeed all HETF shell had been fired off by the 4.7s. Patrick Satow continues:

> Alas, as the gunfire ceased, it became obvious that the Old Lady was sinking. A final SOS message was given to the radio operator, in the hope that it could still be transmitted to someone on shore. It evidently was received, not by any station in the British Isles, but nearly one thousand miles away in Gibraltar.
> As the ship settled lower in the water, the captain gave the order to 'abandon ship'. All available boats were swiftly lowered, and

rafts were released. In an orderly manner that is expected from an experienced and well disciplined crew, the men climbed over the side and took the Spaniards with them. Fortunately there was only a moderate sea condition, with no great Atlantic swell, otherwise more casualties might have occurred at this critical time.

If a ship goes down rapidly, there is great danger of men being sucked into the swirling waters, and so everyone got clear. Whilst abandoning ship, some of the officers and men had been partly or wholly immersed in the sea. Although every effort had been made to haul them quickly into boats or onto the rafts, individuals had little resistance to the cold after their immediate past service in the tropics.

At times likes these the strangest priorities occupied men's minds. The ship's captain recalled one such example as it affected him:

While at Freetown shortly before returning home, I had met an old shipmate aboard the battleship *Malaya*, Lieutenant-Commander I.W.T. Beloe. He had not liked my beard at all, and said so forcefully, promising to even buy me an electric razor if I shaved it off. He did and I did! But I did not like it much. Yet the last thing I did before leaving the ship after everyone had left, was to dive into my cabin and grab this infernal contraption. Goodness knows why and it never worked again after immersion in the Atlantic. Silk stockings for my wife and other far more important valuables remained with the ship!

Wally Harrison:

Once the planes had gone, the engineering officer came up to the bridge and reported that the ship was in a bad way. She was slowly but surely breaking in two, and her stem and stern were rising. Shortly after receiving the engineering officer's report the captain shouted to the first lieutenant, 'abandon ship'. On hearing that order I went to the port side of the bridge and jumped into the water some twenty-five feet below.

After a few moments in the water I met up with Ted Mallory and then others began to join us from the ship. As the numbers in the water grew larger we swam further from the ship. The weather was good and the sun was shining as we looked back on the ship.

Andrew Rippon:

I was trying to make my way forward to the engine room hatches
when Mr Derbyshire told me to help launch a Carley float and we
got off the ship. Eventually we were established on our respective
rafts and boats and attempted to stay close to one another.

Wild Swan had an obvious broken back, the bows were almost
vertical and the after end barely above the water. This was my last
sight of the ship. Sometime before midnight I could still see the
bows pointing skyward.

Owen Pugh:

After the firing ceased I made my way as best I could to the radio
office, and ascertained from the Yeoman of Signals, CPO Yates,
that he had got a Mayday signal away, and this had been acknow-
ledged by Gibraltar Radio.* We also placed all confidential books
and cyphers in a weighted box and threw them overboard.

It was only too apparent that the ship's end was near, and No 1
and I stayed aboard as long as possible, throwing anything that
would float overboard.

At the last a young Irish steward named Kealey remained aboard
with him. Turning to him, Owen Pugh asked him if he could swim.

He said he could a little, and I then told him to put his clothes back
on, which he had been taking off. I told him that we would swim
across to a cork rope mat, called a Floatnet, which we had previously thrown overboard, and which was floating nearby. Unfortunately when we got to it, we found that it had been rolled up and
stowed on the side of a gun turret for so long, that it had lost its
pliancy and would not unroll. We sat astride it for a few minutes,
but it kept rolling over and tipping us back into the water. I told
Kealey that we would swim over to a raft, as the ship's whaler,
motor boat and all the Carley rafts were full and overcrowded.

Before I reached the raft I looked back for Kealey, but could see
nothing of him. I swam back and searched without success. Eventually I had to give up and swim on to the raft and climbed
aboard. It was grossly overladen, so much so that it was floating
underwater, and we sat up to our thighs in the sea.

---

* And not just Gibraltar. By some quirk it was picked up by Liverpool Radio, who
onpassed it to the Admiralty. Another recipient was the destroyer *Worcester* off the
NE coast of England. Serving aboard her was Bill Wellman, a close friend of TGM
Albert Timpson and he thought his mate was finished.

Donald Lingard:

The order to 'Abandon Ship' came after we had been near-missed on our starboard side and cracked open on our port side. Our aerials were damaged and we had to rig the jury to continue making signals up to the last possible moment. We jumped over the side and swam to the nearest Carley float, all of which were very crowded. Our motor boat got away with the navigating officer and plenty of survivors.

We, with the whaler and the Carley rafts grouped together as best we could, knowing that it would be easier to be sighted if rescue came. The Carley float was very overloaded and practically submerged.

The engine of the motor boat would not start. Being higher out of the water than the rafts, it drifted more freely in the surface wind and thus became separated from the others during the night.

F.R. Burrett:

After going to my mess to get a couple of tins of cigarettes, I got into a Merchant Navy type raft (battens and oildrums) we had found abandoned the day before, and which, in common with most of the Carley rafts, had been punctured by gunfire. We paddled it away from the sinking ship, picking up men from the water as we went. Eventually there were about 25 in the raft. (The sight of men fending off their erstwhile shipmates with kicks and paddles to prevent them boarding rafts was one I will not forget.)

A.G. Linford:

Towards dusk the order was given to 'Abandon Ship'. The whaler had been holed, the motor boat floated and the rafts thrown in, some (at least two), were split. The Spanish trawlers were long gone. There was not enough room in the motor boat or rafts for all, some had to hang on to the raft ropes and maybe drifted away during the night. I managed to hang on until there was room in one during the night.

Linford then watched while the captain dived from the starboard side of the *Wild Swan* and was taken on board a boat.

A leading seaman, I think his name was McLeod, spent all the day and night swimming from raft to raft, cheering up the boys. But later he just drifted off and no one had the strength to help him. Another of the crew who died of exposure was an ex-captain of

Bradford City FC, name not recalled. The ship's Petty Officer Cook, who lived in Gosport, died in my arms from exposure during the day. A good many others also died from the same cause and more died some time after the rescue because of it.

Commander Sclater later recorded:

The whaler held 41 men, the motorboat 31 and the remainder were on Carley floats of which the ship fortunately had three in excess of establishment and a large Merchant Navy pattern raft which had been recovered at sea.

A heavy swell was running and an uncomfortable night was spent. Many of the men were thinly clad and their resistance was lowered by a year's service in the tropics from which the ship had just returned. I endeavoured to keep the boats and rafts together, and keep the men paddling, singing, etc, to keep their circulation going, but I regret to say that 31 in all died from exposure.

Commander Sclater later recalled to me that:

Myself and Sub-Lieutenant Revill were in the whaler, Lieutenant Satow and others in the launch. Patchett, the ship's coxswain, shouted 'Three Cheers for the Captain' or 'Three Cheers for the old *Swan*' or something similar, but the exposure soon started to get everyone. Strangely it seemed as if it was the single men who died, those you would expect to be the youngest and fittest, while the married men all survived in the main. Perhaps it was the will to live was stronger in these cases, I do not know.

And so the long night passed.

*

Back in France the aircraft were returning to their bases. It had *not* been a very successful sortie on the whole. Too many crews had not come back to make it a mission worthwhile celebrating. Among the Junkers Ju88-A4's which did not return was 5779 of KGrl/106 (commanded by Uffz Heinrich Hendrich, a 37-year-old pilot from Saarlautern); 0717, (commanded by Ltn Helmuth Hayner, a 22-year-old from Kronberg), also from the First Staffel. From KGr2/106 were missing 0728, (commanded by Uffz Ferdinand Jäger, a 23-year-old from Gorspen-Vahlsen); a second commanded by Feldw Bordsch. Joachim Zwick, a 29-year-old from Alt-Beelitz Friedeberg and a third commanded by Günter Gahr, another 23-year-old from Osterode/Allenstein belonging to the 3rd Staffel, along with 2366, a Ju88A-5 of KG106, (commanded by Uffz Rudolf Zepf).

Nor was the end of their losses in sight this day. While returning home to base another aircraft from KGr106 was shot down in error by their own flak gunners over Caen and destroyed along with her crew. This was 2116, commanded by Karl Spengler. As a final seal to a bad day yet an eighth bomber, 8552 from 111/KG77, developed engine trouble over France and had to crash-land.

In consolation they claimed to have inflicted a crushing blow on HG84 and the Naval War Diary listed their reported destruction in some detail next day:

> The first attacks by KG77 failed to hit their target and met with no success, but KG106 reported that they had sunk two merchantmen of 2-3,000 tons, damaged severely three more merchantmen of 2-3,000 tons. They also reported they had seriously damaged and probably sunk a two-funnelled destroyer.

The last part was correct, but the 2-3,000 ton freighters were of course, really 150-ton Spanish trawlers, three of which had been sunk, in addition to *Nuevo Con*, and others badly damaged. It was not long before a hint of the truth began to percolate back to Luftwaffe HQ. A Reuters' News Agency report was picked up and its summary was duly recorded by the Naval Staff: 'a group of fishing boats was confused for the convoy from Gibraltar which was actually 50 miles to the west or more.'

By later on the 18th complete disillusionment had arrived. In Part VI of the War Diary (p 348) was recorded under the main heading: *Luftkriegführung; Raumen-England*.

> On 17/6 armed long-range reconnaissance of *Fl Füehr Atlantik* located a convoy of 21 steamers 300 nautical miles West of Brest. All the aircraft, with one exception, attacked in error a fishing flotilla in BF1418 instead of the convoy and sank several fishing steamers and an English destroyer in the vicinity.
>
> Only one aircraft of the second wave intercepted the convoy at 2236 hours in BE 3628.

This entry was heavily scored in the margin, with two exclamation marks beside them, which conveys the German Navy's opinion of the Luftwaffe's 'victory' with eloquent brevity.*

*

* It is not known to which ships the so-called only correct attack was directed. No mention is made of even a sighting from HG84 at this time, or later. The last known aircraft to attack *Wild Swan* was at 2156, and that was destroyed.

If the Germans were disillusioned by their mistakes and heavy losses, then the men of HG84 and its escorting warships were oblivious of their lucky escape for some time. Only later was it realised how *Wild Swan* had saved their bacon. As the report on the convoy concluded: 'It seems that the unfortunate loss of *Wild Swan* at least served to divert the Luftwaffe's attention from their main object, the convoy, and *Wild Swan* had the great satisfaction of seeing six of her opponents crash under her gunfire.'

Vessels were diverted to their aid and air searches were planned for the morning. The destroyer *Vansittart* (Lieutenant-Commander T. Johnston) was proceeding up the Irish Sea towards Londonderry when she received instructions to reverse course and proceed to the aid of her former flotilla mate in 49°52′ N, 10°44′ W, her last signalled position. The Polish destroyer *Krakowiak* was much closer, being still with HG84, but C-in-C, Plymouth, was told to send her to that position, 'only if lack of fuel prevents her from remaining with HG84'. She had fuel, and she stayed.

Vansittart still had a long way to go early on the 18th when she received further information:

Admiralty to Vansittart: Sunderland a/c will search area around 49°52′ N, 10°44′ W at daylight and will then direct you as necessary. After completing rescue make Fastnet and proceed via QZ118 to Milford Haven.

Meanwhile, far to the south, *Wild Swan* had died, and her crew were dying.

*

Almost lost to sight to most of her crew, the old destroyer took a dignified exit from their lives at 2315 that night. Few saw her go. Signalman Harrison wrote:

As she sank further into the water the bows and the stern lifted clear and the ship formed a 'V'-shape just before she went right down. I distinctly remember thinking it looked like a defiant 'V' for 'Victory' sign.

Owen Pugh in his report noted:

The *Wild Swan* sank . . . the stern half first. The bows remained pointed vertically upwards for a few seconds, and finally she slipped beneath the waves.

Patrick Satow added later:

The sun had now set and as darkness closed in, *Wild Swan* broke her back. The bow and stern rose almost defiantly as she finally sank beneath the waves in latitude 49 degs 52 mins north, longitude 10 degs 44 mins west. Fortunately, owing to the gathering darkness little was seen of this tragic moment by the ship's company, who were mainly preoccupied with their own salvation.

Not only the precise location of her grave, but its depth, were recorded:

Immediately before the ship's final encounter with a squadron of Ju88's, she was on an easterly course heading for the English Channel. She was leaving the very deep seas of the North Atlantic, and crossing the well-defined Continental Shelf, where the depth of water decreases sharply from over a mile to less than 100 fathoms (600 feet). As a means of checking the ship's position, the echo sounder had been switched on. Along with many other items of equipment onboard, such as the radar set and much of the machinery, the echo sounder was still running when the ship foundered; but it would have stopped for all time as soon as the green waters of the ocean rushed in. The last reading of depth, taken just before the final SOS message was sent, gave 84 fathoms (504 feet). So, unlike many of the ships sunk in the shallower seas closer to land, the wreck of the *Wild Swan* will never be a hazard to navigation, even for the greatest of super tankers or other ships built for maritime use in the future.

Thus passed *Wild Swan*.

And now men began to die also. Lieutenant-Commander Sclater recalled in a talk given a few weeks later how this happened:

The wireless set had been mended and I knew our distress signal had been picked up so there was nothing to do but wait to be rescued. We had two boats and nine floats and everybody got safely out of the ship. However it was a cold night, the sea got rough, many of us were thinly-clad and our resistance was reduced by a year in the tropics. We kept together and tried to keep our circulation going by singing and so on. By morning we were in a bad way.

F.R. Burrett, PO, TGM, wrote later how:

The ship soon broke in halves, which drifted apart and then sank. The PO telegraphist had rigged a jury aerial after the mast collapsed and used his battery transmitter to radio our position, so that some of us knew it was just a matter of time before we were picked up, always provided we were not attacked by patrolling Focke-Wulf reconnaissance planes first.

However, I was surprised to find that after a few hours men began to lose consciousness and then die. We lost five such men from our raft and a total of 32 died in the night although none had physical injuries.

There was a slight swell and light rain about dawn, not a worry as we were all chest-deep in water. There was some anxiety, when it was realised the raft was sinking. I do not know whether any rafts did sink, because by daylight we were scattered over about five miles of ocean despite our efforts.

Sub-Lieutenant Pugh:

Those in the two boats were I think fairly comfortable, and even those on the Carley floats, well off compared to ourselves. The sea was not unduly rough, but as we were partially under the water to start with, any sort of wave completely immersed us and we were wet, cold, shivering and hungry the whole time. Three men on my raft died of exposure during the next desperate twelve to fifteen hours, and we had no option but to let them go to lighten the raft, which was in danger of sinking. I was in pretty bad shape, I often wonder how much longer I could have lasted. I know I suffered from salt water sores for several weeks afterwards, from continually rubbing my legs to try to restore the circulation, and to keep warm, if that is the right word.

Wally Harrison gives another detailed account of that terrible night:

An hour or two after abandoning the ship it had grown dark and we realised that to keep ourselves going we had to keep active. We did this by verbally amusing each other, telling jokes, obscene jokes, corny jokes, ancient jokes, *anything* to keep talking. We would insult each other but it was fully understood that it was merely to keep our vigour. If somebody was becoming drowsy, the person holding on next to him would have a mock scrap with him. Both would feel more awake and alert after such a brief encounter.

In this situation one might expect the night to be interminably long, but, strangely, to me it seemed to pass quite quickly. However at times you could not feel your arms and legs and had to thrash about in the water to get your circulation going. I was part of a long chain of people, one holding the other and as dawn broke I did not realise that the end of my chain was attached to the whaler.

During the night my chum Ted Mallory who had been at my side right from the very beginning, became quiet and did not respond to us. We soon realised that he had quietly passed away. After a while we released him and rejoined the chain without him. At times I felt my own consciousness fading and had to snap myself out of it with a flurry of activity to get back to a more alert state.

I do not know whether I had periods of delirium but I distinctly remember being comforted by my mother on three or four occasions that night. She would say, 'Don't worry, Wally, you will be all right!' My mother had been dead twenty-six years. She had died when I was about two years old.

Patrick Satow writes:

During that rather miserable night, nobody said much: thoughts were mainly centred on the chances of being found next day. Few of us survivors actually knew that the final SOS message had been cleared before the ship went down, and her position was therefore known accurately to British Naval Authorities at home.

In an interview before his death many years later, Albert Timpson gave the following account of this last transmission:

The ship's proper radio was destroyed, but in a last desperate effort, an SOS was sent out on a small battery set used for inter-ship gunnery contacts.

It was a complete freak that the radio message was picked up. If it had not been, we would all have had it.

*

The morning of 18th June dawned, and air searches got into their

stride. Two Sunderland long-range flying boats from No 10, RAAF
Squadron, based at Mount Batten, near Plymouth, were assigned to
assist the destroyer *Vansittart* in the search. The Luftwaffe was also
early astir in the vain hope that some survivors from the six lost bombers might somehow have survived. It was a hopeless search in that
respect, but it brought new fears to the *Wild Swan*'s survivors that
they might be machine-gunned from the air.* These fears were made
almost manifest when the Luftwaffe, as usual, beat the RAF to the
scene of the action.

Lieutenant-Commander Sclater recalled:

About 6 o'clock in the morning we saw a plane coming towards us
but it was a Focke-Wulf. It cruised round evidently looking for
survivors from the German planes but fortunately took no notice
of us.

Of the Sunderlands despatched one, W4004Z, piloted by Flight
Lieutenant Dave Vernon, aborted its mission without any success
and returned to her base. The second, Y/10, piloted by Flight
Lieutenant Maurice Leopold 'Buck' Judell, had better fortune. His
Sunderland, W3999/Y, was airborne from Mount Batten on this
Air/Sea Rescue Search in their Mark III aircraft at 0300 on the 18th.

At 0610 they commenced a square search with visibility based at
four miles and at 0815 they altered course and a further square
search was commenced with visibility based at two miles. At 1005 a
destroyer, Pendant Number I.64 (*Vansittart*) was sighted and they
exchanged visual signals, Lieutenant-Commander Johnston enquir-
ing whether the Sunderland had sighted anything yet of HMS *Wild
Swan*, Judell was forced to reply, 'No, nothing seen'.

The search was continued. At 1030 wreckage and a large patch of
oil approximately five miles square was sighted and the destroyer
was called up by visual signal and directed to the oil and debris. Two
lifeboats and four rafts were then sighted about one mile down-wind
of the oil patch and a further message was sent to the *Vansittart* giving
position of that sighting.

When *Vansittart* reached the first boat she was informed that the
motor boat had drifted to the north on its own earlier and the
destroyer signalled to Judell, 'Search to north for motor boat'. *Vansit-*

* There were the usual press stories that *Wild Swan*'s survivors had been machine-
gunned in the water, but these accounts were journalistic fabrication.

tart commenced picking up survivors at 1100. Y/10 meanwhile took herself off to the northward and duly sighted the motor boat, returning to direct the destroyer towards it in turn and taking photographs all the while of the rafts and boats in the water. HQ signalled that the Sunderland should remain in the area while the rescue was underway until fighter cover arrived. By 1215 Beaufighter X/235 had arrived and took over aerial protection, circling *Vansittart* while she picked up the men on the motor boat. Judell and his team then returned to base after a long, but very rewarding, day's operations, being waterborne at Mount Batten at 1500 that afternoon.

*

Wally Harrison recalls the last hours:

> As the sun came up we felt a little bit better. As it rose higher in the sky we even derived a tiny amount of heat from it. It was a beautiful morning. Some time in the morning a plane came into view and all our hopes rose. We waved and shouted but the plane flew past at some distance from us. In fact it was quite a long way from us and we felt dejected as it disappeared into the distance. I feel sure that if he had seen us he would have altered course and done a circuit round us. We did not know if it was a friendly or enemy aircraft.
>
> Sometime later I recall a dark shape looming up in front of me. I recall nothing else until I woke up lying on the deck of a vessel. I was lying alongside the torpedo tubes so I knew it was a destroyer. I felt absolutely *wonderful*. Firstly it was so good, at long last, to feel something *solid* below my back. (I remember periodically banging my fist on the superstructure just to relish the feel of something solid). Secondly I felt the warm glow of Navy 'grog' inside me. In fact they had poured a considerable amount of rum into us. I felt gloriously intoxicated and I can also recall others around me in a highly elated condition. Being alive felt *good*!
>
> On the question on which station picked up our last message I did eventually talk to some of the communications ratings aboard *Vansittart*. They told me that it was Gibraltar W/T that had picked up our last SOS and re-transmitted it.

Aboard the *Vansittart* was one old 'Wild Swan' who had last seen her in July 1938; in his diary he recorded the day thus:

We sailed from Devonport on a routine patrol and received a signal to the effect that the destroyer HMS *Wild Swan* was being bombed south of Ireland. It was not until the following morning that we were able to locate the first of the survivors. The rough sea hampered rescue operations but most of them were picked up and landed at Milford Haven.

Andrew Rippon recalls:

At first light it was difficult to see the other carley floats and our spirits were at a very low ebb. Sitting with water up to the waist and bobbing around like a cork and talking about the lost presents and the chances of reaching Portsmouth and singing, all gradually raised our hopes. After about sixteen hours in the water and several false alarms from enemy aircraft the eventual sight of a sister ship approaching was the most tremendous relief.

I had been trying to comfort a young OD who seemed very ill and, despite all efforts, died while aboard our saviour. His name, O'Rourke, was tattoed on his arm.

F.R. Burrett:

At about 1100 next day a low flying plane was seen on the horizon. We kept down, not knowing its nationality, but it was flying in wide circles and gradually closing, eventually being recognised as a Sunderland flying boat. They flew over low, when they sighted us and fired a Very signal to a destroyer, as yet unseen by us. Soon *Vansittart* approached at speed and we survivors were picked up and taken to Milford Haven, arriving at about midnight.

Lieutenant-Commander Sclater:

One episode comes back to me of this time. Before abandoning ship Lieutenant David Revill, who was also my correspondence officer, went below to the ship's office and brought out the money, several hundred pounds in notes, but he didn't have time to rescue the large number of coins. (Our accounts were kept at Gibraltar or Freetown but a large 'Float' was kept on board also.)

At Milford Haven the money was handed in and a paymaster there was detailed to reconstruct our accounts. Of course they didn't work out right. Much energy was wasted and it would have really been better if *all* the money had gone down with the ship!

Hiram Morgan was one of those who were later awarded for his part in the rescue of survivors. His son wrote that, as he recalled it:

> My father was a petty officer steward, but served the guns with the after ammunition supply party aboard the *Swan* and in the last action helped keep the guns fed until there was no more ammunition to load. But he got his award while he was the senior survivor on a Carley float in the water for over fourteen hours before they were picked up. He recollected that he had to knock out a couple of chaps who were going crazy and were therefore endangering the lives of the others on the float.

A.G. Linford:

> We were picked up by *Vansittart* the next day. The ship's petty officer cook who lived in Gosport, died in my arms from exposure during the day. A good many others also died from the same cause and more died after rescue.
>
> Following on after the pick-up by *Vansittart*, we were fed hard rations and hot tea, rum, and eventually landed at Milford Haven, late at night, fed soup and boiled eggs by some wonderful ladies (volunteers). We were allowed to buy toothbrushes and paste at a local shop but forbidden to send telegrams or communicate to relatives (because we were told that the Germans did not know if the ship was sunk or which one it was!) Apparently, and luckily, we had not been seen in the water on the morning after the sinking by German planes in the area who were sweeping for their own men.
>
> We boarded, or rather were herded on to, a train for Portsmouth via Bristol and Bath. Someone obtained a daily paper at Bristol and we were headlines! After argument, we were allowed to send telegrams home. We arrived at Portsmouth late evening and were shoved in barracks and not allowed to go home until kitted up. I arrived home the next afternoon.

Patrick Satow:

> The survivors were landed at the port of Milford Haven, at the south-west tip of Wales, at about midnight. Temporary accommodation was provided, before they were sent on by train in the morning of 19th June. Everyone was attired in the clothes they

were wearing, with the rest of their worldly possessions lying 84 fathoms (500 feet) down on the sea bed in the North Atlantic.

Also lost with the ship were the special items of clothing which had made life bearable at sea. The survivors reached dry land clad only in what they were wearing when 'Action Stations' had sounded during the last evening aboard. Undismayed, the families set to work yet again to replace articles which had been lost, and thus provide these treasured additions to standard issues of clothing.

Lost, too, with the ship were the many gifts being brought home at the end of a 2½-year commission, including all those exotic fruits and carefully chosen items of clothing which were unobtainable in wartime Britain. On the long journey by train, with steam haulage up to the Paddington terminus in London, many of the weary crew slept in their seats. A few left at stations *en route*; but the majority went on to cross London for other mainline departures.

Thirty-two men died of exposure according to Lieutenant-Commander Sclater's later records, 31 of the *Wild Swan* and one Spaniard.

The fact that the British national papers were blaring her destruction to the whole world while the crew were not allowed to communicate with their families caused much resentment, both then and later. In a typically ham-fisted way officialdom made a tragic situation worse. Particularly hard was it on the wives, children and loved-ones of those who did not survive. Even those whose husbands did return were left to worry and fret for many long hours.

> *NOIC Milford Haven to Admiralty*: 2335B/13. *Vansittart* arrived with 10 officers and 123 ratings, survivors of *Wild Swan*. Eleven Spaniards, survivors of later trawler, landed by *Vansittart*.

Typical headlines were: 'HMS *Wild Swan* sunk' 'Her Swan-song was 6 bombers down' 'Convoy veteran goes down after great last fight' 'Destroyer's 6 Nazi bombers: half attacking force wiped out'.

Mrs Beryl Sandal recalled the anxiety of waiting for news of her father, Albert Timpson, after the news story had broken:

> I remember as a small child all the events of the war and particularly when *Wild Swan* sank – the worry and heartache for my mother in particular while waiting for news. We waited all day for

him to arrive home – then we received a telegram. When he did arrive at last, it was in a taxi, somewhat scruffy, in borrowed clothes.

His stomach suffered a lot during the time he was in the water waiting to be rescued and at the end of the war he was invalided out of the Services.

Mrs Ada Townsend remembers one who did not come home: 'My brother lost his life in that action. He was Leading Seaman G. Marsh, son of Lieutenant Marsh, RN.'

Lieutenant-Commander Sclater's wife, Helen, had been through the agony of that interminable wait before, after the loss of *Royal Oak* when the Admiralty had prematurely announced there were only eight survivors. She can recall the anguish. This time however, strangely enough, she was spared it, for she had not seen the newspapers or heard the broadcasts!

So the Wild Swan's came home at last.

*

The old ship had gone, but the war, and their lives, continued without more than a pause. Of those that recovered, not all survived for long, the insidious workings of exposure caught up with some later rather than immediately. They soon went their own ways and few saw each other again. Patrick Satow recalls visiting Mr Derbyshire at his home. Owen Pugh received letters from Dr Hutter and Kenneth Holland. He was to meet the former again, after the war when both were playing rugger in London. The latter's letter makes sad reading. It is full of enthusiasm, for Lieutenant Holland had been appointed to the brand-new destroyer *Loyal*: 'This is a magnificent vessel with plenty of useful guns and a great deal to keep me busy!' Alas, within a short while he was dead, the sea had caught up with him.

The others were dispersed, most to new ships. Owen Pugh went to the destroyer *Fame* and saw out the war in the North Atlantic and, with her, 'was able to avenge *Wild Swan* many times over' with her string of U-boat sinkings. Lieutenant Satow, Lieutenant-Commander Sclater and Lieutenant Revill all went to new 'O' class destroyers, and found themselves, very shortly, in hot action. At the New Year's Eve battle in the cruel Arctic five British destroyers out-fought and defeated the pocket battleship *Lützow*, the heavy cruiser *Admiral Hipper* and six German destroyers, each one twice their size, and sent Hitler into a towering rage during which he threatened to scrap the entire German surface fleet!

Owen Pugh and Commander Sclater met briefly towards the end of the war at Antwerp, but Lieutenant Revill did not survive and was lost in Arctic waters later in the war. Lieutenant Satow survived, serving with the *Kempenfelt* and *Wager* in the British Pacific Fleet, later in two cruisers and then a carrier off Korea as a navigation specialist. Albert Timpson served as a draughtsman at the *Collingwood* shore establishment near Portsmouth for many years, retiring in 1970 and dying in retirement. Duncan Hutter left the Royal Navy after the war, re-joined, but this time in the lighter blue of the junior service, and rose to the top of his profession before retirement.

Many of the survivors still live in Portsmouth, for so long *Wild Swan*'s home! 'Florrie' Ford, F.R. Burrett, when not on frequent excursions abroad, A.G. Linford; Owen Pugh runs a successful business in Northumberland, Patrick Satow still works in nearby Kendal. Donald Lingard lives at Macclesfield, Air Commodore Hutter in South Devon. Commander Sclater went to live at Fleet in Hampshire after serving with the Navy in HM minesweeper *Hound*, and as Resident Naval Officer at Lyness, in the Orkney Islands, with memories of *Royal Oak*. He worked as Bursar of King's College, Cambridge, becoming a Fellow and MA before retiring.

For those who did not survive Lieutenant-Commander Sclater distributed the money raised by the Borough of Surbiton, receiving touching replies in return via the Family Welfare Section at Portsmouth Barracks. Of Leading Seaman George Marsh for example it was recorded: 'He was particularly attached to his little sister and he had wished her to be apprenticed to hairdressing on leaving school, and had promised financial help.'

There were many similar poignant stories. Able Seaman Francis O'Rourke, who had died while aboard the rescue ship, so close to safety, had a crippled sister to whom he was also devoted, his father recalling that he had written in one letter, 'Don't worry, I will look after her when I come home again.'

In his final report Lieutenant-Commander Sclater wrote to Their Lordships: 'All officers and men behaved with great courage and cheerfulness and entirely in accordance with the traditions of the service.' He made many recommendations for bravery. Alas, as always, not *all* his recommendations were followed, but many of the deserving Wild Swans were decorated for their courage in this gallant fight.*

*

What of other players that have passed briefly across the background? Their fates are equally diverse. The Sunderland crew for example, who found them in the wide waters of the Atlantic. Patrick Satow wrote:

A few days after reaching home, the navigating officer wrote a letter to the Commander of the Royal Australian Air Force squadron at Plymouth. This was to express heartfelt thanks and appreciation for the work of his crew who had found the survivors 220 English land miles due west of Land's End in Cornwall, and some 140 miles to the south-west of Ireland. It was distressing to learn from a reply that these thanks could never be passed on to the aircrew for whom they were intended. Only a few days after the 18th June, the same crew had gone on another mission and failed to return.

What of the eleven survivors from the *Nuevo Con?* Silence descended on their fate, and the loss of *Nuevo Con* and three of her sisters. Despite the fact that many of the Spanish fishermen must have been killed, others wounded in the Junkers 88's later attacks, not a word was breathed of their loss by the Spanish authorities. As late as 1948 *Nuevo Con* was *still* listed as being afloat and serving in Lloyd's Register of Shipping. In 1947 the Spanish Official List noted she had been 'Wrecked' and this was noted in *Lloyds Mail Advice* on 19th February 1947, when the reasons given were amended to read: 'Sunk through war causes while fishing on Great Shoal Bank in 49°45' N at 8.30 p.m. on 17.6.42.' There is no further information and no reference to the other three trawlers. Many other trawlers had been sunk by both German and Allied military action, and their loss had been admitted openly and full lists published. But those lost with *Wild Swan* seem to have been treated as something special, and never admitted.

Details of how the survivors of *Nuevo Con* fared and were subsequently treated in this country first drew the concern of the British Naval Attaché in Spain, Captain A.H. Hillgarth, OBE, RN, and the Assistant Naval Attaché, Lieutenant S.A. Gomez-Beare, RNVR, following meetings with the Spanish Minister of Marine, Admiral D.

* Decorations etc are listed in Appendix 5.

Salvador Moreno Fernandez. In signals sent in July, this interest is revealed:

Naval Attaché, Madrid to DNI: 1529/13. Ref. loss of *Wild Swan* and Spanish trawlers. Can I inform Ministry of Marine that Spanish survivors will be repatriated and that Spanish Embassy knows about them? Minister informs me that Spanish vessels are forbidden to fish on the Gran Sol Bank where presumably action took place, but they go there just the same. This does not mean any action will be taken against survivors on repatriation.

'*M' Branch, to Naval Attaché, Madrid*: 2144/14. Your 1529/13. Spanish Embassy are looking after survivors and are trying to obtain passages for them. It is believed that they have already secured two.

Patrick Satow wrote that he later heard that several declined the offer to return to Spain for some time, and that a trawler was made available to them, 'provision was made for them to earn their keep by making a fishing vessel available. (No doubt it had quite a limited range of operation, so they could not reach the Continent). They evidently made a useful contribution to Britain's meagre food resources. I do not know when these Spaniards were returned to their homeland; but it is possible they might have been released after the Second Front in June, 1944.'

The Times, indeed, commented upon the matter in a report from Madrid, datelined 21st June 1942:

Madrid Press, quoting the announcement by British Admiralty on Friday under a London date line through Official Spanish News Agency, gives prominence to the loss of the *Wild Swan*. The Admiralty's references to the trawlers which became involved in this action was evidently considered an unimportant item here and was omitted!

By coincidence, on 1st July 1942 the *Segundo* and *Primier Enrique* were arrested by the destroyers *Antelope* and *Westcott* close astern of the next HG convoy to sail, HG85. The *Maria Luisa* was also pulled in as she was boarded and found to have a powerful W/T. They were sent into Gibraltar and *Segundo Enrique* was found to have H/F, W/T equipment aboard as well as, 'suspicious documents'. By another remarkable co-incidence *both* these ships later foundered under tow of British warships on the way back from Gibraltar to the UK, the *Segundo Enrique* astern of the trawler *Stella Carina* and the *Primier*

Enrique in company with the corvette *Geranium*, on 3rd September 1942 in position 36°23′ N, 8°43′ W.

*

The *Wild Swan* died gallantly. Her last fight was as brave and as noteworthy as any air/sea action of World War II, yet, while many other ships received their due, *Wild Swan*'s demise has been over-looked by history. It is hoped the record is now set straight.

Yet the final word must belong to one of the many old Wild Swans; one who knew her years before, in happier times, as a trim, sleek warship in her hey-day; Arthur Manton:

In 1942 I was serving in the Flower class corvette *Hydrangea*, when a grizzled, three-badge LTO joined. I asked him his last ship. 'The old *Wild Swan*', he replied. 'She's had it at last, out in the Bay. She went down fighting!'

A fitting epitaph for any warship.

EPILOGUE

I am commanded by My Lords Commissioners of the Admiralty to inform you that they have read with admiration the account of this very gallant action which reflects credit on the Commanding Officer and all his ship's company for their very spirited defence of their ship.

Flag Officer in Charge, Milford Haven.

APPENDICES

HMS *Wild Swan* (1919-42)

Name: Second of the name; First a sloop of 1876, renamed *Columbine* in 1912, sold in 1920. *Job Number:* 1105
Builder: Swan Hunter & Wigham Richardson, Wallsend-on-Tyne. *Engined by:* Wallsend Slipway and Engineering Co.
Order: 14th Emergency War Order. *Class:* Modified 'W' Class. *Date of Order:* April 1918.
Laid Down: 11th July 1918. *Launched:* 16th May 1919. *Completed:* 15th October 1919. *Commissioned:* 14th November 1919.
Pendant Number: D.62 (I.62 in 1940). *Dimensions:* 300ft (pp) 312ft (oa) x 29½ft x 10ft 8ins (min) 11ft 7½ins (max)

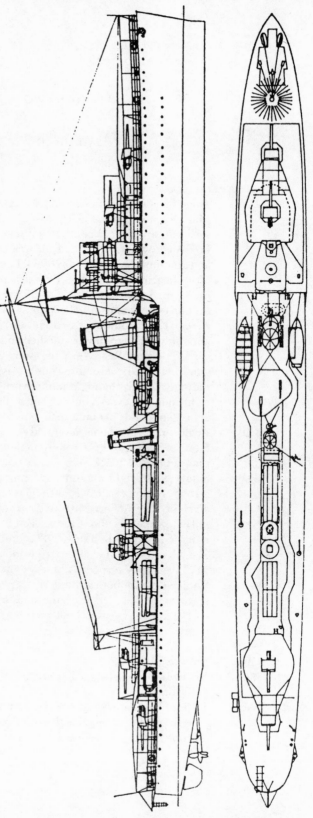

Profile and Plan as completed.

Armament

As Commissioned January 1940:

FOUR – single 4.7-inch Breech Loading, Mk.I guns on Central Pivot Mark VI mountings. Each gun fired a 45-lb shell with separate shell and cartridge. Maximum elevation 30°, guns were therefore Low Angle weapons (L.A.). Total weight of each gun, mounting and ammunition was 11 tons 8 cwt. Each gun barrel had rifling of one turn in thirty calibres (30 cal.) and about 30 grooves to each gun. A small 'Half-Shield' offered limited protection for the gun crew against the elements and almost none against the enemy. Each mounting cost about £2,250. 190 rounds of ammunition, 50 rounds of starshell and 21 practice rounds were carried per gun. Ready-use rings were built adjacent to each gun where shells were stored nose-up while others came up from the magazines by hand. Maximum range was 16,000 yards. An eight-man team was required, and a good rate of fire would be about ten rounds per minute.

TWO – single 2-pdr Pom-poms, mounted en-echelon between the funnels. Stowage for 500 rounds per gun with an effective height range of 10,000 ft. Mk.IIC.

TWO – Single .303-inch Lewis guns, with muzzle velocity of 2,440 ft per second. Height range of 1,900 ft. Gas and spring operated and air cooled. Rate of fire 250 rounds per minute and weight with full magazine was about 30-lbs. Mounted on a pedestal. Drum mounted ammunition supply 47 rounds per drum.

SIX – 21-inch torpedo tubes in two triple mountings, firing either a Mk IV or Mk V torpedo. These weighed 3,357-lbs or 3,492-lbs. Total weight for both sets and six torpedoes was 32½ tons. No re-loads were carried. Each torpedo had a 320-kilo charge and cost £1,200. Range was 3,000 metres at 43 knots speed or 10,000 metres at 30 knots speed.

As Modified in Summer of 1940:

TWO – Bren guns were 'liberated' from the Army at Boulogne and kept in the bridge.

ONE – 12-pdr High-Altitude gun replaced the *after* set of torpedo tubes. This fired a 14½-lb shell with a 5¾-lb charge and was a 50-cal weapon, with a rate of fire of 30 r.p.m.

Captains

Lieutenant-Commander Deforest J.D. Noble:	1919-20
Lieutenant-Commander Cecil R.E.W. Perryman, DSC:	1920-22
Lieutenant-Commander David B. Nicol:	1922-23
Lieutenant-Commander Percival P.W. Mainwaring:	1923-25
Lieutenant-Commander A.M. Donovan, DSC:	1925
Commander C.G. Stuart, DSO, DSC:	1925-27
Commander Louis H.K. Hamilton, DSO:	1927-28
Lieutenant-Commander E.L. Berthon, DSC:	1928-29
Lieutenant-Commander A.L. Pears:	1929-30
Reserve	1930-31
Lieutenant-Commander P.N. Walter:	1931-32
Commander P. Todd:	1932-33
Commander F.J. Wylie:	1933-34
Commander Stephen H.T. Arliss:	1935-36
Lieutenant-Commander R.C.M. White:	1936-37
Reserve	1937-39
Lieutenant-Commander J.L. Younghusband:	1939-40
Lieutenant-Commander C.E.L. Sclater:	1940-42

Summary of Pre-War Career

Lack of space necessitated the omission of the first four chapters of the book which contained the full details, and many stories, of *Wild Swan*'s career from 1919 to 1939. Its loss is regretted. The following is a brief outline of events.

1919:   3rd Destroyer Flotilla, Atlantic Fleet. Commissioned 8th October, Chatham-manned.

1920:   January-February: Rosyth-Chatham. March-July: Baltic-Copenhagen, Libau, Danzig, Helsinki, Riga etc. July-August: Summer cruise-Douglas, I.O.M., Swansea, Falmouth-Chatham. Refit. September-October: Harwich.

1921:   Winter Cruise: January-March: Ferrol, Vigo-Arosa Bay-Gibraltar. April-June: Port Edgar/Rosyth/Scapa. June-Newcastle-Sheerness. July: Leave Chatham-Torbay. Reduced size flotilla (from twenty to eight ships, two leaders to one). August-Chatham. Refit. October-Invergordon, Rosyth. December: Chatham, Leave.

1922:   Re-Commissioned May. Mediterranean-'Chanak' Crisis-Dardanelles-September-December.

1923:   Med until August. Re-commissioned-Med. Aegean and Greek crisis.

1924:   Med.

1925:   Gibraltar January refit. Med.

1926:   3rd D.F. Med. Refit Chatham January. February-July Med. August sent to China Station due troubles in Far East. Arrived Hong Kong and sent to Kiukiang.

1927:   February: Boarded the *Kiang-Wo* which had been seized by Nationalist troops and ejected them, holding Chinese General hostage.

1928:   May: Returned Home. Re-Commissioned Chatham October. Med.

1929:   Med. October: Visit to Constantinople.

1930:   Relieved by new 'A' class in 3rd D.F. April. Returned to Chatham. Paid off into reserve, Portsmouth then Rosyth.

1931:   May Refitted Portsmouth for 8th DF China. Portsmouth new home port. October collided with motor boat Portsmouth, no damage. Sailed for China, arriving Hong Kong December.

1932:   8th D.F. China Station.
1933:   Re-Commissioned Hong Kong.
1934:   December, changed crews with H.M.S. *Delight*, Became 1st
            D.F. Singapore.
1935:   Arrived Aden. February at Malta, 1st D.F. Med. Abyssinian
            crisis at Malta.
1936:   1st D.F. Malta. July sailed from Malta for home. July Spanish
            Civil War commenced while flotilla at Gibraltar. Sent to
            Huelva to evacuate civilians between 25th/28th July. Arrived
            Spithead 31st July 1936. Reduced to Local Defence Flotilla,
            Portsmouth.
1937:   L.D.F. Portsmouth. Coronation Review Spithead, May.
            Reduced to reserve for major refit and re-boilering, plus fitting
            of ASDIC equipment.
1938-39:   Reboilering etc at Portsmouth Dockyard.

APPENDIX FIVE

Honours and Awards

From 'London Gazette' Supplement of 15th September, 1942 (H & A-24.9.1942)

For bravery and skill in action against enemy aircraft while serving in H.M.S. *Wild Swan.*

To be a Companion of the Distinguished Service Order
Lieutenant-Commander Claude Edward Lutley Sclater, R.N. (Captain)

The Distinguished Service Cross
Lieutenant David Haigh Revill, R.N.R. (Main Armament Gunnery Control)

The Distinguished Service Medal
Acting Leading Seaman David Scott, P/JX.150146 (Starboard Pom-pom)
Able Seaman John George Fisher, P/SSX.21571 (12-pdr H.A. gun)

Mention in Despatches
Lieutenant Kenneth Talbot Holland, R.N. ('X' and 'Y' guns)
Temporary Sub-Lieutenant Owen Sidney Pugh, R.N.V.R. (12-pdr H.A. gun)
Chief Petty Officer Steward Hiram Wyndham Morgan, P/L.14753. (After supply)
Petty Officer Arthur Wells, P/JX.126158 ('Y' gun)
Acting Leading Seaman Alexander McLeod, P/JX.134063 ('B' gun)
Able Seaman Leslie Dennis Amos, P/SSX.26583 (Starboard Lewis gun)
Able Seaman Harold Reuben Pearce, P/SSX.30650. (Port Pom-pom)

*

Recommended for Awards had been:
Acting Petty Officer Ty. John Derrick, D.S.M., P/JX.13198.
Acting P.O. Telegraphist Robert C.E. Clement, P/J80581.

SOURCES

1 Mining of ss *Westmorland*, including extract from deposition made by Master, on 5th February 1941. FOIC Liverpool No 218/367/26. 6th February 1941. ADM199/239

2 Report of an Interview with Master of ss *Urla*, 6th February 1941. Shipping Casualties Section, Trade Division. ADM199/2155.

3 Report of and Interview with Master of ss *Bassano*, 17th January 1941. Shipping Casualties Section, Trade Division. ADM199/2135.

4 Report of an Interview with Master of ss *Clytoneus*, 18th January 1941. Shipping Casualties Section, Trade Division. ADM199/2135.

5 Damage Report on mining of HMS *Warwick*, 7th January 1941. ADM199/2064. Western Approaches Diary, ADM199/372.

6 Operation *Specimen I*, Report of Proceedings of HMS *Pegasus*, 23rd December 1940. ADM179/160.

7 Dover Command War Diary, 1940. ADM199/360.

8 Operation on Night of 10th/11th September 1940. Report of Proceedings of Captain (D) 16th DF No. 940/190.

9 Evacuation of Dunkirk. Report of Proceedings of HMS *Wild Swan* 7th June 1940.

10 Report of Proceedings of HMS *Wild Swan*, Operation *XD* 1 and Evacuation of Boulogne 23rd May 1940. ADM199/607.

11 Operation XD, The Hook. Report of Proceedings of HMS *Wild Swan*, HMS *Codrington*, HMS *Hyperion*. ADM199/795.

12 Board of Enquiry into the bombing of HMS *Registan* – Findings and Minutes, Plymouth letter No 2634/M.595, 14th July 1941. ADM1/11298

13 Report of Proceedings of HMS *Wild Swan*, 30th May 1941. ADM1/11298

14 Analysis of U-boat operations in the Vicinity of Convoy HG84 9th-20th June 1942. Anti-Submarine Warfare Division, 29th July 1942. ADM199/2006

15 Report of air attack on HMS *Wild Swan* on 12th May 1940. ADM199/100

16 Attacks on OG, HG and SC Convoys, 1941. ADM199/1142.

17 Director of Torpedo & Anti-Submarine & Mine Warfare 1940-45. Analysis of attack on ss *Scottish Maiden*. ADM199/1790.

18 Naval Staff War Journal (German), June 1942. PG. 32054, roll 1673. T1022, *et seq.*

19 Admiralty Fleet Orders 3rd September 1942. 4231. Summary of Report written to Naval Gunnery Department, Bath and published as AFO.

20 Admiralty Fleet Orders 15th Septembr 1942, 4580. Honours and Awards for bravery and skill in action against enemy aircraft while serving in HMS *Wild Swan*.

21 Admiralty Weekly Internal Summary, 127. July 1942.

22 Combat Report Book No 10 Squadron, RAAF Mount Batten, Plymouth for 18th June 1942. AIR27/151, pps 607/610.

23 Returns of the Quartermaster General Luftwaffe for aircraft casualties, June 1942. IWM Documents film GER/MISC/MCR 18, Reel 6.

24 Last Fight of the *Wild Swan*, by 'A Naval Officer', Broadcast of Friday, 2nd October 1942. DLO 28738. BBC Archives.

25 Nore Command War Diary July-October, 1940. ADM199/375.

26 'Batiments Espagnols perdus 1939/45' (official Spanish Archives).

27 'La Guerra en el mar, alcanza a una par eja de Bouzas', *Industrias Pesqueras* magazine.

28 GAF Locations on Western Front, 18th June 1942. Coastal Area: Bordeaux-Aalborg. GAF Notes Western Front. 'The attack on HMS *Wild Swan*, 120' SSW of Bantry Bay on 17th June was carried out by Ju.88 aircraft from units K.Gr106, IIKG.77 and III KG.77, based at Dinard, Rennes and Vannes respectively. (Graded A.1). ADM 223/94, 67458.

INDEX

Index